NJORD AND SKADI: A MYTH EXPLORED

NJORD AND SKADI

A MYTH EXPLORED

SHEENA McGRATH

Published by Avalonia
www.avaloniabooks.co.uk

Njord and Skadi

Published by Avalonia
BM Avalonia, London, WC1N 3XX, England, UK
www.avaloniabooks.co.uk

Njord and Skadi: A Myth Explored
© Sheena McGrath 2015
All rights reserved.

First Published by Avalonia, October 2016
ISBN 978-1-910191-03-3

Typesetting and design by Satori
Cover Art by Laura Daligan ©2016. www.lauradaligan-art.com

British Library Cataloguing in Publication Data. A catalogue record for this book is available from the British Library.

This book is sold subject to the condition that no part of it may be reproduced or utilised in any form or by any means, electronic or mechanical, including photocopying, microfilm, recording, or by any information storage and retrieval system, or used in another book, without written permission from the author.

Njord and Skadi

DEDICATION

To Nash, Dana, and Mark,
who all encouraged me in their separate ways.

ACKNOWLEDGEMENTS

I would like to thank the librarian at the College of the North Atlantic for all his help, Simon Ross for sending me several papers only available in England, and Terry Gunnell, Triin Laidoner, and John McKinnell for their generous assistance.

ABOUT THE AUTHOR

Sheena McGrath lives in northern Canada. She has a degree in medieval studies, and is the author of four other books: *The Sun Goddess, Asyniur, Sun, Moon and Stars*, and *Brigantia*. To catch up with what she's doing now, check out her blog, *We Are Star Stuff*.

Other books by this author:

The Sun Goddess: Myth, Legend, and History (Cassell: 1997)
Asyniur: Women's Mysteries of the North (Capall Bann: 1997)
Sun, Moon and Stars (Capall Bann: 2006)

Table of Contents

Abbreviations 8

Introduction: Why this myth?
and, What's with all the questions? 9
The Story 12
Three or Nine? How long in Thrymheim? 33
The Main Characters 37
Asgard, Jötunheim, Midgard: Where Are They? 93
Are there any stories similar to this myth? 101
Theories About This Myth 113
What is a Giant? Or, Risar and Thursar
and Trolls, oh my! 122
Why do the Gods and Giants Interact at all? 140
Who are the Vanir? 143
Who is Njord's sister? 156
What about Gerdr and Freyr? 163
What is it that Giantesses Want? 170
Why Could Skadi Claim Atonement and Compensation? 183
Sami Parallels 196
Why is Njord so passive? 207
What is a Hostage? 213
Why did Skadi have to choose by their feet? 218
Why is Loki so vulgar? 222
Why does Loki borrow a shape if he's a shape-shifter? 228
Why Does Loki Keep Getting Stuck? 232
Conclusion 235

Bibliography 239

Index 262

Abbreviations

Flt	*Flateyjarbok*
Gylf	*Gylfaginning*
Grm	*Grimnismal*
Hly	*Haleygjatal*
Harb	*Harbardsljod*
Hst	*Haustlöng*
Hkr	*Heimskringla*
Hynd	*Hyndluljod*
Lks	*Lokasenna*
Skld	*Skáldskaparmál*
Skr	*Skirnirsmal*
Thrym	*Thrymskvida*
Vaf	*Vafthrudnismal*
Vsp	*Voluspa*
Ys	*Ynglinga saga*
Yt	*Ynglingatal*

CHAPTER 1

Introduction: Why this myth? and, What's with all the questions?

Roughly 20 years ago I wrote a book called *Asyniur*, which covered the Norse goddesses and also looked at women and women's roles in medieval Scandinavia. After I'd finished, the Skadi myth stuck with me, and at one time I even attempted a novel based on what I saw as its themes. The novel never really got off the ground, but my interest in the myth remained.

Usually, I write about something because there isn't much on that topic, and I want to learn more about it. In other words, I write the book I wanted to read. (I suspect this happens to a lot of nonfiction writers.) A little bit of research showed that there was a good deal being written about the Vanir gods and the giants in academic circles, and also among popular writers, but not an in-depth study of my particular myth. (*Prolonged Echoes* by Margaret Clunies-Ross came closest, as part of her book is a close analysis of the Skadi myth and the myth of another giantess - Vanir marriage, that of Gerdr and Freyr.)

Within and without the field of Norse mythology, it seemed like the giants were finally getting the attention they deserved. Lotte Motz had been a pioneer in that area, establishing that the giants did receive worship and were more important than most had realized. Others, from John Lindow and John McKinnell to Marlene Ciklamini and Else Mundt, Armann Jakobsson and Preben Meulengracht Sorensen, also contributed to understanding the giant-god dynamic.

From a completely different direction, the book *Monster Theory* also helped to focus interest on the "other" of the myths, the aberrant, chaotic giants. And, outside academia, there were cults of Loki and of the Rokkur (giants and other such beings) springing up on the internet. Once again it seemed that popular culture was doing with gusto what academia does rather more respectably.

The interest for me in the myth of Njord and Skadi came from several features:

- it had no obvious moral or meaning
- it has a downer ending (the Divine Divorce, anyone?)
- it has a lot to say about the relations between gods and giants
- it is both comic and deadly serious
- it shows Skadi and Loki at a crossroads in their relationship with the gods
- it brings out the power relations in the Norse mythic universe
- it gives the giants a much bigger role in the story than usual

The myth as a whole has both the usual back-and-forth between the gods and giants as Thiazi kidnaps Idunn and pays with his life in the first half, and then a much different second half when Thiazi's daughter brings in legal norms in place of mythic necessity, demanding compensation for her father's murder - and getting it. We see a giant acting more civilized than the Aesir, and getting what she wants - sort of. Both parties try to step outside the endless cycle of theft and murder that mark relations between the two groups. This effort is ultimately doomed, but even when Njord and Skadi separate, she remains a goddess (Snorri tells us) and is invited to the Aesir's feasts. It needed Loki's efforts to provoke the final breach between gods and giants.

The structure of this book is somewhat unusual. If you have looked at the table of contents, you will have noticed that most of the chapter headings are in the form of questions. I wanted to write this book in that form, to take the reader along the paths I followed as I tried to figure out what this myth might be about, and why it interested me so much.

I call this the Perceval method, after the young knight in Arthurian legend who, confronted with the bleeding lance and other mystical items at the Fisher King's castle, fails to ask the saving question: what is the meaning of these things? When he wakes the next morning, the castle and everyone in it has vanished, and he must go searching for them to atone for his mistake. The moral, as far as I am concerned, is don't be afraid to ask questions. You may not save anyone, but you will learn something.

In the end, this method led me to write far more than is actually in here - E. M. Forester may have said "only connect", but in the end, with over 100 000 words of manuscript, the looser connections had to go. Some modern Heathens see the magpie as Skadi's bird; this may explain why I found it so hard to resist every shiny bauble of neat facts that I found. Peter Orton said that the *Poetic Edda* is so interconnected it is like a commentary on itself[1], and if you add in the *Prose Edda*, which essentially explains and expands on the myths, then it can feel difficult to stop making connections.

(Should you be interested in some of the pieces that were too out-there to fit in this book, they will be appearing, after some surgery, on my blog, *We Are Star Stuff*.)

At any rate, I hope you enjoy the book, and its somewhat unusual format. It's been a labour of love for me; I hope you like it too.

---

[1] Orton 1998-2001: 226.

CHAPTER 2

The Story

The myth of Thiazi and Skadi is a story in two acts. The first part involves Thiazi and the kidnapping of the goddess Idunn, while the second is about Skadi's revenge after the gods rescue Idunn and kill Thiazi.

The first half we know mainly from the poem *Haustlöng*. (See the chapter entitled Thjodof of Hvin for more on the poem itself.) Odin, Hoenir and Loki were out wandering and they decided to stop and make dinner. They tried to cook an ox, but for whatever reason it stayed raw. Then they noticed an eagle, which was watching them from a tree. It made a bargain with them: in return for a share, it would cook their food. (What the gods did not know was that the eagle was the giant Thiazi in his bird-shape, and he was preventing the food from cooking.) The hungry gods agreed, but regretted the deal when the eagle took three of the four quarters.

Loki, who had served up the meat, was angry, and struck at the eagle as it flew away. Unfortunately, his stick stuck to the eagle, and Loki stuck to the stick. The eagle, indifferent or perhaps malicious, flew on, with Loki bumping along the ground. He, "crazy with pain", according to the poem, begged Thiazi to stop, and the giant seized the opportunity to make a deal. He demanded that Loki brings him the goddess Idunn, who held the apples of immortality, in return for his freedom. Loki agreed.

Thiazi brought Idunn to Jotunheim, and the giants now enjoyed the benefit of the apples, while the gods began to age. They bound Loki, and ordered him to get Idunn back. Loki used a "hawk's flight-skin" to bring him to Jotunheim. Once there, he turned Idunn into a nut and brought her back clutched in his claws, with Thiazi in close pursuit.

The rest of the Aesir were waiting for them, and had prepared a bonfire on the walls of Asgard. They lit it just as Loki flew past, so that Thiazi would fly right into the flames. He did; and died.

It seemed that was the end of the matter, since Thiazi had no sons, only a daughter. The Aesir had reckoned without Skadi's formidable nature; she took up armour and weapons and travelled the long distance to Asgard.

She must have presented a threat to the Aesir, for they offered her compensation: she could choose a husband from amongst the gods, but she could only choose him by looking at his feet. Skadi chose one pair of feet, notably attractive, saying, "I choose that one; few things on Baldr will be ugly."[2] But the feet were those of the Vanir god Njord.

She then imposed another condition: they must make her laugh, which she was sure they could not do. Loki, however, came out with his testicles tied to a nanny-goat's beard, and the two of them had a tug-of-war, with Loki yelping and the goat bleating, until the rope broke and he fell into Skadi's lap. She laughed, and the settlement was complete. As a bonus, Odin threw Thiazi's eyes up into the sky, where they became stars. Some say these stars are Castor and Pollux in the constellation Gemini. (It should be noted that Thor takes the credit for Thiazi's eyes in *Harbardsljod*.)

Then she and Njord were married, and worked out a deal between them. They would spend nine nights at Thrymheim (Noisy-Home), Skadi's realm in the mountains of Jotunheim, and then nine at Noatun (Ship-Harbour), by the seaside. Each hated the other's abode, and they went their separate ways. Skadi, however, seems to have retained her station as a goddess.

How the Two Halves Relate

There are many similarities between the two halves of this story, Thiazi's half and Skadi's half. Although some authors go so far as to speculate that Snorri may have invented the story of Skadi to account for existing verses (which he quotes) about her unhappy marriage, I can't help but think that if he did, he made a good job of it. Since we have no other source for the Skadi story except the verses that the couple speak about how unhappy they are, it's hard to know how much Snorri invented, or whether it was a cut and paste job.

---

[2] Byock 2005: Loc. 1720.

The many parallels between Thiazi's story and his daughter's, however old either one is, are very satisfying, and make for a unified whole which seems fitting for a story which is about the adventures of a giant family who wish to take advantage of the powers of the gods. Some of these parallel motifs are:

1. a giant wants a god/dess for a partner
2. both father and daughter aim (too) high
3. travel between Jotunheim and Asgard
4. unsuccessful pairing
5. Loki involved in both stories
6. in each a passive character whose fate is determined by others
7. quest to take that which the Aesir hold precious (revenge?)

Both halves can be said to be about how giants try to gain access to the precious things of the gods (7). Thiazi succeeds briefly, but it costs him his life, and Skadi has conditional success: no husband, no Baldr, but she attains goddess status. (See Does Skadi Win? for more on this.)

Numbers 1 and 2 go together. Thiazi wants Idunn, and either her apples or the rejuvenating power implied in her name. Skadi wants Baldr, the next generation of the Aesir, son of the senior god, and one of the few we know will survive Ragnarok (although she may not know that). Both are playing for very high stakes. If nothing else, considering how the gods normally treat interloping giants, including her own father, Skadi was running a risk going to Asgard at all. It takes a lot of courage to then try for Odin's only heir as a husband.

Travel between Jotunheim and Asgard (3) is always depicted as difficult, and the giants' home as far away from that of the gods. Loki seems to do it all the time, but mainly Jotunheim is seen as remote wilderness, much the way that Alaska is for most of us. In this story, however, both gods and giants whiz back and forth. In the first half it is Loki who does all the travelling, out to Jotunheim with Idunn, and then back again, in addition to his journey with Odin and Hoenir, and presumably home from wherever Thiazi dragged him.

In the second half, Skadi travels to Asgard, then she and Njord visit her home and then his in Vanaheim, and then she leaves him and returns home. (This last bit may be metaphorical, simply meaning that she went back to her old status.) So there's quite a lot of toing-and-froing in this story. Many of the Norse myths are about someone's journey but this one is a travel agent's dream.

As for Number 4, it seems pretty obvious to say that the Thiazi-Idunn pairing was not a success. When a woman's friends and family burn you to death, it hasn't worked out. The results were less severe for Skadi; she gets to keep her status as a goddess, although it seems that she and Njord became the proverbial example of a couple who couldn't stand each other's company.

As noted above, Loki is instrumental to both halves of the story (5). He is the one who strikes Thiazi, who helps him kidnap Idunn, and who brings her back. In part two, he is the one who saves the situation after Skadi is disappointed in her new husband, by making her laugh. In fact, he and Thiazi are the liveliest characters in the story, making mischief and magic, and then scheming together, before it all turns dark.

Idunn and Njord are the passive objects (6) that suffer the attentions or lack thereof of others. Idunn gets kidnapped, and Njord is forced into a marriage that almost immediately turns sour, a humiliating experience for anyone. (See Idunn and Why is Njord So Passive for more.)

With regard to number 7, it is interesting that while the Aesir usually steal objects from the giants, the giants usually try to kidnap or marry people they consider to have certain characteristics. (Although you could argue that if you want the apples, you need Idunn.) Skadi doesn't want the beauty and radiance of a god; she wants Baldr. (The fact that he's Odin's sole heir probably doesn't hurt, either.) The other instances of giants trying to take things from the gods always involve either Freya or Freya and Sif, in other words fertility and affinity. It is unclear whether the giants view them as simply the embodiment of a particular quality, or if they just have a different world-view. (Also, the Aesir already have Idunn, Baldr, Freya and Sif; presumably the giants lack their qualities.)

Þjóðólfr of Hvinir: Haustlöng

The poem *Haustlöng* no longer exists except as a quotation. What we have is what Snorri gives us in the *Prose Edda*, but whether we're seeing it in the form that Þjóðólfr of Hvinir composed it is open to question. We know very little about the poet, except that he was probably from southern Norway, home of the river Hvinga.

Other than that, we know that he was at the court of Haraldr hárfagri ('Fine-Hair') who was the first king of a united Norway, reigning from about 872 CE.[3] Þjóðólfr was one of his court poets, along with Þórbjörn hornklofi ('horn-blast'). Both of them composed poetry that used many mythological references. Þjóðólfr apparently composed a poem in Harald's honour, which hasn't survived, but *Harald's Saga* says the poet was a "good friend" of the king.[4] Unfortunately, we don't know anything about Þjóðólfr's own religion or any other biographical details. (According to *Heimskringla*, Þjóðólfr interceded with Harald on behalf of his four sons by the Finnish woman Snaefrith, after he banished them. The story is in chapter 26 of *Harald's saga Hárfagra*.)

Þjóðólfr also is credited with another poem, *Ynglingatal*, which describes the illustrious ancestry of the Norwegian petty king Ragnvald the Mountain-High, giving him a long list of Swedish and Norwegian kings as his forebears.

(We will be looking at *Ynglingatal* later, since it traces Ragnvald's ancestry back to the Vanir god Frey, and by extension to Njord.) It is assumed that Ragnvald was a patron of Þjóðólfr's, which seems likely, as he was Haraldr's cousin.[5]

Haustlöng was composed around the beginning of the tenth century, and like several other famous skaldic poems, it describes artworks with mythological scenes, in this case a shield. Þjóðólfr was probably following the pattern laid down by Bragi Boddason 'the old' - his most famous poem is *Ragnarsdrapa*, which describes the images painted on shields hung around an aristocrat's hall. That poem survives as fragments again, but Abrams says it's easy to put them

---

[3] Abrams 2011: Loc. 1302.
[4] Ibid: Loc. 1308.
[5] Ibid: Loc. 1308.

back together if you know the story of Thor and the Serpent[6]. Like Þjóðólfr's poem, it describes several scenes, four in Bragi's poem, while *Haustlöng* juxtaposes two narratives. (*Husdrapa* is usually included in this group, although it describes painted wall panels rather than shields.[7])

Haustlöng means "Autumn-Long", and it is thought that this is a reference to the length of time it took to compose the poem, with its elaborate kennings and double structure. (Heather O'Donoghue thinks it may be a reference to how long it takes to understand its meaning.[8]) As mentioned, *Hst* is a shield-poem, although in this case the shield was a gift from Thorlief (see below), rather than just a description of shields in a hall.

This seems to have been a popular form for poetry in medieval Scandinavia, perhaps inspired by the shield-poems attributed to Homer and Hesiod.[9] Þjóðólfr is careful to mention the gift in the first verse of his poem, no doubt wishing both to repay Thorlief by vaunting his generosity, and to brag about his high-status gift. (Although Heslop, among others, doubts whether there were ever actual shields, on various grounds.[10]) The two halves of the poem end with a comment about the images painted on the shield, once again crediting Thorlief for giving the gift.

Thorlief is usually assumed to be Thorlief the Wise, who was the organizer of the Gula-Thing, and one of the consultants in forming Iceland's constitution, which was based on the laws of the Gula-Thing. He was also an adviser to Haakon the Good, and related to the later Orkney earls. (The poem *Hyndluljod* was created for one of his relatives, so the interest in the arts ran in the family.)[11]

The poem itself is composed in *dróttkvætt*, a verse form that was heavy with multi-layered kennings, and complicated to follow. You will see as you read the translation below that some of the kennings are quite involved, and not at all obvious to a modern reader. (Maybe not to Snorri Sturluson's audience either, since one purpose of *Skld* was to teach

---

[6] Ibid: Loc. 616.
[7] Heslop 2009: 1.
[8] O'Donoghue 2007: 53.
[9] Kurman 1974: 1-2.
[10] Heslop 2009: 2.
[11] Vigfússon and Powell 1883: 19.

Njord and Skadi

readers the way to write skaldic poetry and the myths behind the kennings it used.) Snorri gives the poem in two pieces, although oddly enough he tells the story of Thiazi in prose at the beginning of *Skld*, then gives the verse version much later, when listing kennings for Idunn.

The oddity of this is underlined by the fact that poem and prose go together in the Thor story that is the basis of *Ragnarsdrapa*; Snorri quotes the poem right after he relates the myth. It may be something as simple as him not having a copy of Þjóðólfr's poem when he was writing the earlier portion of his book, or it may have been a deliberate decision. At any rate, thanks to Snorri, we have the poem to puzzle over:

> 1. How shall I make repayment
> For the war-wall-bridge [shield]
> ....
> For the voice-cliff [shield]
> Which I received from Thorlief.
> I can see the unsafe journey
> Of three gold-bold deities and Thiazi
> On the finely-wrought cheek of Hildr's drum [shield].
>
> 2. The lady-wolf flew long ago
> To meet the commanders [Aesir]
> In an old old-one's [eagle] form.
> The eagle perched
> Where the Aesir bore
> The harvest-Gefn-horse [ox]
> The rock-Gefn [giantess] -refuge [cave] god [giant]
> was not guilty of cowardice.
>
> 3. Not free from malice
> the giant was slow to serve the gods.
> Who causes this, said
> The helmeted wisdom-teacher [Odin] of the fetters [gods]
> The much-wise-worded giant-eagle
> Began to speak from the fir-tree.
> The friend of Hoenir [Loki] was not friendly to him.
>
> 4. The mountain-wolf [giant] to Step-Meili [Hoenir]
> Asked for his fill
> From the holy trencher/table.
> The raven-god's friend [Loki] had to blow the fire
> The battle-bold Rognir [Odin/chief] of land-whales [giants]

let himself sink down
Where the trick-sparing defenders of the gods
Were sitting.

5. The fair lord of the earth [Odin]
bade Farbauti's son [Loki]
To share quickly
the bow-string-Var's [Skadi's] whale [ox] among them.
But the cunning foe of the Aesir
Snatched up four parts
From the broad table.

6. Morn's hungry father [the giant]
Then greedily ate
The ox at the tree-root.
That was long ago,
Until the deep-minded war-booty-withholding god [Loki]
Struck the very bold foe
Down between the shoulders
With a pole.

7. Then set fast was
the burden of Sigyn's arms [Loki]
whom all the gods eye in his bonds
to the foster-father-of -the-ski-goddess [father of Skadi: Thiazi].
The pole stuck fast
To Jotunheim's mighty spectre
and the hands of Hoenir's friend [Loki]
to the end of the pole.

8. With a wise deity now
The voracious bird of prey flew
Over a long way; the wolf's father [Loki]
must be torn in pieces.
Odin's friend [Loki] grew exhausted,
Lopt [Lofty = Loki] grew heavy
Odin's companion
Begged the giant's meal-companion for peace.

9. Hymir's kin-branch [giant] demanded
that the rouser of tales,
mad with pain,
to bring him the maid
who knew the Aesir's old-age cure.
Brisingamen's thief [Loki]

*Got the gods' lady {Idunn}.
to the rock-Nidud's [giant's] courts to Brunnakr's Bench.*

*9. The bright-shield-dwellers [giants] were not sorry
After this had taken place,
Since from the south
Idunn was now among the giants.
All Invgi-Frey's kin,
At the Thing, were old and gray -
ugly-looking in their form.*

*10. - Until they found the hound of the falling sea of
corpses [bloodhound: Loki]
of the ale-Gefn [Idunn]
and bound the thief, that tree of deceit
"You shall be tricked out of your mind with trickery",
spake the angry one [Thor]
"unless, also with trickery, Loki,
you lead the glorious joy-increasing girl of the gods
[Idunn]
back here."*

*11. I heard this, afterward,
the trier of Hoenir's mind [Loki]
In a falcon's flying-fur flew;
And with deceitful mind
Betrayed the playmate of the Aesir [Idunn] back,
And Morn's father's, with the wings of an eagle,
Sped after the hawk's offspring [Loki].*

*12. The shafts soon began to burn -
The powers had shaved kindlings -
And the son of Greip's wooer [giant] was scorched.
This is said in memory
of the mountain-Finn's [giant's: Hrungnir's] sole-bridge
[pedestal: shield]
A shield painted with tales
I received from Thorlief.*

*13. And yet one may see on the ring of fire [shield]
Where the giant's dread [Thor]
To Grjottunggard, to the giant Hrungnir,
In the midst of encircling flames. (grave-mound of stone-
enclosures [sea-bed's gold: of rings, Hringa-giant:
Hrungnir])
The son of Jord drove to the game of iron [battle]*

and the moon's way [sky] clattered beneath him.
Wrath swelled in Meili's kinsman [Thor].

14. All the sanctuaries of hawks/falcons [skies] did burn while down below,
thanks to Ullr's step-father
the ground was battered with hail,
when the goats drew the easy-riding-chariot of the temple-deity forward
to the encounter with Hrungnir
(Svolnir's widow [Odin's widow: Earth] split asunder.
15. Baldr's brother did not spare then
the greedy enemy of men.
(mountains shook and cliffs shattered;
heaven burned above.)
I have heard that the watcher [Hrungnir]
of the dark-bone of Haki's land [witness for the rock-whales, for the giants, Hrungnir]
saw his warlike bane ready to kill him.

16. Swiftly flew the battle-pale [gleaming] ring-ice [shield]
beneath the soles of the rock-guarder [giant]
(the bonds [gods] wanted it so,
the ladies of the fray [valkyries] wished it.)
The eager rock-gentleman
did not have to wait long
for a swift blow from the
valiant friend of the hammer-face-troll [Mjollnir].

17. The life-spoiler of Beli's bale-troop [Thor]
made the bear [giant] of the hide-out of the high sea-swells
on the island of his shield [shield-boss];
The gully-land [mountain] prince [giant] sank
Before the sharp hammer
and the rock-Dane-breaker [Thor] (or: Agdir-men of mountains: North)
Forced the defiant one back.

18. And the hard flint-stone
of the visitor to the woman of Vingnir's people [giants]
whizzed at Ground's boy [Thor],
into his brain-ridge,
so that the steel-pumice
still stuck in Odin's boy's skull,
spattered with Eindridi's [Thor's] blood.
19. Until ale-Gefiun of the wounds [Groa]

began to enchant the red boaster of being rust's bale
[whetstone]
from the sloping hillsides
of the wound-god's hair.
I see these deeds in Geitir's fence (or fortress) [shield].
A shield painted with tales
I received from Thorlief.
                (My own translation, following Faulkes, North and Adams)

As you can see, *Haustlöng* incorporates two myths: how Thiazi stole Idunn, and how Thor killed Hrungir. The two myths have their similarities, as shown below:

Thiazi steals Idunn, and Hrungnir threatens to steal Freya and Sif (he may also have had designs on Thor's daughter Thrud, see below).

Both giants threaten the Æsir through over-consumption, in one case of food, in the other of drink. (Abuse of hospitality.) Hrungnir takes beer from Thor's large cups, threatening to drink Asgard dry, and Thiazi eats three-quarters of the ox.

Also, they take all the Æsir's goods; in one case Thiazi stops them cooking their meat and then steals most of their dinner, while Hrungnir threatens to drink all their beer, so they won't have it for hospitality or for Odin to seek inspiration in.

Odin travels to Jotunheim and encounters giants who desire/compete with his possessions. (Thiazi wants his food; Hrungnir takes a bet that his horse is better than Odin's.)

At first, both seem friendly, but that soon changes. (In Hrungnir's case, Odin provokes him, but Thiazi is out to annoy, it seems.)

In both cases, someone else has to get Odin out of trouble. (Loki, Thor)

The victories are equivocal; Hrungnir's flint-stone wedges in Thor's forehead, and Skadi comes to avenge her father and is incorporated into the Aesir's aett.

Both of the giants are tricked; by either Thialfi or Loki.

Finally, both giants end up dead.

These two must have been well-known tales, since the artist who painted the shield expected viewers to recognize the pictures. They are also the first two tales of *Skáldskaparmál*, showing that they were both important stories. And of course Bragi is telling Aegir the stories, so perhaps the story of Idunn was foremost in his mind. The giants vs. gods theme predominate in *Skld*; the first four tales are their battles, followed by two on the theme of gods vs. dwarves, just for a change.

The prominence of the Thiazi story may also owe something to politics. In *Ys* we're told that after Skadi left Njord she had many sons for Odin, including Saeming, the first of the earls of Hladir (rulers of east Norway from the ninth through the eleventh centuries). The skalds Kormak and Eyvind both refer to this mythical line of descent, so it was well-known. [12] Snorri could count on his audience knowing this, and that may be why Thiazi and Skadi come first in *Skaldskaparmál*.

Snorri Sturluson: Skáldskaparmál, Gylfaginning, and Ynglinga Saga

The poem *Haustlöng* gives us the first half of the story, Thiazi's attempt to kidnap Idunn. Snorri Sturluson's *Skáldskaparmál* gives us the second half, Skadi's were-gild. As usual with Snorri, he gives us an explanation of Thjodolf's poem, and fills in details that the brief and elliptical poems often leave out.

His book, *Skáldskaparmál*, is a guide for would-be poets, or skalds, who in the post-Christian period might not understand the stories behind various kennings and allusions to pagan myth. Snorri himself was an Icelander of aristocratic lineage, who also wrote the story *Gylfaginning*, which is another guide to Norse myths, and the *Hattatal*, which lists various poetic terms. (You can get all three in Anthony Faulkes' translation of the *Prose Edda*, unlike most which only tell the stories of the Aesir and other heroic or aristocratic figures.) He also wrote the *Heimskringla*, which is made up of various stories, including the *Ynglinga saga*, based on the earlier poem the *Ynglingatal*, which traces the ancestry of the Yngling dynasty.

---

[12] Clunies-Ross 1987: 172-3.

Njord and Skadi

All three sections of the *Prose Edda* have references to Skadi and Njord and their story, as well as various kennings for them both, such as "wrangler-with-Loki" for Skadi, and "ship-god" for Njord. But the story of Thiazi's death and Skadi's demand for compensation, and resulting unhappy marriage, is told in *Skáldskaparmál*. (The first section, *Gylfaginning*, tells the story of their marriage and its end.)

In this version it is given as a story Bragi the deified skald is telling Aegir, a giant who had made his way to Asgard and was being made welcome there. Let's just pause for a minute and consider this. The Aesir are being hospitable to a giant, and welcoming him at their feast. Snorri's description of this is interesting, because it echoes the display put on for King Gylfi at the beginning of *Gylfaginning*, and suggests that the gods impressed him with both their wealth and power of illusion. Presumably this was a literary conceit of Snorri's.

Aegir's visit also has implications for the cosmological myth that underlies all Norse mythology. We know from this myth that Aegir visited the Aesir; *Lokasenna* tells us that he in turn hosted them. The poem appears in the *Poetic Edda* after *Hymiskvida*, which tells how the Aesir decided to have a feast, and demanded that Aegir hosts it. (This was common royal behaviour, right up through to Elizabeth I, who sometimes bankrupted her courtiers by visiting them.) Aegir told them he needed a special cauldron to brew the ale, and Thor and Tyr are duly despatched to bring it back from Hymir, who owns it. They get the cauldron, but Hymir gets his head hammered.

The myths do not see this as detrimental to the hospitable relation established between Aegir and the deities. He holds his feast, but Loki arrives to disrupt it. (Note that *Hymiskvida* features Thor in his giant-killing role, while in *Lks* he is "off east", until he turns up to threaten Loki. You can't help but feel the exclusion was a deliberate one; it would be difficult to keep Thor and Aegir in the same room.[13]) Sorensen thinks that the feast in *Lks* was an attempt at incorporating the giant's realm peacefully; Loki's mission is to spoil it.[14]

---

[13] Sorensen 1998: 245.
[14] Ibid: 255-6.

Njord and Skadi

However, the first feast, which is the frame of *Skld*, goes off well, although since the first four tales Bragi tells are of gods killing giants, it might not have. Aegir proves a good audience, however, and listens politely. In fact, he is as much Bragi's "feed" or straight man as Gylfi was for High, Just-as-High and Third, asking questions at the appropriate moments and inserting admiring comments.

The first story Bragi tells him is that of Thiazi kidnapping Idunn; perhaps the theft of his wife was uppermost in his mind around giants. (Which Bragi begins without any prompting; perhaps the presence of a giant in Asgard focussed his mind.) The inclusion of the settlement reached with Skadi may be intended to emphasize the accord between gods and giants that Aegir's presence implies.

Brage began his tale by telling how three asas, Odin, Loke and Honer, went on a journey over mountains and heaths, where they could get nothing to eat. But when they came down into a valley they saw a herd of cattle. From this herd they took an ox and went to work to boil it. When they deemed that it must be boiled enough they uncovered the broth, but it was not yet done. After a little while they lifted the cover off again, but it was not yet boiled. They talked among themselves about how this could happen. Then they heard a voice in the oak above them, and he who sat there said that he was the cause that the broth did not get boiled. They looked up and saw an eagle, and it was not a small one. Then said the eagle: If you give me my fill of the ox, then the broth will be boiled. They agreed to this. So he flew down from the tree, seated himself beside the boiling broth, and immediately snatched up first the two thighs of the ox and then both the shoulders. This made Loke wroth: he grasped a large pole, raised it with all his might and dashed it at the body of the eagle. The eagle shook himself after the blow and flew up. One end of the pole fastened itself to the body of the eagle, and the other end stuck to Loke's hands. The eagle flew just high enough so that Loke's feet were dragged over stones and rocks and trees, and it seemed to him that his arms would be torn from his shoulder-blades. He calls and prays the eagle most earnestly for peace, but the latter declares that Loke shall never get free unless he will pledge himself to bring Idun and her apples out of Asgard. When Loke had promised this, he was set free and went to his companions again; and no more is related of this journey, except that they returned home. But at the time agreed upon,

Njord and Skadi

Loke coaxed Idun out of Asgard into a forest, saying that he had found apples that she would think very nice, and he requested her to take with her her own apples in order to compare them. Then came the giant Thjasse in the guise of an eagle, seized Idun and flew away with her to his home in Thrymheim. The asas were ill at ease on account of the disappearance of Idun,—they became gray-haired and old. They met in council and asked each other who last had seen Idun. The last that had been seen of her was that she had gone out of Asgard in company with Loke. Then Loke was seized and brought into the council,[157] and he was threatened with death or torture. But he became frightened, and promised to bring Idun back from Jotunheim if Freyja would lend him the falcon-guise that she had. He got the falcon-guise, flew north into Jotunheim, and came one day to the giant Thjasse. The giant had rowed out to sea, and Idun was at home alone. Loke turned her into the likeness of a nut, held her in his claws and flew with all his might. But when Thjasse returned home and missed Idun, he took on his eagle-guise, flew after Loke, gaining on the latter with his eagle wings. When the asas saw the falcon coming flying with the nut, and how the eagle flew, they went to the walls of Asgard and brought with them bundles of plane-shavings. When the falcon flew within the burg, he let himself drop down beside the burg-wall. Then the asas kindled a fire in the shavings; and the eagle, being unable to stop himself when he missed the falcon, caught fire in his feathers, so that he could not fly any farther. The asas were on hand and slew the giant Thjasse within the gates of Asgard, and that slaughter is most famous.

Skade, the daughter of the giant Thjasse, donned her helmet, and byrnie, and all her war-gear, and betook herself to Asgard to avenge her father's death. The asas offered her ransom and atonement; and it was agreed to, in the first place, that she should choose herself a husband among the asas, but she was to make her choice by the feet, which was all she was to see of their persons. She saw one man's feet that were wonderfully beautiful, and exclaimed: This one I choose! On Balder there are few blemishes. But it was Njord, from Noatun. In the second place, it was stipulated that the asas were to do what she did not deem them capable of, and that was to make her laugh. Then Loke tied one end of a string fast to the beard of a goat and the other around his own body, and one pulled this way and the other that, and both of them shrieked out loud. Then Loke let himself fall on Skade's knees, and this made her laugh. It is said that Odin did even more than was asked, in that he took Thjasse's eyes and cast them up into heaven, and made two stars of them. Then said Æger: This Thjasse seems to me to have been considerable of a man; of what kin was he? Brage answered: His father's name was Olvalde, and if I told you of him, you would deem it very remarkable. He was very rich in gold, and when he died and his sons were to divide their heritage, they had this way of measuring the gold, that each should take his mouthful of gold, and they should all take the same number of mouthfuls. One of them was Thjasse, another Ide, and the third Gang. But we now have it as a saw among us, that we call gold the mouth-number of these giants. In runes and songs we wrap the gold up by calling it the measure, or word, or tale, of these giants. Then said Æger: It seems to me that it will be well hidden in the runes.

(*Skáldskaparmál*: ch. 2 & 3, Anderson's trans.)

Both Skadi and Aegir come to Asgard and survive. They actually come away having established a relationship with the Aesir, and if that relation seems a little unequal, what did you expect?

The other interesting thing that we learn here is that Thiazi was rich. Presumably, since Skadi inherited his domains, she inherited his money, too. That might just constitute the one thing she has in common with Njord, who was sometimes described as "the Wealthy".

The story of their marriage, and Thiazi's wealth, is told in *Gylfaginning*, the Deluding of Gylfi. This was a king who went in disguise to Asgard, only to be met by Odin and his two brothers, also in disguise, who instruct Gylfi in the lore of Norse mythology. *Gylf* forms the first section of the *Prose Edda*, and as is usual with Snorri, it explains and expands on bits of skaldic verse and lore. Snorri relates the story of Njord and Skadi's unhappy marriage to explain verses supposedly spoken by the Van and the giantess.

> *Njord took to wife Skade, a daughter of the giant Thjasse. She wished to live where her father had dwelt, that is, on the mountains in Thrymheim; Njord, on the other hand, preferred to be near the sea. They therefore agreed to pass nine nights in Thrymheim and three in*

Njord and Skadi

> Noatun. But when Njord came back from the mountains to Noatun he sang this:
> *Weary am I of the mountains,*
> *Not long was I there,*
> *Only nine nights.*
> *The howl of the wolves*
> *Methought sounded ill*
> *To the song of the swans.*

Skade then sang this:

> *Sleep I could not*
> *On my sea-strand couch,*
> *For the scream of the sea-fowl.*
> *There wakes me,*
> *As he comes from the sea,*
> *Every morning the mew.*
> *Then went Skade up on the mountain, and dwelt in Thrymheim. She often goes on skees (snow-shoes), with her bow, and shoots wild beasts. She is called skee-goddess or skee-dis.*

(*Gylf* 23)

We know that the verses that Skadi and Njord spoke were from some earlier poet, but unfortunately Snorri doesn't tell us who. (He may not have known.) As we shall see, they were well-known enough for Saxon Grammaticus to import them into the story of Hidings and Reginald.

The last part of the passage, about Skadi returning to her mountains has been interpreted two ways: either the two move back and forth between the two places, while others read it as saying they went their separate ways. Skadi left Njord "fór upp á fjallið og byggði i Þrymheimi", which seems to imply that she now stays at Thrymheim instead of rotating between two dwellings. Certainly the Norse seem to have read it that way.

In the *Ys*, a more historical work that tells the story of the kings of Norway (although it starts with Odin, Njord, and Freyr), Snorri himself says that:

> Njorth married a woman who was called Skathi. She would not have intercourse with him, and later married Othin.

Which seems pretty final. The skald Thórdr Sjáreksson also wrote a verse about it:

> *Gudrun's self by ill*   *Her sons did kill;*
> *The wise God-bride*   *At the Wane's side Grieved;*
> *men tell*   *Odin tamed steeds well;*
> *'T was not the saying*   *Hamdir spared sword-*
>   *playing.*
>   (quoted in Skld XIII, Byock)

which seems to suggest that Skadi's lack of love for Njord was proverbial, or at least widely known.

After Skadi married Odin (if she did) they had a son, Saeming. Eyvind skaldaspillir wrote a poem, the *Haleygjatal*, tracing the earls of Lade back to Saeming:

> *2. That scion*
> *his sire gat, of*
> *Aesir's kin*
> *with etin maid,*
> *the time that*
> *this fair maiden,*
> *Skathi hight,*
> *the skald's friend [Odin} had.*
> *3. ...*
> *Of sea-bones,*
> *and sons many*
> *the ski-goddess*
> *gat with Othin.*

Snorri explains this by saying:

> "Earl Hakon the Mighty reckoned his pedigree from Saeming." (Ys. 2)

I can't help but wonder if the non-consummation has to do with the fact that Odin then fathered numerous sons - not just Saeming - with Skadi. It seems a very pointed contrast. Of course, the motive may once again have been political - Saeming would have been the oldest son, with no older brother to overshadow him. (And no Vanir brother to dispute the Aesir claim.)

The *Ys* is concerned with genealogy and kingly dynasties, in this case the Ynglings, who traced their linage back to Yngvi-Frey, and before him Njord and ultimately Odin. Snorri wrote it to expand on the poem *Yt*, which does not mention any gods, but lists the human members of the dynasty, who seem to have had a talent for unusual deaths. Skadi's son Saeming mentioned above, however, is from another dynasty, the earls of Hladir in Norway, who traced their descent from Odin and Skadi. For more on the Hladir, see the section on the Sami, as well as the discussion of Skadi and Thorgerd Holgabrudr, and see under Njord for more on the Ynglings.

Did Snorri invent the story of Skadi?

Which brings us to an interesting point - was there a myth about Skadi prior to Snorri's Edda? Several people have suggested not, on the basis of either "fairy-tale motifs" or else because Snorri felt he had to justify Skadi's presence in Asgard, so he invented a story to get her there. De Vries, for example, is dismissive of both halves, saying that the Thiazi myth is full of folktale motifs and echoes of other Norse myths, so it can't be original.[15]

Ulf Drobin, on the other hand, said that while the way Snorri knits the episodes together into a flowing whole is very literary, it doesn't mean the units themselves cannot come from earlier times. It just means Snorri was good at putting them together.[16] We know that certain elements existed prior to Snorri: *Hst*, the stanzas by Eyvind and others, various kennings for the main characters. It is frustrating to know that apart from Snorri there's no source for the Skadi-story, but it is good that we have that much, considering what has been lost.

Also, as Preben Meulengracht Sørensen points out:

> *A glance at the investigations of this question, however, reveals that it cannot be answered definitively, and this is perhaps because the question itself has been put in the wrong way. The reason why we cannot say how old an eddic poem is in that we do not know what the poem was like before it was written down in the form in which it is now extant. In other words, we do not know what it is we are trying to date.*[17]

---

[15] de Vries 1937: 37.
[16] Drobin 1968: 31.
[17] Sorensen 1998: 240.

So we don't know how much of the Skadi-myth existed before, and in what form. It may be that Snorri invented a revenge motif to get Skadi to Asgard so she could be unhappily married to Njord, or maybe someone else decided that the *Hst* tale cried out for a sequel. In a certain sense, we'll never know, and trying to eliminate a myth because it has "wonder-tale" characteristics will end by cutting out most of the myths, especially those of Thor. (And Loki.)

Also, I think that there should be (if there isn't already) a Fallacy of the Older Form. There seems to be some idea that old is authentic, while anything new, any innovation on what came before, has to be ersatz. Perhaps I notice this because I was raised a Catholic, and two doctrines that everyone associates with the Church, papal infallibility [18] and the bodily assumption of the Virgin Mary[19], aren't actually very old. So if the Pope can be divinely inspired to invent new dogmas, why couldn't the ancient Norse poets?

In our times we have UPGs, which tell us a great deal about the concerns that modern understanding of the old myths tries to meet. (It's no surprise that gender, class, and outsiderness are in the forefront of how we interpret myths these days, considering how much attention we pay them in the wider culture.) To my mind these are signs that the myths were still living and growing. When they stagnate and can't be changed or improved upon, that's when people lose interest in them. (In modern terms, think about Superman and Batman, who've died, come back, been irrevocably injured, come back, etc. They've evolved, especially Superman, and been retconned[20] more times than any of us have had hot dinners.)

Thiazi's Eyes: The Final Atonement

The last part of the gods' atonement is entirely gratuitous, and consists of one of them throwing Thiazi's eyes up into the sky as two stars. Both Thor and Odin claim the honours for this deed. As we've already seen, Snorri's version gives Odin the credit for doing this. (I wonder if he was

---

[18] http://en.wikipedia.org/wiki/First_Vatican_Council
[19] http://www.vatican.va/holy_father/pius_xii/apost_constitutions/documents/hf_p-xii_apc_19501101_munificentissimus-deus_en.html
[20] http://tvtropes.org/pmwiki/pmwiki.php/Main/Retcon

already sizing her up for when she left Njord?) In *Harb*, however, Thor says that he did it, and Odin doesn't correct him.

> *19. 'I killed Thiazi, the powerful-minded giant,*
> *I threw up the eyes of Allvaldi's son*
> *into the bright heaven;*
> *they are the greatest sign of my deeds,*
> *those which all men can see afterwards...."*
>
> (Hard. 19, Larrington's trans.)

You'll notice that Thor is equally quick to claim credit for killing Thiazi, although Loki typically claims credit in *Lks*, telling Skadi he was "foremost" in the fight against the giant. (He also tells Frigga that he's the reason Baldr isn't there among the deities; clearly rubbing salt in wounds was the order of the day.)

Naturally, the story of the two stars has spawned various astral speculations as to exactly which stars. The obvious candidates are Castor and Pollux: Alpha and Beta Geminorum. These two stars form the heads of the twins in Gemini, and are easy to see in the night sky. (Another take on this whole story is a cartoon at Happle.tea that points out the inherent gruesomeness of this whole act, and the spookiness of having your dad's eyes up there in the sky.[21] The stars of Gemini reach their highest point in the sky in January, which associates nicely with Skadi's wintry nature.[22] (The section on Thiazi has more on this.)

---

[21] http://www.happletea.com/2011/07/08/watchful-eyes/
[22] http://www.timothystephany.com/constellations.html

Chapter 3

Three or Nine? How long in Thrymheim?

Njord and Skadi spent nine nights at Thrymheim, then nine nights at Noatun. Right? Fair and square.

What if I told you that out of the four manuscripts we have of the *Prose Edda*, three say that the couple spent nine nights at Thrymheim, and only three at Noatun? Also, that the manuscript that says nine and nine refers to them as "winters", not nights, unlike the other three.[23]

Considering the near-universal agreement among translators that it is nine and nine, not nine and three, this is rather surprising. Even quite serious scholars such as Jan de Vries and Gabriel Turville-Petre keep up with the agreement that this is a settled matter.[24] This is strange considering that three out of the four sources for this information say something else.

The four manuscripts for *Gylf* are known as the Codex Regius, the Codex Trajectinus, the Codex Wormianus, and the Codex Upsaliensis. Regius has nine and nine, but it says winters, not nights, which suggests a rather longer stay in each abode. It is very clear that the time spent in each place was the same, saying "nine winters at Thrymheim, then nine at Noatun" (my translation from Dillman's French).

Dillman and Jesse Byock both think that nine and three are correct. Byock explains his reasoning in his notes to his translation of the Prose Edda:

> *The Codex Regius says 'nine winters.... and another nine', but the other three main manuscripts, Codex*

---

[23] Byock 2006: Loc. 3692.
[24] Dillman 1991: 175.

> *Upsaliensis, Codex Wormianus* and *Codex Trajectinus*, say 'nine nights... and another three'.

Which seems pretty straightforward. So the Regius manuscript not only changes the number of nights but it also introduces another change: from nights (*nætr*) to winters (*vetr*).

However, the manuscript still quotes the verse where Njord says "nine nights only" he spent in Thrymheim, without doing anything about the discrepancy. Regius (or his source) did tidy up the grammar, however, to match the grammatical gender of *vetr*, which is masculine where *nætr* is neuter, and then presumably tidied up again by equalizing the nights.[25]

He also notes that this chapter of Regius has other oddities; while all the mss. list Njord as the third god, after Odin and Thor, Regius fails to mention that Njord isn't one of the Æsir. Dillman thinks that perhaps the scribe forgot or was unaware that *áss* has two meanings, 1) a god generally, and 2) a member of a particular group of gods, the Æsir. Trajectinus notes that Njord is not one of the Æsir, but doesn't go on to specify what he is.[26]

Another discrepancy is less significant: the Codex Upsaliensis has Thrudheim ("Power-Home") for Skadi's home instead of Thrymheim ("Noisy-Home"). This was probably written in confusion for Thor's home, Thrudvangr[27] ("Power-field").

Dillman comments that it is strange that all these translators and editors would fix the winters/nights problem and leave the problem of how many untouched. He grants that it is not earth-shaking, but it does tell us something about the relations between the Vanes and the giants' daughters, which he figures probably goes back to Indo-European myth. It also tells us something about the translators and editors, of course.

This raises the question of what a medieval Icelandic audience would have expected Njord and Skadi to do, since the gods and giants do, for the most part, exhibit recognizable human behaviour. Lindow sums it up like this:

---

[25] Ibid: 179.
[26] Ibid: 178.
[27] Ibid: 176.

> *A contrast between male and female is also drawn, and it is implied that the differences between the sexes can be reconciled through the institution of marriage. This resolution, however, only gives rise to another question: Where to live? And, as the narrative proceeds, the attempt to mediate between matrilocal and patrilocal patterns of postmarital residence fails. After nine days by the shore and nine in the mountains, all the oppositions are put back in place, Njord and Skadi having decided that they are as incompatible as ships and skis, summer and winter, seagulls and wolves.*[28]

The fact that Njord spends more time in Thyrmheim could suggest a pattern of male relocation, or that he was the less powerful partner. That would once again suggest the power of Thiazi's family, and his daughter, the "ring lady".[29] Anthropologists call this uxorilocal marriage, meaning the husband has to relocate. I'm sure Njord had some less polite words, especially after several nights awake listening to the wolves howl.

Ian Miller has a more down-to-earth approach, looking at how real couples sets up house. The sagas frequently show new households being established at marriage, especially among wealthier families. However, he also mentions two proverbs about what was the best type of household. Naturally they cut in different directions: "a house shall have a married couple", and "It's best for the property of brothers to be seen together". The first could favour simple households, based on neolocality or moving away from mom and dad. The second proverb favours complex households, with several families making up one unit, usually living in several buildings on one property.[30]

He points out that the ability of people to relocate to their own farm would depend on how much land was available, which would require an active land market. Unfortunately, we don't know anything about this, either how Icelandic markets operated or what the demographics were. Miller does say that it is possible that the amount of land available was shrinking, which would squeeze young couples that might

---

[28] Lincoln 1999: 172.
[29] Clunies Ross 1994: 126 n. 24.
[30] Miller 1990: 125-6.

otherwise set up on their own.[31] The sagas exhibit a great deal of variation, however, as people work out all sorts of solutions to the problem of accommodating a new household.

Of course, deities aren't subject to these sorts of pressures, and both Njord and Skadi had homes of their own already. (Skadi and Freyja being among the few Norse goddesses who have a home of their own, along with Frigga, Saga and possibly Gefjon.) So the visits back and forth might have seemed like a reasonable solution. For deities, and people, keeping close to your kin made sense, and newlyweds expected to be able to call on their respective families for support.

The difference between Njord and Skadi, and their homes, has been discussed in the section on Theories. One idea, however, deserves comment here. John Lindow puts forward the idea that the nine nights Freyr has to wait before he can be with Gerdr was meant to echo the nights Njord and Skadi spent together. In that reading, Freyr's affair with Gerdr (see their chapter) was as doomed as that of his father and his giant-bride. The poem, after all, ends on a note of separation, just as Njord and Skadi go their separate ways, and Freyr is not made any better by the news that Gerdr will meet him - the poem ends with him lamenting over the delay.[32]

Note also that he does not choose their meeting-place, she does, just as Njord goes to Thrymheim first, and spends more time there than at home, if we follow Dillman. Gerdr's words are significant, too: she names Barri, and says: "and after nine nights, there to the son of Niord/ Gerdr will grant love"[33]. Once again the giant *aett* is setting the terms.

---

[31] Ibid: 126.
[32] Lindow 2008: 171.
[33] Skr. 39, Larrington's trans.: 67.

Chapter 4

The Main Characters

Njörðr

> *The third asa is he who is called Njord. He dwells in Noatun, which is in heaven. He rules the course of the wind³⁴ and checks the fury of the sea and of fire. He is invoked by seafarers and by fishermen. He is so rich and wealthy that he can give broad lands and abundance to those who call on him for them. He was fostered in Vanaheim, but the vans gave him as a hostage to the gods, and received in his stead as an asa-hostage the god whose name is Honer. He established peace between the gods and vans.*
>
> (Gylf 23, Dasent)

Chapter 23 of *Gylf* is probably the best summary answer to the question "who is Njord?" The rest of that chapter is concerned with his failed marriage to Skadi, which is his major myth. Chapter 24 tells us that "afterward" he begat two children in Noatun, Freyr and Freya. This has caused much speculation as to who their mother was, especially since it seems unlikely that it was Skadi. *Hkr* says he had them before he went to Asgard, which seems more likely.

In the *Poetic Edda*, however, *Skr* refers to her as Frey's "mother". Most understand this as referring to her role as his step-mother. Njord gets several mentions as Frey's father, in the prologue and stanzas 38, 39, and 41, the latter using "son of Njord" as a kenning for Freyr. Similarly, in *Thrymskvida*, Freya is referred to as "the daughter of Njord" (22).

Vaf has a stanza describing Njord, as the giant Vafthrudnir matches his knowledge of lore against Odin's. The god asks the giant where Njord came from, and how he came to be among the Aesir:

---

³⁴ The Wikipedia entry for Njord has a lovely picture of him letting the winds out of a bag.

Njord and Skadi

> 'Tell me this tenth thing, since all the fate of the gods
> you, Vafthrudnir, know,
> from where Niord came to the sons of the Aesir,
> he rules over very many temples and sanctuaries
> and he was not raised among the Aesir.'

Vafthrudnir replies:

> "In Vanaheim the wise Powers made him
> and gave him as hostage to the gods;
> at the doom of men he will come back
> home among the wise Vanir."
> (Larrington's trans. 38-9)

So we know that Njord had an active cult, and that he was one of the Vanir (see chapter on the Vanir for more on them). We also know that he goes back to his people at the apocalypse. *Grimnismal* describes Njord's residence:

> 'Noatun is the eleventh, where Niord has
> a hall made for himself,
> the prince of men, lacking in malice,
> rules over the high-timbered temple.'
> (Grim. 16)

Lks also gives us some information about Njord, although of a somewhat doubtful nature. Loki has been insulting Freya, and her father steps in, saying:

> 'That's harmless, if, besides a husband, a woman has
> a lover or someone else;
> what is surprising is a pervert god coming in here
> who has borne children.'

Loki said:

> 'Be silent, Niord, from here you were
> sent east as hostage to the gods;
> the daughters of Hymir used you as a pisspot
> and pissed in your mouth.'

Niord said:

> 'That was my reward, when I, from far away,
> was sent as hostage to the gods,
> that I fathered that son, whom no one hates
> and is thought the prince of the Aesir.'

Loki said:

> 'Stop now, Niord, keep some moderation!
> I won't keep it secret any longer:

with your sister you got that son,
though you'd expect him to be worse than he is.'
(Lok. 34-6)

The fact that Njord was married to his sister appears in *Hkr* as well, where we are told that he wed his sister and they had Freyr and Freya, but that when Njord came to live with the Aesir, they forbade such marriages. As for Hymir's daughters, they are generally assumed to be rivers running into the ocean, although some translations have Njord sent as a hostage to the giants as well, which implies that giantesses humiliated him while he was there. (See the chapter "Why is Njord so passive?" for more on this.)

(Hymir appears in two myths, both involving Thor. In *Thrym* he goes fishing with Thor, who hauls up the Midgard-Serpent until Hymir panics and cuts the line. The other story, *Hyrmskvida*, turns out less happily for Hymir, as Thor and Tyr steals his cauldron so Aegir can brew ale in it. Neither poem mentions any daughters.)

The statement in *Vaf* 39 that Njord will return home at Ragnarok is one of the biggest teases in Norse myth - up there with the battle between Heimdall and Loki.

"In ragnarök (aldarrök means simply 'doom of the age') he (=Njörðr) will return home". This statement explains why, in the battle on the field of Vigriðr where ragnarök culminates, Njörðr does not appear at all. He obviously has nothing to do there and, when the world of the Æsir must collapse, he can return home, free of his obligation to stay in Ásgarðr as a hostage.[35]

Słupecki also thinks that Snorri considered Freyr to have been born after Njord came to Asgard. In those circumstances, even though Freyr was of the Vanir line, he fought and died at Ragnarok just like all the other Aesir gods.[36] This could possibly mean that only the world of the Aesir is destroyed - that the Vanir survive, along with their home. And of course, there's Hoenir, who stays on in Vanaheim, while Njord returns there, so that both can outlive the attack of the giants.

---

[35] Słupecki 2012: 289.
[36] Ibid: 289.

The late poem *Solarljod* also mentions Njord, saying he had nine daughters:

> *Here are runes*
> *which have engraven*
> *Niörd´s daughters nine,*
> *Radvör the eldest,*
> *and the youngest Kreppvör,*
> *and their seven sisters.*
> *(Sol. 79)* ³⁷

The "nine sisters" seems to be a reference to waves, just as Heimdall was the son of nine sisters, often identified as Aegir's daughters, the waves of the sea.³⁸ There is a list of Aegir's daughters in the *Prose Edda*, and *Hynd* give the names of Heimdall's mothers, all giantess-names. (Simek is dubious about this³⁹, but Lindow thinks there may have been two different traditions about them.⁴⁰)

Neither list mentions Radvör and Kreppvör; perhaps yet another tradition produced Njord's daughters, although they're not mentioned anywhere else.

In *Skáldskaparmál* we are given kennings for Njord:

> *" How should one periphrase Njördr? By calling him God of the Vanir, or Kinsman of the Vanir, or Wane, Father of Freyr and Freyja, God of Wealth-Bestowal."*
> *(Byock: Chap. 13)*

Snorri goes on to quote a verse by Thórdr Sjáreksson about the marriage of Njord and Skadi:

> *Gudrun became herself her sons' slayer; the wise god-bride [Skadi] could not love the Van; Kialar [Odin] trained horses well; Hamdir is said not to have held back in swordplay. (Faulkes's trans.)*

The verse is interesting because Gudrun sent Hamdir into battle, and thus became the slayer of her son, which implies a connection between the other two verses - that Odin seduced Skadi after she married Njord.⁴¹ (Kialar being one of Odin's many names.) The first story in *Skld* is that of

---

³⁷ http://shadowlight.gydja.com/solarljod.html
³⁸ See Young 1933: 79ff.
³⁹ Simek 1996: 136.
⁴⁰ Lindow 2001: 169.
⁴¹ Frog and Roper 2011: 34.

Thiazi's death and Skadi's vengeance, including her choosing Njord by his feet. He is also mentioned as the father of Frey and Freya, and in various kennings for "warrior".

In *Hkr* Njord appears in three of the stories. The main one is the *Ys*, which gives us the euhemerized version, telling the story as if Odin and Njord were simply outstanding men rather than gods. In the *Ys* version of the Aesir - Vanir war, the Aesir were the aggressors, but the Vanir fought back, and the two armies ravaged each other's lands, and neither side could win a lasting victory. This being so, they met and established peace, exchanging hostages. The Vanir gave Njord the Wealthy and his son Frey in exchange for Hoenir. (See the chapter on Hoenir.) The Vanir also sent Kvasir, their wisest man, in exchange for Mimir, "a man of great understanding"[42].

The Vanir appointed Hoenir and Mimir to their councils, but Hoenir would not speak without Mimir, so the Vanir cut Mimir's head off and sent it back to the Aesir, thinking that they had been tricked. The Aesir, for their part, made Njord and Frey sacrificial priests, *diar*, although Njord had to give up his wife because she was also his sister, and the Aesir forbade such unions.

Ys goes on to tell us that Njord married Skadi, but they separated and she went on to marry Odin and have many sons. Later, Odin died, and Njord was king after him,

> *Niord of Noatun then took the rule over the Swedes and upheld the sacrifices; then the Swedes called him Drott (or Sovereign) and he then took scot from them. In his days there was peace, and the seasons were so good that the Swedes believed that Niord had power over the crops and the well-being of mankind. In his days most of the diar (or priests) died and all were burned, and afterwards they sacrificed to them. Niord died in his bed; he also had himself marked for Odin before his death. The Swedes burned him and wept much by his grave.*[43]

Frey took over afterward, and he was a popular king as well, fortunate in the weather and wealth.

---

[42] Laing: 218. (available here: http://www.sacred-texts.com/neu/heim/02ynglga.htm)
[43] Hkr (trans. Monsen and Smith): 7.

Njord and Skadi

Of the other two stories that mention Njord, the *Saga of Hakon the Good* describes the Yule celebrations, including drinking toasts, first to Odin for victory and power for the king, then toasts to Frey and Njord, for good harvests and peace (ch. 14). A kenning for a sailor in the same saga is "Njörðr-of-roller-horses" (ch. 28).

Finally, in the *Saga of Harold Graycloak*, Njord is used as a kenning for "warrior" in a verse by Einarr skálaglamm called *Vellekla* ("Lack of Gold").

Egils saga also has a reference to Njord, in a verse composed by Egil praising Arnbjorn, who gives out the wealth Njord and Freyr bestowed on him generously. Clearly Njord's power to enrich his worshippers was on people's minds.

Apparently even into the 18th and 19th centuries people were still giving Njord credit for good catches. In an account collected by a folklorist in Norway, we're told:

> The old people (the people of old times) always had good luck when they went fishing. One night, old Gunnhild Reinsnos (born in 1746) and Johannes Reinsnos were fishing in Sjosavatn. They had brought a torch and were fishing with live bait. The fish were biting on the hooks, and not much time passed before Gunnhild had enough fish to boil for all week. So she rolled the line around the rod and said: "Thanks to you, Njor, for this time."[44]

Not quite the king of the Swedes or one of the great gods, but still bringing plenty to the people.

Etymology, or Was Njord a Goddess?

So now that we've established that Njord was a god of sailors and fishermen, who fathered two children, and married two women, would you believe that he was originally an earth-goddess? This may seem like an extremely odd question. But, even casual research on Njord will bring up this topic and variants on it time and again:

> It may be that Skadi was originally a god, while her consort, Njord, was a goddess, whose sex changed because the name appeared to be masculine.
> (Turville-Petre)

---

[44] quoted in Dumézil 1955: 215. (my translation)

> ...but also by the linguistic identity of the name Njordr with prot-Gmc *Nerthuz Nerthus, an earth goddess, for whom Tacitus describes a cult as taking place on an island in the Baltic in the first century A.D. The change of sex from Nerthus to Njordr can presumably be explained by the fact that with *Nerthuz either a hermaphrodite deity was meant, or else, more likely a divine brother and sister (like Freyr and Freyja).
> (Simek)
>
> In any case, the story of Skadi's compensation makes some kind of historical sense, given the sex change Njordr himself almost certainly underwent.
> (Lindow)
>
> The name Njördhr is said by some scholars to be an Old Norse equivalent of the (possibly) female Nerthus, the German fertility Goddess mentioned by Tacitus in his Germania, who was also connected with islands. Maybe this is the twin sister left behind in Vanaheim. Or perhaps, as some have thought, Njördhr was once a Goddess who somehow underwent a sex change through the years. The other alternative is that the fertility Goddess of the Germans was really a God all the time.
> (Karlsdottir)

After reading all this you might be excused for assuming that Njord had originally been a goddess, or at least had a twin who was a goddess. Some have even gone so far as to trace this feminine tinge to the lack of any active participation in the few myths he's mentioned in, and assume that his marriage to Skadi is a carnivalesque riot of gender inversion.

Some of you, who are not entirely familiar with Norse myth, may be wondering who this Nerthus is who apparently shares Njord's name. The chapter on Njord's sister deals with Nerthus at greater length, including the question of whether she is the mysterious sister that Njord was with before he joined the Aesir.

Briefly, however, Nerthus seems to be a north Germanic or south Danish goddess (Tacitus calls her Terra Mater) who was worshipped in the form of an idol, which every so often went on pilgrimage in a wagon to "visit" her worshippers. The wagon was enclosed, however, since no mortal could see the goddess and live. We have these details from the Roman writer Tacitus, who recorded them in his *Germania*, written in the first century A.D. This is the only mention of Nerthus that we have, and how or if she is connected to Njord is not obvious, since Tacitus does not mention him, and the Eddic and skaldic sources do not mention her.

However, the identification of Njord and Nerthus is more contentious that it might at first seem. While we know that Tacitus mentioned her along with many other Germanic deities otherwise unknown, like Tamfana and the Alcis, Tacitus' own work has not survived, and we have only copies made much later. As Lotte Motz says about the manuscripts:

> *There are in fact reasons why the equation Nerthus-Njordr should be questioned. Nerthus, i.e., nertum, is only one of the several forms transmitted by the manuscripts: the others are necthum, neithum, herthum, Neherthum, Verthum. The variant nertum was chose by Grimm because it corresponds to Njordr.*[45]

Grimm is pretty up-front about this:

> *if the idea of Thor's mother at the same time passes into that of the thundergod, it exactly parallels and confirms a female Nerthus (Goth. Nairđus, gen. Nairđaus) by the side of the masculine Niorđr (Nerthus), just as Freyja goes with Freyr.*[46]

(He is referring her to the Fjorgyn - Fjorgynn question, the first being a by-name of the earth-goddess Jord, and the second the name of Frigg's father. Fjorgyn's son was a common kenning for Thor, and some have seen Fjorgynn as connected to the name of the Baltic thunder-god, Perkunas. This would suggest that Frigg's father was another thunder-god, or perhaps Grimm is suggesting that he was Thor.)

Another problem in identifying Nerthus and Njord is that while an idol of Nerthus did travel round in a wagon, we don't know of Njord doing the same, although the cult of Freyr had a similar custom:

> *In Sweden it was Freyr, son of Niordr, whose curtained car went round the country in spring, with the people all praying and holding feasts; but Freyr is altogether like his father, and he again like his namesake the goddess Nerthus.*[47]

---

[45] Motz 1992: 3.
[46] Grimm: 256.
[47] Ibid: 252.

John McKinnell offers a way out of the confusion, however, pointing out that the "readings shared by the best manuscripts...are thought likely to be correct." These manuscripts come in three groups (or stemma, to be technical), and the best of group X read Neithum, group Y, Nerhtum, and group Z, Nertum. McKinnell points out that the Italian scribes we owe these manuscripts to were unlikely to introduce a "th" sound since Italian itself usually goes the other way (e.g. Tomasso for Thomas, Teodorico for Theodore). He figures that Nerthum is probably more correct therefore than Nertum, and that it could represent a grammatically masculine Nerthus or neuter Nertum.[48] (If Njordr were derived from Nerthus, it would go: Nerthus > *Njarduz (breaking) > *Njorduz (u-mutation) > Njordr (syncope).[49])

Nerthus/Njordr has usually been construed as connected to Old Irish *nert, "strength", giving us something like "the Powerful One". McKinnell suggests that Njord ("Strength"?) and Freyr ("Lord") might well be associated with political authority. Since both gods are divine ancestors of royal lines, this is an interesting idea.

Polomé, on the other hand, insists that they are two separate derivations, and two separate deities:

> *a) Nerthus and Njordr are two separate divine entities, whatever similarity their names show; as Dumézil (1959) had already recognized, the latter is a sea god [which also explains his particular wealth], and the former is typically a fertility goddess; b) in spite of the similarity of their names, they reflect different derivations: Njordr belongs to the root *ner- "plunge and emerge" with the suffix *-tu-\ Nerthus is rather to be linked to Celtic *nerto-.*
> (Polomé: Njord and Nerthus)

Other ideas, which McKinnell mentions, is that Njord is connected either to the idea of contentment, as in Old English geneorð 'contented' and neorxnawang 'paradise' (literally 'field of contentment'), or to the word 'north' (i.e. 'deity of the northern people', cf. Greek νερτερος 'belonging to the underworld').[50]

---

[48] McKinnell 2005: 51.
[49] Ibid: 50.
[50] Ibid: 51.

Further to Polomé's assertion that the two are different deities, with different names, Dumézil has a way of reconciling the two, names, gender, and all:

> As for the difference of sexes -- Nerthus goddess, Njord god -- it has been explained in many, rather unsatisfactory ways. Perhaps this simply further testimony, and a very ancient one, of a common fact in Scandinavian marine mythology: most of the stories that tell of a sea spirit are known in variants where the spirit is masculine as well as in others where the spirit is feminine.
> (Dumézil: Gods Northmen 76)

So we may well have two different cults, one with a goddess and one with a god. Another theory is that the place-names found in Sweden, which are mainly coastal, reflect a cult of Njord, while those in Norway are mainly inland, and might belong to Nerthus. Simek thinks that the two are a pair based on grammar: "The usage of the plural of the god's name, Njordr, which occurs in several skaldic poems, points to [that] solution."[51] If so, we have another pair, like Freyr - Freya, and possibly Fjorgyn - Fjorgynn, a feminine personification of earth, and the father of the goddess Frigg[52].

I cannot leave this section without mentioning another theory, which Richard North puts forward: that Nerthus and Njord are the same person, and the masculine ending is no mistake, because Njord and Nerthus are the same god, who marries Terra Mater. He ties this to Njord's later marriage to Skadi by endorsing the Skadi = Scandinavia theory (see next section), which would make Skadi a version of the Terra Mater figure whose wedding with Njord was the object of a cult celebration.[53] I can't say that I find this a particularly convincing theory, but it does get full points for ingenuity.

Wagon-God

How shall Niord be referred to? By calling him god of chariots or descendant of Vanir or a Van and father of Freyr and Freyia, the giving god.

---

[51] Simek 1996: 230.
[52] It should be noted that this last pairing is not in universal favour; some, like Simek (1996: 86), think Fjorgyn is a late invention.
[53] North 1997: 20-1.

The "wagon-god" (*vagna guð*) reference is often used to connect Njord and the ancient Germanic goddess Nerthus. Part of her cult involved her statue being paraded around in a wagon. There is no need for it to be connected to Nerthus, however, since we also know from *Olaf Tryggvarsson's saga* in *Flateyjarbok* that a statue of Freyr received similar treatment, only accompanied by a priestess rather than a priest.

One problem with this reading is that some versions of the Edda, including the original Codex Regius manuscript have *vana guð*, Vanir god. I can see how a translator might feel that since the manuscript goes on to refer to him as a Van and a descendant of the Vanir, *vagna guð* would make more sense. It would make the manuscript very repetitious, however.

Perhaps one solution is found in not focussing so closely on the Nerthus/Freyr issue, and noting that Thor is also designated "wagon-god", and possibly Odin (Reiðartyr).[54] We know that Thor rides in a wagon drawn by two goats, while Odin, like Njord, is a bit more of a puzzle.

Odin usually rides Slepnir, his magical horse, while Njord does not have any animal that we know of. You imagine him travelling in a boat, but perhaps like his son he had two transports, one for land and one for sea. Once again, we're probably missing some bit of myth, although it's tempting to speculate as to what sort of animals would draw Njord's chariot if he had one.

Skadi

We know that Skadi is the giant Thiazi's daughter, which makes her a giantess, and we know that she marries Njord as part of her settlement with the gods. (She is the only giant who achieves this; whether the story explained Skadi's anomalous status or merely reflected it, to some extent she succeeded where her father failed.) We also know that the marriage didn't work; while she kept her status as a goddess, she does not live with Njord, but rather in her father's old home at Thrymheim. In fact, as Welshbach points out,

---

[54] Orchard 1998/2002: 412. (But see http://en.wikipedia.org/wiki/Talk%3AList_of_names_of_Odin)

Njord and Skadi

nowhere in the sources is Skadi actually called a giantess[55], although since she is Thiazi's daughter, and referred to as "Morn", which is a common name for a giantess, there is little doubt that she is of jotunn stock.

Her relationship with her father is emphasized in *Hst*. Two kennings for Thiazi call him the father of the "bow-string Var" or "ski-goddess", and another refers to Thiazi as Mörn's father. It may be, too, that the poet is gesturing towards the sequel to his story - Skadi's trip to Asgard. (While some think that the Njord - Skadi myth isn't very old, these references to Skadi would suggest that Thiazi's daughter at least was a well-established concept by the 800s.)

I have already quoted the passage from *Gylf* about Skadi and Njord's marriage. After Snorri tells that story, he finishes the 23rd chapter (on Njord) by telling us a little more about Skadi, quoting *Grimnismal*:

> 'Thrymheim the sixth is called, where Thiazi lives,
> the terrible giant;
> but now Skadi, the shining bride of the gods,
> lives in her father's ancient courts.
> (Grim. 11)

It is in *Gylf* that we also learn of Skadi's final revenge on Loki after the gods bind him under the earth:

> 'Then Skadi took a poisonous snake and fastened it above Loki so that its poison drips down onto his face...'
> (Gylf ch.. 50)

This is also mentioned in the prose section at the end of *Lks*, which also tells how the gods bound Loki as punishment for his part in Baldr's death: "Skadi took a poisonous snake and fastened it over Loki's face; poison dripped down from it." She may have had reason to be so angry, after she and Loki exchanged words earlier in the poem:

Skadi said:

> 'You're light-hearted, Loki; you won't for long
> play with your tail wagging free,
> for on a sharp rock, with your ice-cold son's guts,
> the gods shall bind you.'

---

[55] Welshbach: 48.

Njord and Skadi

Loki said:

> 'You know, if on for on a sharp rock, with your ice-cold son's guts,
> the gods shall bind me,
> first and foremost I was at the killing
> when we attacked Thiazi.'

Skadi said:

> 'You know, if first and foremost you were at the killing
> when you attacked Thiazi,
> from my sanctuaries and plains shall always come
> baneful advice to you.'

Loki said:

> 'Gentler in speech you were to the son of Laufey
> when you invited me to your bed;
> we have to mention such things if we're going to reckon up
> our shameful deeds.'
> (Lksn. 49-52)

Apart from this, Skadi appears twice more in relation to family. In *Skr*, she features in the prose introduction. In fact, she also speaks the first lines:

> 'Get up now, Skirnir, and go and ask to speak
> with the young man
> and ask this: with whom the wise, fertile one
> is so terribly angry.'
> (Skr. 1)

This has always puzzled scholars, since Skadi isn't Frey's actual mother, but presumably she's doing step-motherly duty. She does not appear further in the story, having launched the plot.

The other reference occurs in the poem *Hynd*. As you might expect from a poem about a young man learning his lineage, the reference is to Skadi's family:

> 'Baldr's family was heir to Bur,
> Freyr married Gerd, she was Gymir's daughter,
> of the giant race, and Aurboda's;
> though Thiazi was their kinsman,
> the giant who loved to shoot; Skadi was his daughter...
> (Hynd. 30)

Njord and Skadi

We know that Skadi was considered a goddess from Snorri Sturluson, who tells us in the story of Aegir's feast that all the gods were invited, "and likewise the Ásynjur: Frigg, Freyja, Gefjun, Skadi, Idunn, Sif." (*Skld* 56)

According to *Hkr*, Skadi also had sons for Odin, after she left Njord:

> "To Asa's son Queen Skade bore
> Saeming, who dyed his shield in gore, --
> The giant-queen of rock and snow,
> Who loves to dwell on earth below,
> The iron pine-tree's daughter, she
> Sprung from the rocks that rib the sea,
> To Odin bore full many a son,
> Heroes of many a battle won."
> (Eyvind Skaldaspiller, in *Heim.*)

Some scholars regard this as a late effort, however, probably to gain a pedigree for the Jarls of Norway.[56]

This poem is part of *Háleygjatál*, which is written in the same meter as *Yt*, and like it, traces the lineage of the poet's patron back to the gods, in this case Odin and Skadi. What the *Yt* did for the rulers of the Oslo fjord region, this poem was intended to do for the rulers of the Trondheim area.[57]

Another translation of this poem gives us some interesting geographical information (read down, not across):

> Hail, lord!
> The chief was begotten
> By the kin of the god
> With the giantess
> In those days of old
> When the prince's friend
> Was Skadi's mate
> In the Manheims,
> And the fell-sliding
> Ski-goddess
> Begot with Odin
> Many sons.
> (Monson and Smith)

Apparently the Manheims were a part of Sweden; according to the *Hkr*, Greater Sweden was known as the Godheims.[58] Lindow says that according to the *Yt*, Njord and Skadi lived in Manheims[59], so either Eyvind changed the lore to suit himself or there were different traditions about Skadi.

---

[56] Clunies-Ross: 1987: 172-3.
[57] Lindow 2001: 160.
[58] Hkr (trans. Monsen and Smith): 6.
[59] Lindow 2001: 161.

Njord and Skadi

Another reference to Thiazi and Skadi comes from a poem by Kormak. This reference to Thiazi is rather enigmatic, not helped by the fact that we only have part of Kormak's poem, composed in praise of Earl Sigurd of Hladir, who died in 962.[60] The poem was composed after Sigurd, who was a generous man, had a great feast at Lade (the earls' seat) and paid for it himself:

> *No man bore cup* *Who would not with joy*
> *Or basket with him* *Go to the blood offering*
> *To the jarl's feast gave.* *Which the generous prince*
> *(The gods betrayed Tjassi)* *(The king fought for gold.)*[61]
> *(Hkr - History of Hacon the Good)*

It is assumed that this was another reference to Skadi and Odin's son Saeming, who founded the Hladir line.

Another, odder mention of Skadi is in the *Saga of Harald Hardrade*, the section of *Hkr* which tells the story of Harald Hard-Ruler (or Stern-Counsel). Chapter 84 tells of the dream of Thord, who sees the armies of England arrayed against Harald's, and leading the English:

> *a huge witch- wife upon a wolf; and the wolf had a man's carcass in his mouth, and the blood was dropping from his jaws; and when he had eaten up one body she threw another into his mouth, and so one after another, and he swallowed them all. And she sang thus: --*
> *"Skade's eagle eyes*
> *The king's ill luck espies:*
> *Though glancing shields*
> *Hide the green fields,*
> *The king's ill luck she spies.*
> *To bode the doom of this great king,*
> *The flesh of bleeding men I fling*
> *To hairy jaw and hungry maw!*
> *To hairy jaw and hungry maw!"*[62]

The dream was not inaccurate; Harald Hardrada fell at Stamford Bridge in 1066. (Although Harold Goodwinson did not have long to enjoy his victory - William the Conqueror wasn't far behind the Norwegian king. Some have blamed the

---

[60] Hull 1902-4: 261.
[61] Hkr (trans. Monsen and Smith): 87.
[62] www.northvegr.org/sagas%20annd%20epics/kings%20sagas/heimskringla/009_16.html

forced march to Stamford Bridge and back down south for the English defeat at Hastings.)

Dark Goddess from the Dark Island: Etymology

There is a contradiction in what we know about Skadi. We are told that she is the shining bride of the gods, and apart from her initial appearance at Asgard, she does not seem unfriendly towards the gods. Her name, however, hints at a rather darker persona:

> *The origin of Skadi's name has not been found, although many suggestions have been offered. Some have identified it with the Old Norse noun skadi (harm, injury) while others have related it to the Gothic skadus and Old English sceadu (shade, shadow). In either case, it could be implied that Skadi was a goddess of destruction, or perhaps of darkness and death.* [63]

Many people have instanced the binding of Loki episode, in which Skadi hangs a poisonous serpent over Loki's head, as justifying her name. Considering the amount of violence and revenge in the Eddic and saga literature, however, Skadi's actions seem quite restrained.

Considering that not only did he lure her father to his death, but then boasted about it to her, he got off pretty lightly. (Compare the Morrigan's harassment of Cuchullain, or Artemis' punishment of Actaeon for what seems like an honest mistake.) Other than that, however, it is hard to justify seeing her as a dark goddess. Deities usually get the names they deserve, however. For example, Odin definitely lives up to the *odr*, "furious" root of his name, with his patronage of battle and poetry, as well as his involvement in possibly shamanic activity.

Coming at this from a slightly different angle, we can see from Lotte Motz's paper on giantess names that Skadi is not alone. Under the category "Aggressiveness", we have Skadi, and Greip "grasp, grip", Hremsa "to clutch, to seize with claws", and Sleggja, "sledgehammer".[64] In a related category we have words to do with noise, especially animal or battle

---

[63] Turville-Petre 1975: 164.
[64] Motz 1981c: 503.

noise, which would connect with Skadi's home, Thrymheim, rendered as Noisy-Home or Crash-home[65].

Throughout this book we are confronted with the dual nature of giantesses: deformed and ugly, or else beautiful and sexually attractive. Sometimes they alternate between one and the other, although some of these stories may have been influenced by the Loathly Lady motif that appears in Irish and Arthurian stories. (Vargeisa is one of these. She suffers under an enchantment until Hjálmþér kisses her, when she transforms into a beautiful maiden. She has a marvellous sword for him as well; everything a young hero could want.)

Staying with the giantess angle for a moment, another name for a giantess is Morn, and Skadi is referred to by that name in *Hst*. There is a rather odd tale in *Olafs saga helga* (in *Flateyjarbok*) of a ritual involving a preserved horse's penis which was supposedly offered to "Mornir". I will discuss this in more detail further along, but many people have seen a remnant of the darker side of fertility-cults in this and Loki's tug-of-war with the goat.

There is another theory about the origin of the name Skadi. As Georges Dumézil put it:

> *I do not believe that Scadin-avia is etymologically "the Island of the goddess Skaði": the first term of the word must have, or have had, a more positive content, alluding to "darkness" or something else that we cannot be sure of. I believe that the name of the goddess Skaði was abstracted from the geographical name, which was no longer fully understood...*[66]

Dumézil thinks that the identification came afterwards, but others have been more bullish. Gro Steinsland is among them, since if Skadi = Scandinavia it bolsters her sacred marriage theory. Sorn Skald surveys the main proponents of this theory:

> *One of the more lively etymological controversies involving Skadi has to do with origins of the name Scandinavia. Pliny the Elder in his Naturalia Historia describes the land in the north as consisting of many islands, the best-known of which is Scatinavia. One*

---

[65] Orchard 1998/2002: 360.
[66] Dumézil 1973: 35, n. 18.

> *prominent theory whose acceptance has waxed and waned over time (currently, its popularity is rather low) is that Scandinavia comes from *Skadin-awjô, "Skaði's island" or "the island in the shadow." Other scholars prefer an interpretation of "the dangerous island," referring to hazardous reefs around Scania.*
>
> *Proponents of "Skadi's island" include F.R. Schroder and Gro Steinsland. Schroder in his Skadi und die Gotter Skandinaviens argues that the name is a dim survival of a very early importance of the cult of Skadi; though she once ruled the land, her worship was eventually supplanted by worship of the Aesir. Steinsland, on the other hand, claims that Skadi, a giant, represents the earth; the gods she marries represent mortal kings. Their union reflects the bond between land and lord (and incidentally creates a dynasty of Norse chieftains). The views of Schroder and Steinsland are very popular with those heathens who wish to create an identification between Skadi and Nerthus, thereby cleaning up the question of the parentage of Freyr and Freyja and giving Skadi a strong fertility aspect; it also enjoys some popularity with those neo-pagans who subscribe to the idea of a prehistoric matriarchal goddess-oriented utopia that was eventually destroyed by the rise of war gods and their worshippers.*[67]

As Sorn Skald points out, this solves a lot of problems, and once more the neo-pagans rush in where scholars would fear to tread. To see Skadi and Nerthus as the same goddess, however, makes a nonsense of much of what we know about her.

John McKinnell brings together both theories about Skadi's name in a very elegant synthesis, in his book *Meeting the Other*:

> *The name Skadi (and Sca(n)dinavia and Skåney, Skåne) may be related to Gothic skadus, Old English sceadu, Old Saxon scado, Old High German scato 'shadow'. She may thus have originated as either a personification of the land-mass of Scandinavia or an underworld figure.*[68]

---

[67] http://www.koshabq.org/2012/12/30/skadi-building-on-the-old-foundations/
[68] McKinnell 2005: 63.

If Skadi was an underworld figure, that would bring her close to Hel. Régis Boyer in particular seems to see Hel as an emanation of Skadi, and Idunn as the same for Freyja, with all of them being included in a Great Goddess Freyja-Frigga-Skadi. I suppose Hel and Skadi could have things in common, such as being giantesses, and perhaps both having a dark and light aspect (quite literally in Hel's case), and both are described as "brides".

Also, some have seen Skadi as the dark death-dealing aspect of Freyja, whom I would have thought was quite capable of manifesting her own dark side, claiming half the slain and being a sort of Valkyrie goddess. (In an interesting twist, Kvilhaug sees Skadi and Idunn as two halves of an earlier life and death goddess, in the form of Nehellenia.[69])

The Scandinavia theory rests on the account of Pliny the Elder, who in his Naturalis Historia refers to "Scadinavia/Scatinavia" (*Naturalis historia* book IV paragraph 96, book VIII paragraph 39). This led to a hypothesis that there was a form:

> *scaðin – aujo" (Helle 2008, p. 1) or "Scadin-avia" (Dumézil 1973, p. 35) that would have translated as "the dangerous island" (Helle 2008, p.1) or "island of the goddess Skaði" (Dume☐zil 1973, p. 35), with the first syllables 'scaðin' being a reconstructed Germanic form of 'skaði'.[70]

Which sounds wonderfully convincing, especially when put alongside evidence from Sami songs that refer to Scandinavia as "Skadi's Island". The word Skadi appears to be a loan-word, presumably Germanic, so perhaps the idea of Scandinavia as Skadi's land was too.

However, we have three different sources to pour cold water on this theory. First, Jan de Vries, in his *Altnordisches Etymologisches Wörterbuch* was unconvinced of the connection: "Die Etymologie ist zweifelhaft" ("the etymology is doubtful"). Second, Rudolf Simek, who says in his *Dictionary of Norse Mythology*: "Because of her name, Skadi has even been considered as the eponymous mistress of Sca(n)dia (=Schonen) and thus of Scandinavia, but this, however, is not

---

[69] http://freya.theladyofthelabyrinth.com/?page_id=79
[70] Welshbach: 14.

totally convincing."[71] Finally, Welshbach points out in her thesis on Skadi that a work written by a Roman who'd never been north himself is the only source for the Scatinavia/Scadinivia name. Every other source gives an "n" before the "d" in the first syllable.[72]

Which is too bad. McKinnell's elegant synthesis of the two ideas about Skadi's name is very appealing. And, as you can tell by the goddesses and giantesses I compare her to, I think that Skadi does have a dark side. Whether she is an embodiment of Scandinavia is another question entirely, and if she was, you have to wonder how that fact managed to escape the record so totally. I don't think we can blame the Christians for that one, because it sounds like just the sort of etymology that Snorri would have enjoyed.

There is something a little Phillip Pullman-like about the dark goddess from the dark island, and if you believe some, like Else Mundal and Jurij K. Kusmenko, Skadi's nearest comparison would be Serafina Pekkala, who seems to be based on Sami witches. They and others, like Lois Bragg, see Skadi and her father as symbolic of the alien Sami people, rather than an embodiment of Scandinavia.

However, we do know that, as Skadi herself reminded Loki, there were cult places dedicated to her, and place-names in Sweden and to a lesser extent Norway bear this out. Skadavi, Skedvi, Skea and names based on Ska- and Skada- may well bear witness to a Skadi-cult, although Simek cautions that the latter are less trustworthy.[73] Once again it seems that Skadi managed to combine otherness with insiderness in a way that few others did.

Ski-Dis

Skadi, we are told in *Gylf*, is known as the ski-goddess. In the original, ǫndurdis. The word dis connects Skadi, at least by implication, to a broadly defined group of divine females known as the disir. The disir were important enough to have their own festival in the fall, known as the disarblot.

Apart from Skadi, the only major feminine powers known by the -*dis* title are Freyja, who is called the *vanadis*, or lady

---

[71] Simek 1996: 287.
[72] Welshbach: 15.
[73] Simek 1996: 287.

of the Vanir, and Hel, who is called *Jódís* in *Yt*, which is assumed to mean "horse-goddess", perhaps referring to an old idea that the death-goddess rode a horse.[74] (The disir sometimes appear on horseback.)

Apart from these three, there is evidence in the *Poetic Edda* of other beings that are disir. In *Gudrunarqvida in fyrsta* a group of valkyries are called *Herians disir* (Odin's ladies), and in *Atlamal in groenlenzco* a group of dead women are called disir, while in *Grimnismal* the nornir seem to be a stand-in for the disir. "Therefore, calling Skadi ondurdis does not necessarily mean that she was perceived as a goddess but perhaps rather as a powerful female."[75] The primary function of the disir was to protect a person or family, rather like a *fylgur*, or deified ancestors, and if that category could stretch to valkyries, a goddess, and a giantess-turned-goddess, it was a pretty broad one.

The disir and the idises (another group of divine females, from the southern Germanic regions, who are usually linked to the cult of the Matronae and Matres that flourished in Roman times [76]) have both a warlike function (both hampering and helping, depending on which side they're on) and a nurturing, protective one for the person of family that they are associated with. We know that they were called on in a birth-charm (*Sigdrifa*). Their darker side is revealed in the *Greenlandish Lay of Atli:* Glaumvor has dreams in which dead women she calls disir are coming for her husband, the doomed Gunnar.[77]

In the case of Skadi, the -dis title makes me think of her role as ancestress of the Norwegian royal line. Freyja is a little bit less obvious, but her role in *Hynd.* helping Ottar to learn his lineage and claim his inheritance could tie in here. Also, perhaps her title of vana-dis means that just as Snorri describes norns of different aetts, there were disir from the different races/species of Norse myth. (It also makes me think of Thorgerdr and her association with Jarl Hakon.) Hel

---

[74] Abram 2006: 15.
[75] Welschbach 2012: 51.
[76] Simek 1996: 170.
[77] http://www.norsegodsasatru.net/disir.html

is also referred to as *jodis*, "horse-dis", perhaps associated with the darker side of the cult.[78]

Whether Skadi and Freyja were honoured as part of the disarblot we'll never know, but that the disir were so honoured is not in doubt.

Skadi and Hrimgerdr

> 24. 'Wake up, Helgi, and compensate Hrimgerd,
> since you've had Hati cut down;
> if she could spend but one night by the prince
> she'd have compensation for her griefs.'
> (Orchard)

Sound familiar? If I tell you that Hrimgerdr was a giantess, and Hati was her father, killed by Helgi, the parallel with Skadi should be obvious. To underline the point, there is another parallel in verse 17:

> 'My name is Hrimgerdr, my father's name Hati,
> whom I knew as the most mighty of giants,
> many a bride he had snatched from their homes,
> till Helgi hewed him down.'
> (Orchard)

Thiazi, anyone? Hati is an interesting name because it means "Despiser, Hater"[79], and it is also the name of the wolf that chases the moon and will devour it at Ragnarok. So clearly the name is associated with cosmic destruction, and the end times, although since this is the only reference to the giant Hati that we have, it wouldn't be wise to draw too many conclusions. Still, it is likely that Hati is meant to be more the Thiazi sort of giant rather than the big dumb troll type.

In fact, this is yet another Hrimgerdr - Skadi - Gerdr parallel, because we know that the gods killed Skadi's father, and Gerdr makes reference to her brother's slayer when Skirnir arrives. It is nowhere stated that Gerdr's brother was killed by the Aesir, but when a representative of them turns up, it is the first thing she thinks of, which is interesting. So it's speculative, but I think each of them has lost a relative to the same people they are sexually involved with, or in Hrimgerdr's case, attempt a sexual liaison with.

---

[78] http://www.norsegodsasatru.net/disir.html
[79] Simek 1996: 133.

Njord and Skadi

The whole of the story of Hrimgerdr is even more of a burlesque wooing than Skadi's. She makes her proposal to Helgi during a flyting with Helgi's friend Atli, whom she has already insulted sexually. Atli and later Helgi pretend to go along with her, but in reality Helgi gets the information he wanted from her, and keeps her talking until sunrise, when she is turned to stone. (Which is odd, as it's usually dwarves who are affected by the sun's rays.)

Hrimgerdr, like Skadi has a name that betrays her nature. As Simek points out, "Frost-Gerdr" makes a link between the Hrimthursar (frost-giants), and the goddess/giantess Gerdr. The poem makes another connection between Hrimgerdr and Gerdr, in verse 25, when Atli replies to Hrimgerdr's demand for sexual compensation:

> 'He's called Shaggy, and he'll have you,
> since you're loathsome to men,
> the ogre who lives on Tholley;
> the very wise giant, and worst of rock-dwellers:
> he's a suitable mate for you.'
> (Orchard)

And in verse 29, Atli says that since "Helgi has struck you with fatal runes" (Larrington) she will be defeated.

So Hrimgerdr is threatened by runic magic, and the prospect of marriage with a particularly disgusting giant, just as Skirnir threatened Gerdr. The difference is that Gerdr surrenders, and if we believe Snorri, marries Freyr and bears his son. Hrimgerdr suffers a very different fate; she is turned to stone. This underlines the uniqueness of Skadi's case - the Aesir actually do compensate her, whereas it would have been reasonable to expect that her fate would be similar to Hrimgerdr's, or that Thor would have simply killed her, since he has no problem killing giantesses.

Skadi and Thorgerdr holgabrudr

Both Skadi and Þorgerðr Hǫlgabrúðr are giantesses, and both had cults. Both are connected to the Haleygjar (earls of Hladir in Norway) since in some versions Hǫlgi gave his name to Hålogaland, where the Haleygajar originated. Saxo grammaticus says that Þorgerðr was the wife of Hǫlgi, so she is a foremother of the Hákon family. As well as being a supernatural ancestor, she had a cult in Hålogaland, according to *Skáldskaparmál*, *Færeyinga saga* and *Jómsvíkinga saga*.

Snorri, however, gives Hǫlgi as her father, which falls in with the Skadi (and saga) pattern of giants and their daughters.

> They say that a king known as Holgi, after whom Halogaland is named, was Thorgerd Holgabrud's father. Sacrifices were offered to them both, and Holgi's mound was raised with alternately a layer of gold or silver-- this was the layer of earth -- and a layer of earth and stone.[80]
> (Skld, Faulkes trans.)

(Note that both Thiazi and Holgi were wealthy, enough that both could feature in kennings for gold.)

Her sister Irpa, who appears with her in some sagas, could be an embodiment of that dark side. Her name means "Swarthy" or "Dark Brown" and she could very well be an embodiment of the dual nature of giantesses; like Skadi whose name is close to "Scathe" and is associated with winter and darkness, but who becomes the "shining bride".

Þorgerðr is also described as a bride, and McKinnell thinks that -brúðr means just that. He interprets the "Hǫlgabrúðr" as "bride of the (rulers of) Hålogaland" and that Hǫrðabrúðr, a variant of her name, may mean "bride of the (rulers of) Hörðaland.[81] He connects this to the sacred king and dark goddess pattern that he sees in the *Ys*.[82] Most commentators, in fact, assume that the relationship between and Hǫlgi was a sexual one, although Snorri says her was her father. There may have been differing traditions.

There may have been a more intimate relationship between Thorgerdr and Jarl Hakon; Olaf Tryggvason refers to Jarl Hakon as her *bóndi*, husband, when comparing her present state with the protection she had when the Jarl was alive.[83] (*Ólafs saga Tryggvasonar* (Flatey.) ch. 326) The *faldr* or veil that one of Þorgerðr's idols wears is also an indication of married status, which fits with this idea.

---

[80] Faulkes: 112.
[81] McKinnell 2014: Loc. 7546.
[82] McKinnell 2005: 81-5.
[83] Chadwick 1950: 409.

Njord and Skadi

The most obvious thing that Þorgerðr and Skadi have in common is attested cult. Wikipedia has an entry that instances each reference to Thorgerdr and her sister Irpa, many of which either focus on her worship or on some Christian tearing down her image and destroying it. So we know that she had an active cult at the time of Christianization. We know that people offered Þorgerðr gold and silver. We also know that you crossed her at your peril. In *Harðar saga ok Hólmverja*, the godi Grimkell receives unwelcome news from Þorgerðr, and he burns down her temple in retaliation. Þorgerðr had told him he didn't have long to live, and sure enough he dies at dinner that night.[84] For Skadi, of course, we have the much-discussed line from *Lks* about her fields and temples, but no actual accounts of anyone consulting her or giving her offerings.

According to at least one source, Thorgerdr's cult involved human sacrifice, the ultimate offering. In *Jómsvíkinga þáttr*, Jarl Hákon, who was a particular follower of Thorgerdr's, goes into a dark forest and prays to her, but she isn't receptive. He offers her sacrifices, which she refuses, then human sacrifices, which she still refuses. Finally he tells her to choose amongst his own men, except himself and his two sons. It turns out he also has a younger son, Erlingr, who ends up as the sacrifice. (He does win the battle after this, with Þorgerðr coming to his aid with a storm.) Another interesting point is that after Jarl Hákon calls on Þorgerðr and her sister Irpa, thunder comes from the north, and he kneels to the north to invoke her. This ties in with their giant nature.[85]

A final note: H. Munro Chadwick observes that the poem *Haleygjatal* traces Hakon's descent from Odin and Skadi, rather than Holgi and Thorgerdr. He thinks this may be due to three things: first, that *Yt* may have influenced Hakon into emulating it, second, that he may have wished to trace his descent from deities that were popular and known to everyone, and third, he might have wanted to substitute Skadi, a goddess of Sami character, for Thorgerdr, whom Munro describes as "hated" (although he doesn't specify who

---

[84] http://en.wikipedia.org/wiki/%C3%9Eorger%C3%B0r_H%C3%B6lgabr%C3%BA%C3%B0ur_and_Irpa
[85] Røthe 2007: 4.

it was that disliked her so; Christians would presumably dislike Odin and Skadi just as much).[86]

Odin

The very brief version: Odin is head god of the Aesir, and king of Asgard.

His wife is Frigg, and their son is Baldr, the one who was killed by a mistletoe dart.

He is usually described as gray-bearded, and one-eyed. Several of his by-names, such as Harbard, or Hoary-Beard, refer to this. Odin spends a great deal of time wandering the worlds, gathering knowledge and power against the day when the Ragnarok, or Doom of the Gods, comes. Magical knowledge is his speciality, even in his capacity as a war-god. Even the act of flinging a spear, as he does in *Vsp*, has a magical element, as it was a way of dedicating the other side to Odin in advance of actually killing them.

Odin was the patron of warriors, especially berserkers, as well as poets, who owed their inspiration to him, and aristocrats, who saw him as one of their own. This means he turns up in a great many poems and sagas, and is frequently named as a royal ancestor. His name, which means "furious" is connected to both battle-frenzy and poetic inspiration.

Half of those slain in battle went to him (the other half went to Freyja) and this gave him an equivocal reputation. Since Odin needed good warriors to fight at Ragnarok, he was often accused of killing warriors and chieftains he favoured, so that he could have them in Asgard. It should be noted that the myths and sagas do bear this out; a lot of his favourites do come to an untimely (and in some cases, unlikely) end. These often involve trickery of some kind. (The mock hanging of King Vikarr in *Gautreks saga* is an example of this; at the last moment the thin rope and the frail twig it was tied to turn into a stout rope and a strong branch. Vikarr dies.)

He certainly maintains his position. He insults and outwits Thor in *Harbardsljod*, often seen as a duel between the two cults. Odin uses his ecstatic wisdom when the king Geirrod has him hung in front of two fires, so that Geirrod

---

[86] Chadwick 1900: 292.

falls on his own sword, and his son Agnar succeeds him. This assures us that Odin intervenes in human dynasties, too.

To be fair, Odin seems willing to travel anywhere, or sacrifice anything, to gain wisdom and magic power. He learns the "unmanly" art of seidr from Freyja, sacrifices his own eye to gain wisdom, and in *Havamal*, recounts how he hung for nine nights to learn the runes. He wagers his head in a wisdom-contest with the giant Vafthurdnir, although he wins by a trick. (His last question: what did Odin whisper in Baldr's ear on his funeral pyre? The giant immediately realizes he's doomed; only one person knows that.)

Why Does Odin Have Such a Small Part in this Myth?

That's what makes his appearance in the Thiazi myth so odd. He and Loki and Hoenir go wandering, and Thiazi starts using magic on them, and you expect Odin to step in and do something. But then the story veers off in a completely different direction. It may be that those three were chosen for the story because they are in several other stories together (see Hoenir for more on this). Odin does seem to appear as part of a triad a lot, either Odin-Loki-Hoenir or Odin-Vili-Ve.

I think the secret to Odin's participation in the Thiazi myth lies in a more structuralist interpretation. Odin, depending on how you count, is either half or three-quarters giant himself, and despite this spends a lot of his time trying to outwit them and plotting their downfall. In the mythology, he is a force for order, while the giants are forces for chaos.

Why do I say that Odin is part-giant? Because he is. In the Norse creation myth, the first creature was Ymir, a giant, who was born in the space between the ice-world and fire-world. He created a man and woman from his armpit, and another creature from between his feet. So Ymir was the ancestor of all the giants. Meanwhile, the cow Audhumla also appeared, and as she licked the ice around her, she freed a man named Buri, who was beautiful and strong. He had a son Bor, although Bor's mother is unnamed. (Presumably she's a giant, since there's no one else around.) Their son, Buri, married Bestla, whose father was the giant Bolthorn, and they had three sons, Odin, Vili and Ve. So at the least Odin's mother is a giant, which makes him a half-giant, and if Bor had Buri with a giantess, then Odin is three-quarters giant. (Odin is at least half-giant, while Loki is half-god; it would be neat if the "pure as", Hoenir, was all god, but that's another unknown.)

Odin and his brothers killed Ymir, and formed the cosmos from his body. *Gylf* tells us that the blood that gushed forth from Ymir's body nearly drowned all the giants, except for one Noah-like giant called Bergelmir, who climbed up on a wooden box (or coffin) with his wife, and escaped the flood. So the race of giants continued.

As Rasmus Kristensen points out, the line between the gods and the giants isn't so much in the blood, as it is a chosen affinity. The gods decide to be other than the giants, and to create an ordered cosmos, and build first Asgard for themselves and then Midgard to shelter the humans they've made, and to put more space between themselves and the giants.[87] Once Odin has done that, he can't go back. Having set himself against the giants, he has divorced himself from his kin. So he and Frigg create a new aett for themselves, the Aesir. (Maybe that's why Odin has so many sons scattered about - the more kin the better, from his point of view.)

If you accept this, then Odin's many acts of cheating, seducing, and raping giants and stealing their wisdom and goods become necessary, if not ethical, acts. You could say he's carrying on the black ops part of the war against the giants, while Thor is out there battling them in public.

So, naturally, when Thiazi threatens to take away the Aesir's reproductive power, Odin is on the scene, even if only in a bit part. It is Loki who bears the brunt of the action (quite literally). Odin is there as the one who denies his giant ties, while Loki finds that not denying his has put him in a bind. His shifting loyalties are a problem in this story, as in all the myths, until finally in the end Loki chooses for keeps; he goes over to the giants. Thus the two can be seen as inverted parallels; Odin creates the cosmos through denying his gianthood, but Loki destroys it through acknowledging his.

---

[87] Kristensen 2007: 155-9.

Loki

The man seated next to Ægir was Bragi, and they took part together in drinking and in converse: Bragi told Ægir of many things which had come to pass among the Æsir. He began the story at the point where two of the Æsir, Odin and Hœnir, departed from home and were wandering over mountains and wastes, and food was hard to find. But when they came down into a certain dale, they saw a herd of oxen, took one ox, and set about cooking it. Now when they thought that it must be cooked, they broke up the fire, and it was not cooked. After a while had passed, they having scattered the fire a second time, and it was not cooked, they took counsel together, asking each other what it might mean. Then they heard a voice speaking in the oak up above them, declaring that he who sat there confessed he had caused the lack of virtue in the fire. They looked thither, and there sat an eagle; and it was no small one. Then the eagle said: "If ye are willing to give me my fill of the ox, then it will cook in the fire." They assented to this. Then he let himself float down from the tree and alighted by the fire, and forthwith at the very first took unto himself the two hams of the ox, and both shoulders. Eventually the whole ox was eaten, and the two Æsir went home hungry.

This rather abbreviated version of *Hst* comes from *The Prose Edda Minus Loki*, edited by Mikki L. Fraser, from Arthur Gilchrist Brodeur's translation.[88] It shows just how little story there is without Loki. Thiazi gets all the food, and Odin and Hoenir just wander off hungry. There must have been moments when Njord was lying awake in Thrymheim, wishing it had happened like that.

I began with this rather lengthy quote to prove a point - the Norse myths wouldn't be much without Loki. He stirs them up, he makes things happen. Kevin J. Wanner thinks that Loki was a poet's god, the engine for stories. Take a few gods or giants, add Loki, and stand back. Even in *Hst*, he is called *sagna hrærir,* "mover (or rouser) of tales."[89] Wanner goes further than this, and says that:

---

[88] http://www.scribd.com/doc/71470501/The-Eddas-Loki
[89] Wanner 2009: 224.

> *In short, it is Loki who ensures both that Óðinn has an heir to succeed and remember him and that there is something about him that is worth remembering.*[90]

Or, as Michael Chabon describes him: "god of the endlessly complicating nature of plot, of storytelling itself."[91] (I especially liked his description of reading the D'Aulaires version of the Eddas: 'a book whose subtitle might have been "How Loki Ruined the World and Made It Worth Talking About."'[92])

A simple analysis of *Hst* and Snorri's sequel will show this. It is Loki who strikes Thiazi, who helps kidnap Idunn, who steals her back, who makes the obviously displeased Skadi laugh and saves the Aesir's bacon. He is the thread that connects the two halves of the story, because the cast of main characters changes completely from one half to the other. Only Loki remains, as the connecting element. As the god who revels in his half-giant status, this makes sense. He flits between the two worlds, Asgard and Jotunheim.

His place among the gods is an odd one, and Snorri shows open disapproval of it:

> *Also counted among the Aesir is one whom some call Slanderer of the Gods, the Source of Deceit, and the Disgrace of All Gods and Men.*
> *(Gylf 33, Faulkes' trans.)*

As John Lindow points out, this must mean that Loki isn't a true god, or once wasn't a god. Snorri goes on to describe Loki's family, his giant father Farbauti, and his mother, Laufey or Nal, which seems to clarify matters. Loki has a giant for a father, so he isn't of the Aesir's kin originally.

We know about his giant father because Snorri tells us so, both in *Gylf* and *Skld* He was taking his cue from older poems that called Loki as *sonr Farbauta*. *Hst* is one of them:

> *The gracious lord of earth [Odin] bade Farbauti's son [Loki] quickly share out the bow-string-Var [Skadi's] whale [ox] among the fellows.*
> *(Skld Faulkes)*

---

[90] Ibid: 241.
[91] Chabon 2009: 52.
[92] Ibid: 52.

Another is *Husdrapa*:

> *Renowned defender [Heimdall] of the powers' way*
> *[Bifrost], kind of counsel, competes with Farbauti's*
> *terribly sly son at Singastein.*
> *(Skld. Faulkes)*

We don't know very much about his mother, including what sort of what sort of being she was. Laufey or "Leafy Island" seems an unlikely name for a giantess, which has led to speculation that she is an Asynia. Liberman, however, suggests that Laufey simply means "Earth" and so does Nál, the other name given for her.[93] (Snorri, on the other hand, connects it to Old Norse *nál*, "needle".) Liberman sees Nal and Loki as chthonian deities. (Note that it is mainly the older poems that refer to Loki as Farbauti's son.)

According to Simek, "[i]n poetry Loki is always called Loki Laufeyjarson." (Although I found the two kennings referring to Farbauti in his book as well.) Apart from being mentioned as his mother in *Gylf* and *Skld*, Laufey is mentioned in *Sorla thattr*:

> *There was a man called Farbauti who was a peasant*
> *and had a wife called Laufey. She was thin and meagre,*
> *and so she was called 'Needle.' They had no children*
> *except a son who was called Loki. He was not a big*
> *man, but he early developed a caustic tongue and was*
> *alert in trickery and unequalled in that kind of cleverness*
> *which is called cunning. He was very full of guile even in*
> *his youth, and for this reason he was called Loki the*
> *Sly.*[94]
> *(Ch. 2, Kershaw's trans.)*

Loki is mentioned twice in *Gylf* as Loki Laufeyjarson, and once in *Skld* Laufey also appears in the *Thulur*, or lists for poets, in a list of goddesses.[95]

Simek isn't convinced by 'Leafy Island" and suggests she may have been a tree-goddess, from **lauf-awiaz*, "the one full of leaves". [96] He also suggests "the one who awakens confidence", by analogy to the Gothic *galaufs*. However, he

---

[93] Liberman 1992: 109.
[94] http://www.germanicmythology.com/FORNALDARSAGAS/SORLATHATTURKERSHAW.html
[95] Lindow 2001: 208.
[96] Simek 1996: 186.

admits that none of these explanations fit with the sort of family she has.[97] (Clearly he doesn't agree with Liberman, or at least is less sure that she's chthonic.)

But the explanatory power of the Asynia thesis is not to be denied. Lindow notes that Loki is always called Laufeyjarsson instead of Farbautason, and that Laufey isn't a "threatening" name, unlike those of many giantesses. Also, the use of a mother's name can indicate a missing or unreliable father.[98]

It can't be decided for certain, because in Scandinavian society kin was reckoned bilaterally, although in the myths it tended to be reckoned through the father's line.[99] Loki could just as easily claim descent from his mother's side as his father's. But if he's a half-and-half it explains a lot about his actions. Since Lindow first suggested it in *Murder and Vengeance Among the Gods*, the theory has become very popular. (Although it doesn't explain how Tyr, whose father is also a giant, escaped hereditary taint, which is what this theory amounts to.)

The rest of Loki's family are not without interest. His brothers are named Byleistr and Helblindi. There are two kennings for Loki as Byleist's brother, one in *Vsp* and one in *Hynd*. The first has Loki at the head of the giants attacking Asgard, and the second is about his evil offspring. Helblindi, on the other hand, is unknown, although one manuscript gives it as an Odin-name. The *Poetic Edda* first includes it in a list of Odin's by-names, and then tells us twice that Loki can be known as Helblindi's brother. (It's tempting to tidy this up and assume that since Odin and Loki are blood-brothers, Helblindi is always Odin. Not provable, though.) At any rate, "Blind-to-Hel" is an interesting name for anyone to have.

Loki's asynia wife is named Sigyn, and they have two sons: Vali, and Narfi or Nari. (Snorri varies on this; in the chapter on Loki he says one son, but then when he's describing the binding of Loki, he says two.)

The two sons he had with Sigyn seem normal, and they should be at least half-Aesir. However, they aren't his only

---

[97] Ibid: 186-7.
[98] Lindow 1997: 53.
[99] Ibid: 54.

children. The giantess Angrboda bore him three more, and as you might expect from someone named Anger-Boder, they are pretty scary.

The Fenris Wolf, the World-Serpent and Hel are not cute kids. All three of them are involved in the end of things. Hel takes all souls (except those destined for Valhalla) and she receives Baldr after his death, where he has to stay after the Aesir fail to revive him. The Fenris Wolf swallows up Odin at Ragnarok, and his two sons devour the sun and moon. The World-Serpent, who forms the boundary of our world, Midgard, kills Thor and breaks the bounds between civilization and disorder by freeing itself. (*Hst* itself seems to mirror this movement, as its kennings for Loki move from relatively benign ones to calling him the wolf's father, which links back to Thiazi as the "lady-wolf" or kidnapper of Idunn. As Loki is forced into siding with the jotnar, the kennings used for him change.)

Loki's two 'normal' sons also come to a bad end. One is turned into a wolf by the Aesir, and turns on his brother, disembowelling him. The Aesir then take his guts and bind Loki with them. In a sense, these children of his emphasize Loki's own wolfishness, his change from domesticated to savage, from dog to wolf.[100]

So it seems that Loki is constantly going back and forth in his loyalties between god and giant, even in his love-life. The Thiazi - Skadi myth dramatizes this by first making him help kidnap Idunn for the giants, and then get her back for the Æsir, and then wheeling him on to make an angry giantess laugh. As the action unfolds, we see him pulled this way and that, sometimes literally, and getting the gods out of a hole yet again.

The story as outlined in *Hst* and *Skld* has its parallels in other myths as well. As Jan de Vries points out, the story of the giant Geirrod is very similar to this one. In it Loki borrowed Frigga's hawk-form and flew around until he reached Geirrod's hall. There he became stuck; he could not lift his feet from the windowsill. Geirrod locked Loki in a chest for three months and starved him. This time Loki's freedom was dependent on his bringing Thor to Geirrod's hall

---

[100] Larrington 2006: 545.

without magic belt or hammer. In this version, however, Thor deals with the giant, so Loki does not have to betray his kin.

Other tales, such as the story of the Master-Builder who made the walls of Asgard, and Ottar's were-gild in *Reginsmal* (see chapter on Hoenir) have Loki using his guile to get the Aesir out of a hole, after he's got them into it. This seems to be his main function in most of the myths, right up to Ragnarok, where the once-playful motif darkens.

Between two worlds: Loki as Outsider

Loki, unlike Njord, is no mediator. Of course, he never really sought that role. If you wanted to put a positive spin on his activities, you could say he's trying for a balance of power between the two sides, so that neither can prevail. In this he differs dramatically from Skadi, who ends by persecuting him just as much as the gods do. Loki achieved the connection with Odin and his kin that Skadi sought when she asked for Baldr as her husband, but Loki seems to have soured on the Aesir. Loki was blood brother with Odin, which makes it all the more poignant when the two become enemies.

Perhaps his odd status made him feel an outsider. He is unusual among the main deities in having no home of his own. This fits with his constant travelling. Even more so than Odin, Loki is a god on the move. Some would argue that this formed a bond between them, and sets them apart from other deities, notably Njord and Skadi: They are able to adapt and change as circumstances demand:

> *This is also one of the implicit underpinning of the marriage between Njord and Skadhi, for neither is willing or able to transform their nature in order to be able to accommodate the other. Rather than being inexplicable (as some would have it), the blood-brotherhood of Loki and Odin seems both fitting and entirely natural in light of their mutual mutability.*[101]

I have sometimes wondered if this changeableness explains the demonization of Loki. Often in history immigrants have been damned for being versatile, adaptable and clever. And mongrelized, of course. All charges which could be levelled at Loki by those who like their gods more consistent.

---

[101] http://loki.ragnarokr.com/pipindex.htm

Hœnir

> *La multitude d'explications et de théories scientifiques concernant l'essence mythique d'Hœnir, constitue un contraste remarquable avec la maigreur des sources.*[102] *(The multitude of explanations and scientific theories concerning the mythic essence of Hoenir contrasts remarkably with the paucity of our sources.)*

We learn very little about Hoenir in *Hst*. We know that he is annoyed when Thiazi steals their food. He breathes angrily, but unlike Loki he doesn't do anything about it. He then disappears from the story, as Thiazi flies off and events take their course.

However, there is another source of information in the poem. Old Norse poetry preferred not to refer to people and things directly, instead using a roundabout way of naming something called kennings. Hangatyr, for example, is a kenning for Odin, because "tyr" was a god, and the "hanged" part refers to the myth that Odin hung on the World-Tree for nine nights.

In *Hst*, there are four kennings that refer to Hoenir, as follows:

Phrase	Translation
Hoenis vinr	Hoenir's friend
fet-Meila	step-Meili (another god)
holls vinars Honis	Hoenir's loyal friend
hugreyandi Hoenis	Trier of Hoenir's courage/mind

Just to show you how they work in the actual poem, here is a quote from North's translation, with the explanations in square brackets:

---

[102] Strom 1956: 75.

Njord and Skadi

> *The mountain-wolf [giant] asked step-Meili [Hænir] to share out to him his fill from the holy table. The raven-god's [Odin's] friend [Loki] had to blow [the fire]. The battle-bold Rognir [Odin, i.e. chief] of land-whales [giants] let himself drop down where the guileless defenders of gods were sitting.*[103]

Another translation, by Kock, has Hoenir "blowing"; breathing angrily as he has to share out the ox-meat with Thiazi.[104] You'll notice that Kock gives the sense of the kenning for Hoenir, rather than the literal expression:

> *4. Famished, fain would have his fill the mountain-dweller. Snorted the Swift-footed, seated at holy table. Flew the fiend from treetop, fierce in mind, then down to where, unwitting, waited the warders of all godheads.*[105]

"Step-Meili" as a kenning for Hoenir doesn't get us very far. Kock rightly interprets it as meaning "Swift-Footed", since Meili is a god. Unfortunately, he's a very obscure god. We know him mainly from *Harb*, where Thor names him as a brother, and the second half of *Hst* also refers to Thor as Meili's brother. Snorri says he's a son of Odin's, and lists him between Baldr and Vidarr (*Gylf* 75).

The other three kennings that mention Hoenir are all references to Loki, either as Hoenir's friend or trier of his courage, whatever that might be. (I always imagined Loki persecuting Hoenir, who is elsewhere described as "timid" and who is known for his silence.) North puts a positive spin on this, saying that Loki sticks up for Hoenir, and saves him by striking Thiazi. I think that's putting too much gloss on it; it seems more likely that the same tradition that labelled Hoenir timid is at play here. I also think that any description of Loki as Hoenir's "friend" might have to be adjusted for sarcasm.[106] Snorri may have felt the same, since in *Skáldskaparmál* he lists Hoenir second-to-last of the Aesir, the last being Loki.

That three out of four kennings for Hoenir refer to him in relation to someone else (Loki) seems par for the course for

---

[103] http://www.webcitation.org/query?url=http%3A%2F%2Fwww.geocities.com%2Figdrasilas%2Fhaustlong.htm&date=2009-10-26%2000%3A22%3A05
[104] North 1997: 23.
[105] http://forums.skadi.net/showthread.php?t=74157
[106] http://www.gocomics.com/doonesbury/1988/09/08

him. In *Skáldskaparmál* Snorri lists more kennings for Hoenir:

> ...the seat mate, comrade, or trusted companion of Odin, the fast-moving god, the long leg, or the king of clay.

One thing that's interesting is how often Hoenir is someone's friend or companion. It's more usual in kennings to mention someone's family connections, but if Hoenir has family the poets are not mentioning them.

Wandering gods

Hst recounts one of several myths in which Hoenir, Odin and Loki go roaming around exploring. The other two are the story of Otr's weregild and the creation of the first humans. The first story involves a very similar pattern to the Thiazi myth, as Loki kills an otter for dinner, and the otter turns out to be a shape-shifter named Otr, whose brother demands compensation. (Sound familiar?) The gold that Loki gets for them is cursed, and that begins the story of the Nieblungen gold.

The other story is briefly told, since *Vsp* is pretty terse. It tells the story of the creation of the worlds, and the society of the gods,

> *Until three gods, strong and loving,*
> *came from that company to the world;*
> *they found on land Ash and Embla,*
> *capable of little, lacking in fate.*
>
> *Breath they had not, spirit they had not,*
> *character nor vital spark nor fresh complexions;*
> *breath gave Odin, spirit gave Haenir,*
> *vital spark gave Lodur, and fresh complexions.*[107]
> (Vsp 17-8: Larrington)

There are still arguments over who Lodur is, although most people tend to assume he's Loki, which would connect up to the Thiazi story. To make things worse, in another version of this myth, Odin and his two brothers Villi and Ve create the first humans. I suppose in both instances they involve gods who are very close to Odin, whether as family or by choice.

---

[107] Larrington 1996: 6.

Volupsa goes on to tell us that after Odin and Loki have died at *ragna rok*, Hoenir appears along with two other gods afterwards:

> *Without sowing the fields will grow,*
> *all ills will be healed, Baldr will come back;*
> *Hod and Baldr, the gods of slaughter, will live happily together*
> *in the sage's palaces – do you understand yet, or what more?*
>
> *The Haenir will choose wooden slips for prophecy,*
> *and the sons of two brothers will inhabit, widely,*
> *the windy world – do you understand yet, or what more?*
> *(Vsp 62-3: Larrington)*

So Hoenir reappears, along with the two antagonist gods, no longer enemies. (McKinnell calls them the "innocent gods".[108]) There could be a pattern here, since relations between Odin and Loki were pretty fraught.

You will probably have noticed that the wanderings of Hoenir and his friends all take place "early" in the Norse myths. It may be that Odin was still exploring the nine worlds at this stage, or maybe he just hadn't pissed everyone else off yet. Still, Hoenir does appear, which is more than he does in most of the later ones. It may be that he is a deity of first and last, but not middle bits. I can't prove that the story of Thiazi is an early one, but I notice that in *Skáldskaparmál* it's the first story told, which I find suggestive. (The frame in *Skld* has the poet Bragi telling stories to the giant Aegir: was his wife's kidnapping by a giant uppermost in his mind?)

Further evidence of a Loki/Hoenir/Odin triad comes from a later source: a ballad from the Faroe Islands. This is called *Loka tattur* ("Tale of Loki"), and it tells how a farmer lost a bet with a giant, and has to give him his son. The farmer calls on first Odin, then Hoenir, then Loki to hide the boy. Loki, of course, not only saves the child but also kills the giant. Those who see a bird-form for Hoenir will be interested that he hides the child in a swan's feather. There are several

---

[108] McKinnell 1994: 112.

different versions of the song, and it probably dates to the late Middle Ages.[109]

Just as a side note, there's a wonderful cartoon online of Loki, Odin and Hoenir out wandering. The other two naturally dash off to do whatever crazy thing they know will get them in trouble, and poor Hoenir gets dragged along. I think of it when I'm reading the stories of *Reginsmal* and *Hst*.[110] (I especially liked someone's comment that Hoenir was clearly a Greek god who had somehow wandered into Norse myth, where the gods always do things they shouldn't.)

Þiazi

If you are used to thinking of giants as big, slow and stupid, *Hst* will confuse you. It describes Thiazi as "much-wise" and "cunning", adjectives that could be applied to Odin. Again, the poem calls him "most terrible", which implies that as an enemy he was hard to beat.

Leaving the poem aside for a moment, we can see other tributes, grudging or otherwise, in other references to Thiazi throughout Norse literature. Some of this may be the old trick of talking up your enemy to make your victory seem greater, but there is a pattern to the references. Like the giants Odin matches wits with, he is not your ordinary thick troll.

> "I killed Þjazi, the powerful minded giant.
> I threw up the eyes of Olvaldi's son
> into the bright heavens.
> They are the greatest sign of my deeds,
> those which all men can see afterwards.
> What were you doing meanwhile, Harbard?"
> (Har. 19 Larrington's trans.)

> "Thrymheim the sixth is called
> where Þjazi lived, the terrible giant,
>
> but now Skadi, shining bride of the gods,
> lives in her father's ancient courts"
> (Grim. 11 Larrington's trans.)

---

[109] There are several online sources for *Loka tattur*, including Wikipedia, and a version of the ballad at: http://www.boudicca.de/lokkatattur-e.html.
[110] http://ladynorthstar.deviantart.com/art/Loki-Odin-Hoenir-unwise-216806690

The other thing we know about him is that he is rich, although the Aesir don't manage to get their hands on that; presumably that's why Skadi doesn't demand monetary compensation. We are told in *Skáldskaparmál:*

> Þjazi and his brothers Gangr and Idi had a father named Ölvaldi. Ölvaldi was very rich in gold, and when he died his three sons divided their inheritance between them by each in turn taking a mouthful. For this reason the expressions "speech of Þjazi, Gangr or Idi" and "Idi's shining talk" are kennings for gold.
> (Chapter XX, Faulkes' trans.)

(It is hard to know if the detail about taking their gold in mouthfuls is meant to show how odd the giants are, or if there was some story behind it. Norse myth is full of this sort of tantalizing detail.)

Thiazi was also known as the "lady-wolf", a reference to his kidnapping of Idunn, or "snowshoe deity's fosterer", because he's Skadi's father. The first appears in *Haustlöng*, right at the beginning, before he's even had a chance to blackmail Loki, let alone seize Idunn. *Haustlöng* also has several mentions of Thiazi as Skadi's father, most of which are rather complex kennings like: The rock-Gefn-[giantess-]refuge-[cave-]god [giant], or the bow-string-Var's [Skadi's] whale [ox]. Two others, "Morn's hungry father" and "Morn's father", are simpler to parse, once you know that "Morn" is a generic name for a giantess.

The rest of Thiazi's family don't support the stupid giant hypothesis either, at least if we go by their names. (Which is pretty much all we have for them.) His father is variously given as Alvaldi in *Hárbarðsljóð*, which would mean something like "All-Mighty", or Ölvaldi in Snorri's version, "keeper of the beer". Gang ("Gait"[111], or "Wanderer"[112]) and Idi ("the moveable", "the hard-working one") are less easy to understand. Maybe like Skadi on her skis and Thiazi flying through the sky, we're meant to understand them as moving quickly and ranging across the worlds. (Although Idi makes me think of a handle or other mechanical, turning, device.)

---

[111] Simek 1996: 99.
[112] Motz 1987: 311.

Njord and Skadi

They are mentioned briefly in the *Grottasongr*, which is the chant performed by two giant maidens as they work a mill for the Danish king Frodi:

> *Hrugnir was hard, as was his father,*
> *but Thiazi was mightier than them*
> *Idi and Aurnir, our relations,*
> *rock-giants' brothers: we were born from them.*
> *(Grott. 9 Orchard's trans.)*

It's not clear who Aurnir was, although it might be another name for Gang. According to Simek, the name appears in later kennings[113] and in *thulur* (lists of poetic terms), sometimes as Aurnir, sometimes as Örnir. He suggests that it means something like "rock or earth-dweller", like Auregelmir and Aurboda.[114] (Since Thiazi and Skadi are mountain-giants, that would make sense.)

There may be more similarities between Thiazi and Skadi than we think. *The Shorter Voluspa*, interpolated in *Hynd*, refers to Thiazi as "the giant who loved to shoot". Perhaps he hunted in the mountains, too:

> *Baldr's father was heir to Bur,*
> *Freyr married Gerd, she was Gymir's daughter,*
> *of the giant race, and Aurboda's,*
> *though Thiazi was kinsman, the giant who loved to*
> *shoot; Skadi was his daughter.*
> *(Hynd. 30 Larrington's trans.)*

Although, Andy Orchard has it as "the cover-keen giant" and Hollander has "the skulking thurs", and an older translation by Henry Bellows has "The dark-loving giant". Clearly it's a bit obscure.

I have quoted this verse because it establishes the kinship of the two giant families. The kenning "mountain-Finn" implies a connection between the Finns with their skis, bows, and odd religion and the giants, which I will be discussing in another chapter.

We don't know if there was actual existing lore that Skadi and Gerdr were family, but one can see how they would be grouped together: both giantesses who married Vanir gods. It's interesting that Gerdr has two parents, whereas Skadi

---

[113] http://abdn.ac.uk/skaldic/m.php?p=versei&i=1319
[114] Simek 1996: 252.

conforms to the beautiful giantess/ scary dad/ absent mom pattern that crops up in many of the sagas. In *Gylf* Snorri tells us that Aurboda was one of the mountain giants, so perhaps Skadi and Gerdr were related through her.

Another suggestive point, although I don't want to make too much of it, is the kenning "The battle-bold Rognir [Odin, i.e. chief] of land-whales [giants]," which seems to imply that as Odin is to the gods, so Thiazi is to the giants. It's unusual, to say the least, to compare a god to a giant, and Thjodolf must have had a reason for doing it. Rognir means "Chief"[115] and so its application to Odin is obvious, but why Thiazi gets that title is obscure. It might well tie in with Margaret Clunies-Ross's argument that Thiazi and his aett were both rich and powerful, which is why Thiazi was so bold with the gods, and why they don't just kill Skadi.[116]

There is one parallel with Odin, though, that might suggest itself. Odin seduced the giantess Gunnlod, who was supposed to be guarding the mead of poetry. For three nights he slept with her, each night taking a drink of the mead. When Gunnlod's father discovered what he was up to, Odin changed himself to an eagle and flew off, with the angry giants in hot pursuit, also in eagle form.

Once again the giant dies at the hands of the Aesir, and they get to keep the treasure they stole from the jotuns. The difference between Odin and Thiazi is that Odin succeeded, Thiazi failed. The giant may have stolen the apples and (possibly) made Idunn his sexual partner, but unlike Odin he doesn't get to keep the treasure he stole. While Odin's theft was to benefit himself and the skalds he was patron of, Thiazi's attempt brings no lasting benefit to the giants.

The myth of Thiazi's eyes was well-known also. The poet Bragi Boddason, or Bragi the Old, mentions it in his *Ragnarsdrapa*, which like *Hst* is a shield-poem, depicting various heroic feats of Thor's:

> *He who threw into the wide winds' basin the ski-goddess's [Skadi's] father's eyes above the dwellings of the multitude of men.*
> *(Skld 23 Faulkes)*

---

[115] http://www.theapricity.com/forum/showthread.php?t=270, accessed March 22, 2012.
[116] Clunies-Ross 1994: 67.

There's some ambiguity about this feat, however, because while Thor claims credit for Thiazi's death, and throwing his eyes into the sky as stars in *Hárbarðsljóð*, in Snorri's version (*Skaldskaparmál*) Odin is said to have done it, possibly as an additional bit of compensation to Skadi after Loki makes her laugh.

Both Thiazi and the giant Aurvandil end up giving up parts of their bodies to become stars. Aurvandil lost his toe to frostbite when he and Thor were returning from Jotunheim after he fought Geirrod. Thor had broken off the toe and thrown it up into the sky, where it became a star. There has been some discussion of exactly which star, with Venus and Rigel, the toe of Orion, as the top contenders. (One book shares him out: Alcor in the Ursa Major is the legendary toe, while Rigel is the other big toe.[117]) However, if his toe was Rigel, the rest of Orion should also be associated with him, so it must be Venus. (Etymology seems to back this up; Aurvandil comes from *austaz 'east', which is related to words for dawn, and the second half of his name is related to the words "wend" and "wander".[118]) This seems to follow the pattern of giants as embodying natural phenomena. (See the chapter on giant cults for more on this.)

Another point is that when the gods agree to share their ox-meat with Thiazi, the meat is said to be from the "holy table", in other words a sacrificial offering. (For more on a possible sacral role for Hoenir, see the chapter on his character.)

We don't know just what Thiazi's name means, although there have been many guesses, from "Fat, Large" to "Slave-Binder" to something to do with thunder (this last from the 19th century, natch). Simek covers himself by saying "etymology uncertain", while McKinnell says that in modern Icelandic *thjassi* means "giant, fat man" and suggests that it is related to Old High German *tado*, "king" or Greek τιταν "titan, giant" (originally "father deity") and Sanskrit *tatas*, "father". McKinnell thinks that if Thiazi's name does relate to these older words, then his part of the myth must also be old.[119]

---

[117] Allen: 313.
[118] http://en.wikipedia.org/wiki/Aurvandil
[119] McKinnell 2005: 63, n. 7.

Why does Thiazi stop their food cooking?

> Ími steinn heiti!
> Aldri reykr rjúki!
> Aldri seyðir soðni!
> Út yl, Inn kyl!
> Ími steinn heiti!

> 'Imi heated the stone.
> Never shall the smoke smoke.
> Never shall the cooking be cooked.
> Out heat, in cool!
> Imi heated the stone.'[120]

This rather mysterious runic inscription is possibly a spell to spoil someone's cooking. Imi seems to come from *im*, "embers, ashes, dust". The strong form Ímr appears as a giant-name in *Vafþrúðnismál* 5 and elsewhere as a wolf-name, but there is no other instance in the runic corpus of the verb *heita* 'to heat'.

> Then Odin went to try the wisdom
> of the all-wise giant;
> to the hall he came which Im's father owned;
> Odin went inside.
> (Vaf. 5, Larrington's trans.)

There were also other cooking spells, such as:

> Ud, Ølen, og ind Kjølen! I 3de N.
> 'Out, ale, and in, cool! In the third name.'[121]

The authors think that that "ale" olen, has been substituted for *yl*, "heat". They also instance a inscribed bone found in Lincoln, England, which reads (possibly): "B.... heats the stone" or "A stone is called B....".[122]

It might seem like a particularly pointless thing for Thiazi to do, but as always with myth, it's worth looking more closely. The gods, after all, had stepped out of Asgard, the realm they had so carefully set apart from the realm of the giants. This may very well have been Thiazi's way of teaching them who's boss in Utgard. Very little has been made of the gods taking an ox for their meal, although presumably those

---

[120] McLeod and Mees 2006: 129.
[121] Ibid: 129.
[122] Ibid: 130.

oxen belonged to someone, and that someone might mind their cattle being stolen, killed and eaten.

Another theory has it that he was demanding offerings, just as the gods received them. North, in his translation of *Hst*, suggests as much, noting that the "broad table" would be an altar, and the "sacred meal" speaks for itself. I'm not entirely convinced by this, but there is something neat in the idea of the giants turning the tables on the gods like this.

You could interpret this two ways. First, if you follow Kristensen, the tangled relationship between the gods and giants is one of family and those who will not acknowledge family. Thiazi's gesture can be read as a way to make the gods respect their ancestors, and those who are kin through them. Second, Steinsland thinks that it reflects:

> *...knowledge of an old ritual of sacrifice. The story relates that beyond the limits of the blessed homes of gods and men, tribute is to be paid to the powers who are the owners of the land.*[123]

So Thiazi would be the "owner" of this particular area, or at any rate one of them, and he demanded sacrifice or tribute accordingly.

In the story of Thor's journey to Utgard-loki, he has a similar encounter with the giant Skýmir. He was travelling with his two child companions, Thialfi and Roskva, as well as Loki, and he met up with Skýmir on the way. The giant proposed that they pool their food, but no sooner had Thor taken out their share than Skýmir seized it all and put it in his pack. He then set off so quickly that Thor and co. soon lost him. By the time they caught up, and wanted to make dinner, Skýmir was asleep.

The rest of the story is a humorous account of Thor trying to get his food back, and Skýmir not even noticing Thor's hammer-blows because he is so much larger. So the story is only a half-parallel to Thiazi, because while both steal food, and seem to get away with it, and make a god suffer, the outcome is quite different. Skýmir does not suffer any consequences for his deeds. (You could argue that this is the burlesque element of the story: giants make a fool of Thor and he has to take it.)

---

[123] Steinsland 1987: 219.

Clunies-Ross and Jarich Oosten float two more, even more speculative theories. She offers a Levi-Straussian reading on the subject of hypergamy, where the gods do not want to cook their food (let their women marry out), which is why Idunn has apples and turns into a nut (both raw foods). The giants, on the other hand, are only too eager to cook their food with the gods, which is why Thiazi can cook the ox. In the end, though, his giant appetite betrays him, and he eats most of it. (Which gives a sidelight on Freyja's comment that if she married a giant she would be the most *ragr* of women. It may not just be social demotion she fears, but someone whose appetite even she can't satisfy.)

Jarich Oosten, on the other hand, sees it as an origin myth, pointing to the origins of cooking and time.[124] The gods would have had to give eternal time, where things like cooking can't finish, for the passing of time which allows the food to complete cooking. The downside, of course, is that things that exist in time age, as the Aesir do once they enter the stream of time. The cooking is a precursor to the theft of the apples later.

Also, note that when Loki begrudged the eagle his share of the food, he was coerced into giving Thiazi the apples. (These, being a raw food, require no cooking.) Once again, Oosten thinks, the Aesir got the best of the deal, because they got the ability to cook from Thiazi, and were able to escape the consequences of passing time with the apples Idunn held.

While we're on the subject of cooking, it's worth noting that myth begins with Thiazi messing with the cooking fire that the gods have made, and ends with him being roasted alive.

Thiazi and the Eagle

Despite what you might think, not that many beings in Norse myth can fly. Of those who do, they inevitably do it by means of shapeshifting. Odin can turn himself into an eagle and fly. The giants Thiazi and Suttung also can assume eagle shape, but how exactly they do this we are not told. The giant Hraesvelgr, whose wings are the origin of all the winds, takes the form of an eagle. Loki travels through the air, although he

---

[124] Oosten 1985: 50.

often borrows Freyja or Frigg's bird-form to do it. (We never see either goddess fly, though.) The valkyries and Frigg's handmaiden Gna ride through the air on horses. That's pretty much it.

Some gods, in fact, are famous for their more pedestrian nature, especially Thor, who either walks (across Bifrost to the gods' councils) or rides his chariot, drawn by two goats. At other times he wades across fords in rivers (*Harb*) or takes a boat across the waters. Clunies-Ross points out that when Thor ventures into Jotunheimar, he does so to punish the giants or keep them in order. Odin and Loki, however, fly there, usually with the aim of ripping the giants off.[125]

In the story of Thiazi, however, the moral lines are less clear. Thiazi begins the action by keeping the gods' food from cooking, then stealing most of it. Then he tortures Loki into doing what he wants, abetting a kidnapping of a most vital goddess, Idunn. Thiazi must have known he was taking quite a risk. His first appearance, in eagle form, might be a way of indicating that here was a giant whose powers were well-matched to those of Odin and Loki. Thiazi spends most of the myth in eagle form, actually. He first appears in an enormous tree in that form, drags Loki behind him that way, and later chases Loki again when he steals Idunn back. (Loki betrays him, by the way, and by extension his giant kin, when he lures Thiazi into the trap the Aesir have set for him.[126] Skadi is not the only person seeking revenge in this story.)

It also reinforces the in-betweeness of Loki, who can only assume the powers of the greater gods by borrowing a form from a goddess, here and in the myth of Gerrordr, who imprisoned Loki until he agreed to bring an unarmed Thor to him. (See the first section for more on this story, as it forms the other half of *Hst*, and clearly parallels it.) I discuss Loki's use of women's plumage in a later chapter but it is worth commenting here that clearly more than one kind of in-betweeness is intended.

Idunn

Stephen King once observed of Job that he was the Astroturf in a game of football between God and Satan. Idunn

---

[125] Clunies-Ross 2005: 90.
[126] McKinnell 1987-8: 259.

could be said to be the football between Thiazi and the Aesir. In this, her only myth, she plays a remarkably passive role. We never learn if her time among the giants had any effect on her, or if there were any consequences. Idunn is treated essentially as property in this story. (This has affected retellers of her tale; she is often referred to as "stolen" or her kidnapping as a "theft".)

The basics on Idunn are: married to the poet-god Bragi, no known children, accused by Loki of sleeping with her brother's slayer, but no known myth to substantiate it. (Also, since Bragi is exposed as a coward in the same poem, *Lks*, it seems unlikely that he was the guilty party.[127]) Other than that, the most famous thing about Idunn is her apples.

Apples

Idunn's function in Norse myth is to keep the apples of immortality, without which the gods begin to age. As Snorri tells us in *Gylf*:

> 'His wife is Idunn. In her private wooden box she keeps the apples, which the gods bite into when they begin to grow old. They all become young again, and so it will be right up to Ragnarok.[128]

The apples are often said to function as fertility symbols, and indeed in another myth a childless king is visited by Frigg's servant, who gives him an apple for him and his wife to eat. The magic is effective, and they have a son. (More on this story below.)

Apart from that, apples have been found in graves, sometimes along with wooden buckets, and occasionally along with nuts (which are also significant for Idunn). In an eleventh-century poem Thorbiorn Brúnarson says that his wife gives him "apples of Hel", implying that she wants him to die.[129] The apple has a somewhat double-edged meaning in this regard: in Celtic and Greek myths, the apple is the food of immortals, and prolongs life, but only as long as one stays in the otherworld.

---

[127] Since Gerdr greets Skirnir in Skirnirsmal by saying she fears he is her brother's slayer, some (e.g.: Davidson 1964: 164, n. 1) have seen a conection between her and Idunn.
[128] Byock 2005: 36.
[129] Davidson 1990: 165.

Njord and Skadi

There is, for example, an Irish story in which a fairy woman gives a man named Connlae an otherworldly apple that satisfies all hunger and never diminishes. The woman tells Connlae that she comes from *tír inna mbéo* 'the land of the living ones', and eventually he joins her there, thus gaining immortality. [130]

We know of other magical apples in various traditions, usually heavily guarded, such as the apple of the Hesperides, in Greek myth, and the ones in the Irish story of the Sons of Tuireann. Both are far-off, and well protected.

The story of the sons of Tuireann is an interesting one for us, because it has many of the same motifs as the Idunn story, but jumbled about. Shapeshifting is an important part of this story, as it begins with a terrible mistake. The three sons of Tuireann are out hunting, and kill a pig, which as it dies reverts to human shape; the body is that of the god Lugh's father. Lugh then lays a fine on the three brothers, who have to get him various precious objects from all over the world. He disguises this at first by simply saying he wants three apples, a pigskin, etc. But then he explains:

> "The three apples I asked of you are the three apples from the Garden in the East of the World, and no other apples will do but these, for they are the most beautiful and have most virtue in them of the apples of the whole world. And it is what they are like, they are of the colour of burned gold, and they are the size of the head of a child a month old, and there is the taste of honey on them, and they do not leave the pain of wounds or the vexation of sickness on any one that eats them, and they do not lessen by being eaten for ever..."[131]

And of course the other objects will prove equally unusual and hard to get.

The Brothers set sail for the Garden in the East, and when they get there, decide that rather than risk an encounter with the local king's fighting men, they will use their Druid rods, and turn themselves into hawks, and carry off an apple each in their claws. The news spread that the apples were being stolen, and the king's three daughters took the form of ospreys, sending flashes of lighting at the

---

[130] McGrath 2012: 18-9.
[131] Lady Gregory 1904: 56-7.

Brothers, which scorched them. The Brothers turned themselves into swans and took to the water, so losing the ospreys.

The Hesperides, however, were located in the West. (The location of their island was never stated, and sources differ on whether it was a single tree or an orchard that grew there.) The apples were once again golden, and they were a wedding gift from to Zeus and Hera from the earth-goddess Gaia. Hera did not trust the nymphs who guarded the tree to stay away from the fruit, and set the dragon Ladon to guard the tree. The story peters out after this, as there is no shapeshifting or chases involved in Hercules' theft of the apples. He did trick Atlas into getting them for him, and then tricked him again when he returned by fooling him into resuming the burden of the world. (This could be vaguely connected to Loki's back-and-forth with Idunn.)

Another connotation for apple might support Clunies-Ross' contention that it is Idunn, and not the apples, that was the magic rejuvenator:

In Graeco-Roman literature, the apple was used as a metaphor for beauty and love. Sappho likened a young bride to a 'sweet apple' (*gluku'malon*) (Powell 2007, 27). The word μη☐λων *(mēlon)* was a widely-used metaphor for courtship and marriage rites in Greek art and poetry (Winkler 1996, 104). The gift of a fruit (particularly an apple) was a symbol of courtship in many cultures, such as Greek, Roman and Byzantine (Littlewood 1967; 1993). It symbolized fertility, by means of the distribution of seed through the sharing of the fruit.[132]

There are also many instances in Irish literature of apples as love-tokens.[133] One final point about the apple in these stories is that the sweet apple came north with the Romans - native varieties were more like crab apples.[134] I suppose you could choke them down in return for immortality, but a forever of small, bitter apples is not something to look forward to.

Nor has the apple's association with love and fruitfulness gone away. Most of us have twisted an apple's stalk to learn

---

[132] McGrath 2012: 19.
[133] Ibid: 20.
[134] Davidson 1990:165.

the initial of our husband-to-be, and apparently if you take the seeds from an apple in your hand, and then clap your hand to your forehead, you can tell your fortune from the number of seeds that stick to your face. And of course there's peeling an apple as one long piece, then throwing it over your shoulder to see your true love's initial.

Nuts are also associated with Idunn, thanks to Snorri's information. He tells us that Loki brought Idunn back to Asgard in that form, and we can't help but notice that while nuts are small, and easily concealed, they are also fertility symbols. Nuts are, after all, seeds. Throwing nuts at weddings is a common custom, even if rice is less likely to bruise. Fruit and nuts have also been found in graves in southern England and mainland Europe, presumably as food for the afterlife.[135] Incidentally, if Loki turned Idunn into a walnut, as one modern retelling has it, it might be noted that walnuts are the "most masculine"[136] of nuts. In a story where everyone else gets to gender-bend, this could be Idunn's moment.

Notice also, that Loki was thinking very clearly when he turned Idunn into a nut. A nut may be a fruit, same as an apple, but a hard shell protects it.

Rejuvenating One

Both Clunies-Ross and Lindow argue that it was Idunn, rather than any magic apples, which carried the secret of eternal youth. Her name, "Ever-Young", tells us that. In fact, *Hst* refers to her as the "maiden who understood the eternal life of the Aesir" but without any mention of apples.[137]

Kristensen, in his paper "Why Was Odin Killed by Fenrir?" observes that Idunn's loss is treated as seriously as the loss of Freyja and the sun and moon would be in the MasterBuilder myth, and the loss of Freyja in Thrym. The latter is an instructive parallel, since both Thrym and Thiazi try to take from the Aesir some of their most precious powers: the power of sexuality in Freyja, and the power of immortality in Idunn. In both myths, the giants' lust for the goddesses

---

[135] Ibid: 166.
[136] http://symbolism.wikia.com/wiki/Walnuts
[137] Lindow 2001: 198.

motivates the action, and in both myths Loki, of mixed heritage, acts as a go-between.

Clunies-Ross in particular sees Idunn's power as that of sexual reproduction, which ensures the eternal life of the family, even if individuals must die. This would be an extremely dangerous thing to let fall into the hands of the giants, as it would be to the gods' detriment. You will notice that when giants steal one of the goddesses, or threaten to, it is almost always Freyja, the sexual principle incarnate, that they want. Stealing Idunn moves the focus from sex to its probable result, but it is the same thing. The giants would be able to reproduce, while the Aesir would not.

Further, in Grundvig's translation of *Skirnismal*, he changed the relatively meaningless "eleven" (*ellifo*) apples Skirnir offers Gerdr into "of medicine for age" (*ellilyfs*)[138]. A lot of people accepted this emendation because it makes a lot more sense - Freyr, the god who was known for his sexuality, would offer Gerdr the apples of immortality, in both senses: continuation of family and life among the Aesir with an unending supply of such "medicine". *Skld* 22 and *Hst* 9 also use the word *ellilyfs* to describe Idunn's apples.[139]

We've already discussed apples as fertility symbols, but one instance from Norse myth itself illustrates the point I am making. In Chapter Two of the *Volsunga saga*, King Rerir goes to a mound to pray for a son, because he and his wife have no children. Frigg hears his prayer and sends one of the valkyries to drop an apple into his lap. He and the queen both eat some of the apple, and after six years of pregnancy, the queen has a caesarean, and a nearly full-grown boy is cut from her before she dies. He is named Volsung.[140] (Note that the widely-available William Morris translation turns Frigg into Freyja.[141]) The fact that he was sitting on a mound (presumably a burial mound) is suggestive; it makes a very economical point about family continuity, among other things.

---

[138] West 2007: 159, n. 134.
[139] Ibid.
[140] Grimstad 2000: 79-81.
[141] http://www.perseus.tufts.edu/hopper/text?doc=Perseus%3Atext%3A2003.02.0003%3Achapter%3D2

This is precisely the point about Idunn. Whether she herself or her apples are the rejuvenating element is almost beside the point, although to a human audience the continuity of family line would be one of the few forms of immortality they could hope for. If Hoenir stands for eternal life through poetic commemoration, Idunn stands for reproduction and the family.

Given all this, we should not be surprised when, in *Gylf*, Gangleri expresses concern that such power is in the hands of a woman; he says, "Of great importance to the gods it must be, it seems to me, that Idun preserves these apples with care and honesty." (Gylf 26) Motz compares the stories of Idunn and the giantess Gunnlod, who kept the precious mead of poetry. Odin, like Thiazi, deceived the woman and stole the treasure, but unlike the giant, Odin got away with it.[142] Also, we suspect that Idunn was not weeping when she went back to Asgard. Whether Idunn and Thiazi had sex is something that Snorri keeps silent about.

Traffic in Women

If, as Levi-Strauss posited, "the exchange of women [is] a fundamental principle of kinship", then the control of the flow of women is important to make sure the right people are kin.[143] (Levi-Strauss seems to agree with retellers of this myth who view Idunn as merely property to be exchanged or stolen.)

So the Aesir have to make sure that the giants do not get hold of any Asyniur, as that would bring them into a relationship they do not want. Fair exchange is the last thing on the gods' minds. Of course, if you view the giants as unqualifiedly evil, you will feel that this is fair and just. (No doubt that would be Thor's view.) Anyone who's read this far has probably worked out that my view is somewhat different.

I've discussed this theory elsewhere, but briefly, Aesir men marry Aesir women, and no one else does. Vanir cannot marry Aesir, and seem to have shortage of potential spouses, so they marry "down" to the giants. Giant women might marry a Van, but giants can forget about Freyja, and they'd better not even consider an Asynia. (This apparently goes for

---

[142] Motz 1993: 51.
[143] Rubin 2011: 177.

dwarves as well, as Thor shows in *Alvissmal*, where he tricks a wise dwarf into being turned to stone, under the guise of a suitor test.)

Hst expresses the situation when this flow is reversed succinctly:

> The bright-shield-dwellers [giants] were not unhappy after this, now Idunn was among the giants, newly arrived from the south. All Ingi-Freyr's kin [Æsir] became old and grey in their assembly; the powers were rather ugly in form...
> (Faulkes' trans.)

The giants were prospering, and the gods were growing old and feeble. Not too feeble to threaten Loki with dire punishment if he didn't get her back, however. The gods were facing one of their most dangerous moments, with immortal giants ranged against suddenly aging (and presumably weakened) gods.

In this context, it is interesting that Skirnir offered the giantess Gerdr golden apples if she would marry Freyr. It might seem like as much of a capitulation as when Freyr hands over his sword, but it could also be read as an endorsement of Skadi's way of getting what the gods have: marry one. Gerdr refuses, whether because she thinks Skadi got a poor deal, or because she does not want to reproduce the line of the Vanir, is unknown. How Skirnir and Freyr got hold of Idunn's apples (if they are hers, and not just random golden apples) is also unknown.

Balder

Picture this for a moment: a heroic character takes up their armour and weapons and makes the arduous journey to another world. When they get there, they force their way in among alien people, and demand a spouse. Their eye lights on one known for beauty and goodness. The father, however, insists on a test - you have to choose by looking at their feet. Our would-be suitor makes the wrong choice, and everything goes downhill from there, ending in divorce.

Sounds like every bridal-quest narrative you've ever heard or read (except for the ending)? The only thing missing is a dragon or other monster. But it's the tale of Skadi's journey to Asgard, which for a giant was probably just as heroic as Thor and Odin journeying to Jotunheim. And doesn't Balder sound like any attractive young maiden about whom no praise is hyperbole? (Think of the descriptions of princesses in Grimm's tales, for example.) Like those princesses, Balder is completely passive, although unlike them, he was probably hoping to dodge the bullet on this one. (Although you have to wonder sometimes; imagine the king telling his daughter, "Guess what, darling, that smelly swineherd has saved the kingdom, so I've promised him your hand in marriage.")

Because this is known as a myth about Njord and Skadi, it is easy to forget that Njord was never her intended target - she wanted the chief god's only son, Balder. That is presumably part of why the marriage failed; Skadi didn't get what she wanted, and Njord probably didn't appreciate being treated as the booby prize. What woman wouldn't choose a young, good-looking, well-connected husband over a man old enough to have grown children?

The other point to make about Skadi's desire for Balder is that she was trying to accomplish what her father did not. He stole from the gods the power that kept them immortal; his daughter planned to marry the god who would survive Ragnarok, the god who was the only legitimate son of the chief god; in other words, the highest-status god on offer.

She was playing for high stakes. (Of course, there's always John Lindow's theory that she was just blown away by a beautiful foot, just as Freyr was by Gerdr's arms.) So were the Aesir, since it wasn't in their interest to marry their best and brightest god off to a giantess. Clunies Ross thinks that this was the whole point of the Cinderella-style line-up: there is a similar story involving the whitest hand, which turns out to belong to the blacksmith. She thinks that a sea-god would similarly have the whitest feet, and so in both cases occupation trumps gentle birth, and fools the woman making the choice.[144]

In the event, Balder married Nanna, known mainly for dying of grief and being laid on his funeral pyre. Fittingly, like him she exists to die.[145] And, since she is listed among the Asyniur, or goddesses, Odin must have pleased about their marriage.

---

[144] Clunies-Ross 1994: 123.
[145] Lindow 1997: 91.

Oosten notes a structural opposition between the myths of Skadi's marriage and Baldr's death:

> *The opposition between alliance and war, marriage and death is also expressed in the relations between the myth of Balder and the myth of the marriage of Njord and Skadi. Skadi wanted to marry Balder but chose Njord instead. Her condition, that the gods should make her laugh, is in direct opposition to the demand made in the myth of Balder, that all beings should weep. Weeping and laughing express contrary emotions, but the expression of emotions in itself can be considered as an expression of life, while the refusal of emotions can be considered a denial of life. Marriage establishes a social relationship between two groups in order to create new life.*[146]

(He also considers the Saxo version of Balder's death, in which Balder and Hoder are rivals for Nanna, and fight for her. He puts this beside the myth of *Skr*, and points out that when you substitute either Van for Balder, the result is marriage and life instead of death.)

To return to the Cinderella theme, it is usually Njord's feet that get the attention, but surely Balder's feet deserve as much. You would think that the god who was always depicted as "shining" and beautiful would have nice feet. I've always wondered if Odin sent him to rub mud on them or something. I suppose you could say that in this version of Cinderella Skadi ended up with an ugly stepsister, although that seems a little hard on Njord.

One final note on the theme of male passivity: it is interesting that in this myth, all the gods are passive: things happen to them. On the other hand, the giants and half-giants are active, and move the action forward. Thiazi enchants the cooking-fire, Loki strikes him, the two of them chase each other across the sky, then Skadi travels to Asgard, where she gets her pick of a husband (even if the choice is rigged), and later she leaves Njord. Perhaps this is one of the ways in which this myth is meant to be a burlesque, but it is unusual.

---

[146] Oosten 1985: 46.

Chapter 5

Asgard, Jötunheim, Midgard: Where Are They?

This is a question with two answers, broadly speaking. Some of the Eddic poems, and Snorri Sturluson's *Edda*, suggest a model of nine worlds, with various paths connecting them, such as the rainbow bridge Bifrost. Snorri's Edda also has a more earthly version, which locates Asgard, Vanaheim and the rest in the real world.

The Prologue of the *Prose Edda* considers the gods human beings of unusual ability and intelligence who have been deified by those who came after them.[147] Since Odin, Thor and the rest are human, Snorri locates Asgard and all the rest on earth, giving specific locations for each "heim".

The first book of the Edda, *Gylf*, tells a very different version of how the world began, and how the cosmos is laid out. In this story we are told how King Gylfi of Sweden set out for Asgard, where he met three mysterious men named High, Just-as-High, and Third, who describe to him the version of the Norse worlds most of us are familiar with.

According to them, in the beginning there were only two worlds, Muspellzheimr (Muspell-Home) and Niflheimr (Dark-Home). Between them was the abyss known as Ginnungagap (usually translated as "Yawning Void", but also "Void filled with magical (and creative) power"[148]). There the sparks from the fiery world of Muspellzheimr met the ice from Niflheimr and created the first being, the giant Ymir.

As Ymir slept, he sweated, and from under his arm came a male and female, while from between his feet - or legs - came a son. They produced more generations of frost-giants

---

[147] Wikipedia entry "Euhemerism":
http://en.wikipedia.org/wiki/Euhemerism
[148] Simek 1996: 109. (Etymologies for Musp. and Nifl. also come from Simek: 222-3 and 232.)

(although Snorri doesn't specify who did what with whom to produce these giants.)

Ymir meanwhile fed on the milk from the cow Audhumla, who also came from the melting ice. The ice was salty, and Audhumla used it as a salt lick, until finally she freed from the ice another being, Buri. It is not clear what sort of being he was, but we are told he was beautiful.

His son, Bor, married Bestla, a giantess, and they had three sons: Odin, Vili and Ve.

Odin and his brothers killed Ymir, and made the world from his body.

> [The earth] round the edge, around it lies the deep sea, and along the shore of this sea they gave lands to live in to the races of giants. But on the earth on the inner side they made a fortification round the world against the hostility of giants, and for the fortification they used the giant Ymir's eyelashes, and they called the fortification Midgard.
> (Gylf 8, Faulkes)

As the three gods walked along the seashore, they found two pieces of wood, from which they fashioned the first humans, to whom they gave Midgard. They then built themselves a city in the middle of the world, which they called Asgard, and Snorri tells us is also called Troy.

The blood that gushed forth from Ymir's murder drowned all but two of the giants, but fortunately for the giants, they were a breeding pair.

Nine Worlds

Our other main source for cosmological information is the *Poetic Edda*, and in particular the *Vsp*, dealing as it does with the beginning and end of things. The first thing we learn is that there were nine worlds, although they are not named:

> 2. I remember yet | the giants of yore,
> Who gave me bread | in the days gone by;
> Nine worlds I knew, | the nine in the tree
> With mighty roots | beneath the mold.
> (Bellows)

In addition to *Vsp*, *Vaf*, which is a wisdom-contest between Odin and the giant Vafthrudnir, mentions the nine worlds amidst much other lore:

> *"Of the etins' lore and of all godheads,*
> *sooth, and but sooth, I say*
> *for I have seen all the worlds 'neath the welkin.*
> *Nifhel beneath nine worlds I saw,*
> *to which the dead are doomed."*
> (Vafth. 43, Hollander)

One final mention of the nine worlds appears in Snorri's *Edda*, in a rather ominous context. In the section dealing with Loki's monstrous children, we are told:

> *Hel he threw down into Nifhelheim and made her ruler over nine worlds.*
> (Gylf 43, Byock)

So clearly Snorri was aware of the nine worlds model, he just didn't feel the need to discuss it in detail.

I should emphasize here that it's very difficult to map the nine worlds precisely. They overlap, and some of them duplicate each other. Snorri uses the terms Nifhel (Dark Hell) and Niflheim (Dark World) interchangeably, although Niflheim doesn't appear in the *Poetic Edda*. (Simek thinks Snorri invented the name, if not the concept.) There is also confusion about whether Nifhel and Hel are the same, or whether Nifhel is a darker, lower version of Hel itself.[149]

Who Lives in these Worlds?

To learn who lives in these nine worlds, and what they are called, we must look elsewhere. *Alvissmal*, another wisdom-contest, gives us some more information. It is structured as a contest between Thor and a dwarf, Alvis or "All-wise", in which Thor sensibly sticks to questioning the dwarf, delaying until the sun rises and petrifies him.

We can infer the existence of six of the worlds from the answers Alvis gives when questioned about the names of different things, here, the wind:

> *'Wind it's called by men, the waverer by the gods,*
> *the mighty Powers say neigher,*

---

[149] Ibid: 232.

*whooper the giants, din-journeyer the elves,
in hell they call it stormer.'
(Alv. 19-20, Larrington)*

Oddly, he does not mention dwarves, despite being one. Clearly there is no taboo, however, since in verse 14 he says:

*'Moon it's called by men, and fiery one by the gods,
in hell it's the whirling wheel,
the giants call it the hastener, the dwarfs the shiner,
elves call it counter of years.'
(Alv. 14, Larrington)*

So we have seven worlds, presumably as follows:

1. Menn (humans): Miðgarðr.
2. Aesir (gods): Ásgarðr.
3. Vanir (gods): Vanaheimr.
4. Jötnar (giants): Jötunheimr.
5. Álfar (elves): Álfheimr.
6. Náir (corpses, the other world of the dead): Hel.[150]

Add to this Muspellzheimr and Niflheimr and you have nine.

Since this book is not primarily about cosmology, I will leave it at that, and discuss the four worlds that bear upon the subject of this book: Asgard, Vanaheim, Midgard and Jotunheim.

Ásgard

The "Gods' Enclosure", or "Home of the Aesir", where Odin has his residence, Valhalla. Snorri rationalized it by giving it an earthly location. In *Gylf* he placed it in the middle of the world, as a city called Asgard, also known as Troy. In the *Ys* he moved it further east:

*To the east of Tanakvisl [the river Don] in Asia was known as Asaland [land of the aesir] or Asa-heimr [world of the aesir], and the principal stronghold in the land they called Asgard.
(Yngl. Ch. 2, Lindow)*

---

[150] Wikipedia entry "Nine Worlds":
http://en.wikipedia.org/wiki/Norse_cosmology

Asgard mainly appears in Snorri's writing, although it is also mentioned in *Thrym, Hymskvida*, and a verse by the skald Þorbjörn dísarskáld.

> *They travelled far away that day*
> *from Asgard, until they reached Egil's.*
> *He took care of their goats with their splendid horns,*
> *while they turned towards Hymir's hall.*
> *(Hymsk. 7, Orchard)*
>
> *Then said Loki, the son of Laufey:*
> *'Be quiet, Thor, don't speak these words!*
> *The giants will be settling in Asgard*
> *unless you get your hammer back.'*
> *(Thrym. 18, Larrington)*
> "Thor has defended Asgard and Ygg's [Odin's] people [the gods] with strength."
> Þorbjörn dísarskáld, quoted in Skáldskaparmál 4.

All three also stress the danger that the giants present to the Aesir, and Thor's role as defender against them.

There is some ambiguity as to where exactly Asgard is located. Some references, such as the Master-Builder tale, seem to suggest that Asgard is part of Midgard, or at least very close to it. The section of *Gylf* which deals with Ymir's death also states that Asgard was in the middle of the world, presumably Midgard.

Snorri, however, sees it as celestial. The idea of Bifrost, a heavenly bridge, guarded by Himinbjorg, "Heavenly Protection", backs this up.[151] Once again, it is unclear if this reflects a Christian world-view, or if the lore itself was vague.

Vanaheim

"Home of the Vanir", usually imagined as a counterpart to Asgard. We have just one source for it in the older poetry, in *Vaf* 39, where we are told that Njord came from Vanaheim, and that he will return there at Ragnarok. Snorri echoes this in *Gylf*, in the chapter on Njord.

In his other writing, especially *Ys*, he makes Vanaheim part of his euhemeristic schema, adding it to his tripartite model of the earth, with some more local information:

---

[151] Simek 1996: 20.

> To the south of the fells which lie outside all the inhabited land there runs through Sweden the Great a river which in proper speech is called the Tanais; it was formerly called the Tanakvisl or Vankvisl; it flows out into the Black Sea. In the olden days the land between the Vanaforks was called Vanaland or Vanaheim.
> (Yng. 1, Monsen and Smith)

(The Tanais is the River Don in Russia.) The description goes on:

> The land east of the Tana Fork was called the Land or Home of the Aesir, and the capital of that country they called Ásgarth.
> (Yng. 2, Hollander)

(I used Hollander's translation because his version was clearer.) It should be noted, by the way, that some, Rudolf Simek[152] in particular, have reservations about Vanaheim, which they think was made up to match Asgard: one for the Aesir, one for the Vanir. For more on this, see the chapter on the Vanir.

Midgard

There is some ambiguity about "Middle-Enclosure", the world of men. The name sometimes refers to the place, and sometimes to the wall that surrounds it. In *Harb*, for example, Thor says that:

> great would be the giant-race, if they all lived:
> mankind would be nothing, under middle-earth.
> (Harb. 23, Orchard)

which suggests that humanity lived below the enclosure-walls. Snorri's description agrees:

> It [the earth] is disk shaped, and around the outside is the deep sea, and along the edge of the sea they gave lands to the giants to settle, and inside on the earth they made a stronghold around the earth on account of the enmity of the giants, and for this wall they used Ymir's eyebrows, and they called the stronghold Midgard.
> (Gylf Lindow)

The detail about Ymir's eyebrows probably comes from *Grim.* 41, where we are also told that they formed Midgard.

---

[152] Simek 2010.

This may sound a bit strange, but the myths have it that the cosmos was made from the different parts of Ymir's body after his grandsons Odin, Vili and Ve slew him and dismembered him. (It reads a little bit like what would happen if Fergus Henderson and Mike Holmes were gods, and collaborated.) In true nose-to-tail style, every bit of Ymir's body became some part of the world, i.e. clouds from his brain, rocks from his bones, trees from his hair.

In other references, Midgard is a synonym for earth or world, although in Snorri it sometimes seems to be the residence of gods and humans, in opposition to the lands of the giants. Perhaps because of this common usage, Midgard is the only one of the world-names that enjoyed wide currency amongst the Germanic languages.[153] Orchard says the Old English word *middangeard* was used to gloss the Latin *orbis uel cosmus* ("world or cosmos").[154]

Jötunheim

"Giant-Home" is variously located, in some sources being east and in others north. Thus in several places we are told that Thor was "off east" smashing giants, i.e. Lks. (*Vsp*, *Skr*, and *Thyrmskvida* all mention Jotunheim in this sense, as well as *Hst* itself.) It is separated from Midgard by various rivers, such as the Ifing, just as Hel is, and Járnvid.

Simek tells us that as geographical knowledge expanded, Jotunheim moved further and further north, which may also correlate to medieval ideas of hell being in the north.[155] In *Hst*, we are told that Idunn came *sunnan*, "from the south"[156]. Snorri's *Edda* also places it in the north, and Wanner argues that the later sources preserve pagan lore, rather than being influenced by medieval Christianity.[157]

Lindow, on the other hand, thinks that any uninhabited area around the homesteads of men could be conceived of as part of the giants' realms, be it scrub, mountains, forests, or

---

[153] Lindow 2001: 229.
[154] Orchard 1998/2002: 252.
[155] Simek 1996: 180.
[156] Wanner 2009b: 45.
[157] Ibid: 45.

other wild territory.[158] (The quote about Ymir's death, above, states that the giants lived on the peripheries of Midgard.)

Jotunheim survived the demise of paganism, and is mentioned in many later sagas as a remote area, usually in the north or north-east. Glaesisvellir, an otherworldly realm similar to the Irish fairy-realms, was located there.

There are several giant-steads to echo gods' residences like Valhalla, Noatun, and Folkvangr. Thiazi lived in Thrymheim, the giant Geirrod, who kidnapped Loki, lived in Geirrodargard, and Gerdr's father had a homestead, although we never learn its name.

---

[158] Lindow 2001: 206.

CHAPTER 6

Are there any stories similar to this myth?

Hadingus and Regnilda

*"Why do I linger in the shadows,
enfolded by rugged hills,
not following the waves as before?
The challenging howl of the wolf-pack,
the ungovernable ferocity
of beasts, cries of dangerous
brutes ever raised to heaven
snatch all rest from my eyes.
The mountains are desolate
to hearts bent on sterner schemes.
The unbending cliffs and harsh
terrain oppress those whose souls
delight in the high seas.
To sound the straits with our oars,
revel in plundered wealth,
pursue for our coffers another's
fortune and gloat over sea-loot
would be far finer work
than haunting the winding forest-
tracks and barren ravines."*

*"The chant of the birds torments me lagging here on the
shore, disturbing me with their jabber whenever I try to
sleep, and I hear the ceaseless roar and fury of the tide
as it takes away the gentle repose from my slumbering
eyes. There is no relaxation at night for the shrill chatter
of the sea-mew, dinning its stupid screech into my tender
ears, for it will not allow me to rest in my bed or be
refreshed but ominously caws away in dismal
modulations. For me there's a safer and sweeter thing -
to sport in the woods. How could you crop a more
meagre share of peace in light or darkness than by
tossing on the shifting deep?"*
(Fisher and Davidson)

Njord and Skadi

First off, I have to say that I prefer Snorri Sturluson's style to Saxo Grammaticus'. It has the merit of brevity.

Saxo obviously lifted the dialogue from either Snorri or the poet Snorri quotes, and shoehorned it rather awkwardly into the story of Hadingus and Regnilda. Hadingus was a typical Norse hero, who rescued and married Regnilda, and now is pining for his former life of adventure.

There's no suggestion that Regnilda is going to go sailing with her husband - that would be completely unprecedented for a Viking's wife. Nor is she on the sea-shore when she makes her complaint. She says what she says because it balances Hadingus' complaint about living in the mountains. Also, Hadingus is upset because he wants to go sea faring, not because he finds it hard to fit into Regnilda's world, in which he has lived for several years before he starts to get restless.

If you follow Georges Dumézil, Hadingus can't help but say what he did, because he's a human avatar of Njord, the sea-god. Dumézil thought that in certain circumstances the myths associated with gods might be displaced downwards onto heroic figures or even ordinary mortals. In his book *From Myth to Fiction* he made a case for Hadingus following the career of Njord in outline. (He also applied his theory to Roman legendary history, finding several instances of the 1st-function double-act of sovereignty and magic that was a cornerstone of his theory.)

Dumézil thought that Hadingus' career follows two tracks, one Odinic and therefore 1st-function, and an Njord-like one which is obviously more 3rd-function. Dumézil argued that just as Njord went to live with the Aesir, and in the *Ynglingtal* anyway, adopted their way of life, Hadingus chose to follow the Odinic path, in his argument, and thus (ironically) followed Njord. The more Vanic points of Hadingus' career are:

1. incestuous marriage/relationship
2. giant-killing
3. ring sewn up in leg, Regnilda finds him by it
4. both Regnilda and Skadi make free choices
5. complaint in the mountains

Njord and Skadi

I will examine each in turn.

1) Hadingus' first major relationship is with his former foster-mother, a giantess named Harthgrepta. I'm not sure their relationship is properly incestuous in law, although when Harthgrepa says:

> Let this hateful stiffness yield
> let a proper warmth inspire you,
> tie me with the bond of passion.
> For first I gave you the milk of my breast
> fed you as a baby boy,
> performing all a mother's duties
> rendering every necessary service.[159]
> (Fisher and Davidson)

which suggests emotional if not legal boundaries being crossed. Harthgrepa accompanies Hadingus in his travels, until other giants rip her to pieces. The text is unclear, but since a corpse has just cursed her for trying to enchant it, the attack may be the result of her attempt at necromancy.

As we already know, Njord apparently had been married to his sister, although he had to leave her when he went to live with the Aesir, as they did not permit such unions. Unlike Harthgrepa, we have no record of his sister dying violently. (See the relevant chapter for more on Njord's mysterious sister.)

2) The giant-killing episode is a bit confused if we assume it's meant to mirror Njord's career, because Hadingus' eventual wife, Regnilda, has been betrothed to the giant that Hadingus kills, which means she combines Skadi's and Idunn's roles. Hadingus, in fact, performs a much more heroic role, since he determines to rescue Regnilda from the degradation of marriage to a giant, and kills the giant himself. I suppose we could assume that Njord did his bit in setting and maintaining the fires that led to Thiazi's death, as did all the Aesir, but of course in a heroic tale, as opposed to a myth, the hero needs to play an active part.

3) Now we come to a part of the story that definitely echoes the Njord - Skadi myth. Hadingus defeated the giant, but in doing so was injured himself, and lay unconscious, nursed by Regnilda. She wanted to be sure she would know

---

[159] Davidson and Fisher 1996: 22.

him again, and sewed a ring into a wound in his leg. (These days he'd sue her.) As the text has it:

> *Later on, when her father had granted her the freedom to choose her own husband, she reviewed the young men who had assembled at the banquet and handled their limbs in an attentive fashion, searching for the token she had once laid away. Detecting the clue of the concealed ring, she scorned the rest and embraced Hading, consequently marrying the man who had not allowed a giant to possess her as his wife.*[160]

One wonders what thoughts went through their minds as she was feeling their legs. The parallel is clear, however, although Skadi stopped at viewing them.

4) One unusual feature of both the Skadi and Regnilda stories is that both are able to make free choice of their own husband, although Skadi's is somewhat constrained, due to the feet-only rule. I will be discussing elsewhere just how unusual this was, and what an Old Norse audience would have made of it, but it is important to both stories.

In Skadi's case, it is a core part of the story that she is frustrated in her desire for Baldr, and winds up with Njord, in what seems like a free choice of her own. In Regnilda's case, it would be little use her sewing the ring in Hadingus' leg if she couldn't freely choose him afterwards.

5) Both Hadingus's and Regnilda's complaint obviously echo Njord and Skadi's, although they aren't really motivated in the same way. Regnilda's complaint makes no sense; she's nowhere near the sea, although you could argue that she getting in her complaining first.

Hadingus' complaint is a bit odd, too, since he doesn't want to go and live by the sea-shore, he wants to go a-Viking; he misses the adventures he used to have. Presumably Saxo (or whoever told the story he heard or read) knew the verses from Snorri and felt that they fitted Hadingus' discontent with life in the interior.

In conclusion, then, the story of Hadingus and Regnilda was inspired, or at least assisted, by the Njord - Skadi myth. It's hard to know if this is a case of literary borrowing, i.e. Saxo knew the myth, and used it to shape his own story, or if

---

[160] Ibid: 30.

the two had become intertwined at a much earlier stage. (I should note here that in the introduction to Book One of *The History of the Danes*, Davidson and Fischer take apart Dumézil's arguments, although they do note the similarities of the verses. They just aren't convinced that Hadingus and Njord are similar in any other way, including the leg inspection, which they say is a very common folktale motif.[161]) The only dissimilarity is that we know of no breach between the heroic couple, whereas the god and goddess became the most famous exemplars of incompatibility.

Kormak's Saga

> *That evening Steingerd came out of her bower, and a maid with her. Said the maid, "Steingerd mine, let us look at the guests."*
> *"Nay," she said, "no need": and yet went to the door, and stepped on the threshold, and spied across the gate. Now there was a space between the wicker and the threshold, and her feet showed through. Cormac saw that, and made this song:*
> *(1) "At the door of my soul she is standing,*
> *So sweet in the gleam of her garment:*
> *Her footfall awakens a fury,*
> *A fierceness of love that I knew not,*
> *Those feet of a wench in her wimple,*
> *Their weird is my sorrow and troubling,*
> *- Or naught may my knowledge avail me -*
> *Both now and for aye to endure."*
> *Then Steingerd knew she was seen. She turned aside into a corner where the likeness of Hagbard was carved on the wall, and peeped under Hagbard's beard. Then the firelight shone upon her face.*[162]
> *(W.G. Collingwood & J. Stefansson)*

You don't have to strain too hard to see the parallels between *Kormak's Saga* and the Njord - Skadi myth. I might add that in the second verse that Kormak makes, he mentions Steingerd's feet again: "once more I looked at the ankles of the nobly-grown woman"[163]. We have to assume that at this point in the narrative he hasn't seen anything

---

[161] Ibid: 12-3.
[162] http://omacl.org/Cormac/
[163] Poole: 38.

else of her, so the parallel with the line-up of the various gods is strengthened.

As the saga unfolds, we learn that although Kormak and Steingerd were to marry, he doesn't turn up on the day, although there is no doubt that he loves her, and she him. In their case, this is due to a curse an old woman lays on Kormak after he kills her sons and drives her from her home, all unjust and dishonourable actions. So unlike Njord and Skadi, they don't make it past the altar, but like them, they end up separated, although it's by outside circumstances as much as their own natures. (As Steingerd later points out, a lot of what happened is Kormak's fault.)

One interesting point is that Steingerd takes matters into her own hands with regards to her marriage, telling Kormak to ask for her hand. Her choice may not be as free as Skadi's, but both of them do their best to get their man. Steingerd speaks a verse, too, a love-verse, which is unusual in Icelandic sagas. In fact, what happens is that Kormak speaks a half-verse asking her whom she would choose as a husband, and she finishes it, telling him she would choose him even if he were blind.[164] This is a far cry from Njord and Skadi bewailing their situations, but in both cases each speaks a verse giving their point of view, and the one answers the other.

John Lindow saw parallels between Kormak's *coup de foudre* and the love that Frey conceived for Gerdr when he first saw her (and her shining arms). He suggested that Skadi's choice by foot was also less capricious than it might seem - that she too had been struck by the beauty of a clean white foot.[165] Unfortunately, in her case they belonged to the older, unromantic Njord.

Steingerd's name is of significance here, since it echoes Gerdr, Frey's beloved. A kenning that Kormak uses in the same verse where he speaks his love is also interesting: *fall-Gerdr* or *fjallr-Gerdr*.[166] The latter would mean mountain-Gerdr, which given Steingerd, stone-Gerdr, seems reasonable, but it also suggests a giantess-name, which links

---

[164] Eggertsdóttir: 101.
[165] Lindow 2008: 174.
[166] Poole 1997: 47.

back to Gerdr herself and also Skadi, who is a mountain-giantess.

Lindow goes on to point out that feet have potential in Norse myth, since the first giant, Ymir, created life between his two feet. That life was a six-headed giant, who, like Starkadr, was seriously excessive. Lindow thinks that by showing their feet the gods were emphasizing their normality at Skadi's expense. So their act of contrition (penitents went barefoot) was also a subtle act of one-up-man-ship.[167]

Kormak's end, too, seems to parallel the Vanir, but in this case he follows Freyr, rather than Njord. He fights his rival Bersi for the first time with a borrowed sword, and that after he planned to go into battle with an axe. Freyr has to fight Beli with an antler, having given his sword to Skirnir when he sends him to woo Gerdr. Kormak does not follow instructions, and the sword malfunctions. In later duels he uses a sword blunted by a witch, so that he winds up using it like a cudgel. He does have a sword at his final battle, but it obviously fails him.[168]

In all three cases, the marriage does not work or never takes place. We leave Frey in *For Skirnis* longing helplessly for his love, and Kormak is cursed to languish in a similar way. As for Njord and Skadi, the sight of a foot was no augur of a successful marriage, and Njord is left with neither his old wife/sister nor anyone to take her place.

Other Parallels

Folktales and Fairy tales

The play with Loki and the goat resembles a type of folktale like the Grimm tale of the Golden Goose. Whoever touches the goose sticks to it, and whoever touches that person sticks to them, and so on. There are also ruder versions, such as the himphamph, in which a lover tries to distract the cuckolded husband by getting him to construct the himphamph. The husband gets his own back, binding the lover, wife, maid and others in obscene situations.

---

[167] Lindow 2008: 177.
[168] Ibid: 179.

There is also a Nordic version which combines the Golden Goose and the people getting stuck together in embarrassing ways, as well as a version collected in Telemark where:

> *the bird is a magpie, and the persons who get stuck are a beautiful girl, a knight who has dropped his trousers more or less at the sight of the girl, a kitchen maid who, looking for a sausage, has grabbed the knight's penis, and the cook, who tried to hit the kitchen girl on the rear end with a ladle, thereby attaching herself to the himphamph, and who has the outhouse bucket attached to her own rear end.*[169]

When you look at these stories, Loki's trick with the goat doesn't seem so outrageous.

The other folktale motif that the Loki episode brings to mind is the suitor test. This involves a princess or other woman who cannot or will not laugh, and the suitor has to surprise her into laughter. This is similar to many myths in which a god or goddess becomes wrathful, or is in mourning, and is restored to normal through laughter at some obscene display. This is also a common element in folk and fairy tales, so that the Aarne-Thompson index includes it in their tale types, as Types 559, 571-4, 1642.[170]

Skadi, of course, has her own suitor test, which instantly makes you think of Cinderella, although in this case it's the fairest rather than the smallest feet. (Cinderella crossed with Snow White, perhaps?) There are other versions of this sort of story, including an Indian tale in which a father and son choose brides. In this story, they choose their brides on the basis of their footsteps, only to find that the father has chosen the daughter and the son the mother. In the Stith Thompson index this is listed as H365: "Bride test: size of feet".[171]

The final compensation, turning Thiazi's eyes into stars, could be a just-so story that explains how a natural phenomenon came into being. These are common all around the world, and persist to this day. I can remember as a child being shown Father Duffy's well, the water gushing from the

---

[169] Lindow 1992: 132-3.
[170] Clunies-Ross 1989: 8.
[171] Lindow 1992: 131.

place where he struck the ground with his walking stick.[172] Thiazi's Eyes are usually assumed to be the main stars of Gemini, which are bright enough to attract attention and a story.

Chanson de Malmariée and Bridal Laments

The complaints of Njord and Skadi, echoed by Hadingus and Regnilda, are similar to the bridal laments found in many societies; especially ones where the bride is expected to relocate to her husband's home. Another, closely related genre, is the *chanson de malmariée*, which also details a woman's complaints against her husband, the difference being that in the chansons she has been married long enough to really have something to complain about. *Malmariée* literally means "badly married", and the songs are litanies of complaints about inconsiderate and slobbish husbands, who are sometimes violent as well. (Male readers may be pleased to know that there was a subgenre of masculine marital complaint, both comic and serious.)

The bridal lament is the more closely related to Skadi's circumstances, since the new bride or bride-to-be expresses both her fears about her new home and longing for the home and family left behind. Davidson quotes the *Kalevala*:

> *She must bear this without complaint, she is told, and if asked if her mother-in-law gives her butter to eat:*
> *'always say it is given/ brought in a dipper, though you / get it but once in summer / and that from two winters back' (Bosley 1989: 23, 443). The advice to the bridegroom in section 24 as to how to treat his wife helps to complete the gloomy picture of the young bride's subordinate place in the household"*[173]

A Lithuanian bridal laments reflects the weeping a young woman was supposed to perform before the wedding:

> *My heart is broken with grief...*
> *Swiftly to my garden I run,*
> *There shall I weep.*
> *Like streams in spring my tears shall flow...*

---

[172] http://www.nlgeotourism.com/content/father-duffys-well/nflF7D8E6282791E15D9
[173] Davidson 1998: 128.

In my sorrow I am alone, I, a poor orphan...
Farewell my well-beloved flowers,
Farewell my darling garden.[174]

And, at the other end of the Indo-European spectrum, we have the laments of the Indian goddess Nandadevi, who once a year goes on pilgrimage to her native village, and then has to return to her husband, Shiva:

> *At her mother's home life is very different: she has 'butter from seven different places, and breads that are fried with the leaves of the forest' with abundance of milk and rice (Sax 1991: 91), butter once more being regarded as something of primary importance in the diet. Not only do the songs express her reluctance to leave her mait [natal home] after marriage, but also during the pilgrimage it is claimed that when coming down from the mountain, her palanquin drags the men carrying it swiftly towards the village, while on the journey back it is so heavy that they have great difficulty in getting up the slope*
> *(Sax 1991: 58–9).*[175]

Young wives returned to their home villages for this festival, so the goddess' experience echoed their own. Bengal had a similar festival dedicated to the powerful goddess Durga, although the songs contrasting the hard life the bride had in her husband's home with her pleasant life with her family remain consistent.

The bridal laments clearly reflect a pattern where the bride must relocate to her husband's home, usually living with his family. It is not surprising that a young woman might worry about such a change. Njord and Skadi, however, try each other's abodes in turn, but without a satisfactory result.

The *chanson de malmariée*, on the other hand, is a direct complaint about the husband in question:

> *When the boor goes to market,*
> *He does not go there to bargain,*
> *But to spy on his wife*
> *Lest someone seduce her.*
> *In my heart I feel them, the sweet pains,*

---

[174] Paplauskas-Ramunas 1952: 128.
[175] Davidson 1998: 128.

How could I be cured of them?
Boor, get away from me,
For your breath will kill me.
I am certain that your love and mine
Will yet separate.
In my heart I feel them, the sweet pains,
How could I be cured of them?[176]

As you might expect with Provencal songs, there is often a lover waiting in the wings, either real or imagined. They may not have been meant to be taken entirely seriously, although in society where arranged marriages were the norm, and husbands chosen for material reasons rather than sex appeal, many women must have felt a similar way. That women composed many of these songs adds to the interest.

It is easy to imagine the two dialogues of Njord and Skadi or Hadingus and Regnilda as a duet on similar lines. In much the same way the Newfoundland folk song 'A Great Big Sea Hove in Long Beach'[177] is often performed as a duet or with the choir split into male and female halves, so that each of the characters' views are put across by the appropriate gender.

Another, modern parallel

It seems appropriate that the modern variant on the Njord - Skadi story comes from Tolkien. The story goes that two races, the Black Númenóreans and the Gondorians, were at war. The Gondorians and Arnorians were breakaway Numenoreans who considered the others to be renegades.[178] It is not known why the Gondorian king Falastur married Berúthiel of the Númenóreans, presumably as a political accommodation. She went to live in Pelargir, Falastur's home, which was by the sea. She hated the smell of the sea and fish, and the noise of gulls. She wore dark clothing and loathed all ornament. Her name means something like "Angry Queen".[179] She became proverbial, to the point where more than 2,000 years later Aragorn mentions her and her cats in an off-hand remark.[180] Unlike Skadi, she was exiled by the

---

[176] Doss-Quinby 2001:151.
[177] http://www.wtv-zone.com/phyrst/audio/nfld/01/beach.htm
[178] http://tolkiengateway.net/wiki/ Black_Númenóreans
[179] http://tolkiengateway.net/wiki/ Berúthiel
[180] http://en.wikipedia.org/wiki/Cats_of_Queen_Berúthiel

Gondorians and returned home. Tolkien himself commented that Berúthiel was like Skadi, since both disliked their maritial homes.[181]

Perhaps it's just a comment on the sort of people I know, but it is amazing how many people referenced Berúthiel when I told them about this book.

---

[181] http://tolkiengateway.net/wiki/ Berúthiel

Chapter 7

Theories About This Myth

> *it could be argued... that any myth is a neutral structure that allows paradoxical meanings to be held in a charged tension. Indeed, we might argue that this is one of the defining characteristics of a myth, in contrast with other sorts of narratives (such as novels): a myth is a narrative that is transparent to a variety of constructions of meaning.*[182]
> (Wendy Doniger)

Popular treatments of the Njord - Skadi myth seem to focus on a naturalistic explanation, where sea and mountains, or summer and winter, cannot meet. Ideas of this kind often go back to the 19th century "nature-myth" school, which held that all myths were essentially early attempts at science, explanations of the world and how it worked. For example:

> *Skadhi's anger against the gods, who had slain her father, the storm giant, is an emblem of the unbending rigidity of the ice-enveloped earth, which, softened at last by the frolicsome play of Loki (the heat lightning) smiles, and permits the embrace of Niord (summer). His love, however, cannot hold her for more than three months of the year (typified in the myth by nights), as she is always secretly longing for the wintry storms and her wonted activities among the mountains.*[183]

I think it's pretty obvious that this is a pretty reductive explanation of a myth.

The reason it's still popular now is, I think, twofold. First, the economic reason: the books that explain everything in terms of nature are all out of copyright, and so cheap to buy, whether as a paperback or ebook. A lot of them are available free on the internet.

---

[182] Doniger: 119.
[183] Guerber 1994: 115-6.

Second, and this does not apply exclusively to Heathens and Pagans, the emphasis these days is on getting in touch with nature, and the concern over the environment. Paul Birbre is perceptive about this:

> *The ritual marriage of sky and earth has been a popular interpretation [of the Gerdr-Freyr myth] doubtless because scholars wish to think that ancient people thought that way; they wish to think this, because they themselves find it an emotionally significant image. They feel this, I suspect, since they themselves are the product of one religion, Christianity, which involves a sky-god in whom they no longer, perhaps, wholly believe, and of a second, Darwinism, which involves a procreative Earth, Terra Mater.*[184]

No doubt for some a myth that relates directly to nature is emotionally satisfying.

I want to be clear here: I am not denying that there are aspects of the Njord - Skadi myth that are clearly about nature, but I think that if that was all it was, then it would be no more than a primitive tale of little interest. It has to have some resonance in human emotions and behaviour before it's of any worth. In other words, a myth needs to be a good story first.

What aspects of this myth are connected to nature and human activity in nature? In his article on *Gift-Ref's saga*, Bruce Lincoln suggests a set of oppositions:

Njord	Skadi
sea	land
ships	skis
seagulls	wolves
summer	winter
harbours	mountains
fishing	hunting
singing	howling

---

[184] Bibre 1986: 25.

I'm still not entirely sure where the summer - winter one comes from, unless it's the common northern pattern of living on or near shore during the summer, then moving inland once the harbour ices up, and hunting game for food.

No doubt in real life people lived on both, probably depending on what was available at any given time. However, as we will see in later chapters, the Icelanders who lived on the coast saw themselves and their lifestyles as quite different from the inland Sami and Finns, and ships were seen as prestige objects, to the point where people were buried with or in them. The fishing, and later trading and raiding that they allowed were prized above agriculture and hunting, although both were practiced.

The binary that Njord and Skadi seem to embody (from nature-myth to structuralism in a single bound) must have a larger meaning, but what is it? Various authors have different ideas, all related to conditions in northern Europe. Lincoln sees the ship and the possibilities it presents as an embodiment of capitalism, allowing Ref to accumulate money and goods in contrast to Pinchpenny who lives in the mountains, and who is such a miser that even the slightest loss causes him and his family members to commit suicide. The contrast between the sociability and money-making of the shore and the fear and isolation of the mountains couldn't be starker.

Lincoln mentions summer vs. winter, although he doesn't elaborate on it. Guerber, quoted above, also sees Njord as a summer god, although it's not clear why. Perhaps *Hkr*'s account of the good crops during Njord's reign influenced them.

A more modern version from Alice Karlsdottir sees them as light and darkness, as well as the seasons. The ship was a mode of travel for the warmer months, before the ice set in. Skis and skates would be far more useful in winter. Further, she says: "It is interesting to see a variation on the usual theme of winter married to summer, in that it is the male deity who represents fertility and warmth, and the female who is the bringer of darkness and death."[185]

---

[185] Found at the Wayback Machine:
http://web.archive.org/web/20080304171217/http://www.vinland.org/heathen/mt/njordhrskadhi.html

Karlsdottir raises two further points which are worth pursuing in light of this question of male fertility deities. First, is the link between fertility and death, which I will discuss in more detail further on along with Gro Steinsland's sacred marriage theory. The link between fertility and death is evident, however, in everything from compost bins to oil deposits. Second, Njord and his family represent two groups of food sources, one wild and one domestic. Njord, as god of sailors and fishermen, provided one source, while Freyr made the crops grow, and Freya looked after the fertility of humans and animals. So Freyr and Freya complemented each other domestically, while Njord and Skadi did the same for wild food.

McKinnell, on the other hand, sees the seas as full of life, while the mountains are barren. Another way of looking at it is that Njord and Skadi are not dependent:

> *The story of Njord and Skadi shows a mutual break up, as neither of them can be happy in the home of the other (Gylf XXIII Prose Edda 23-4). They are both independent deities, and do not rely on each other to perform their divine functions: indeed, as Skadi is a ski goddess, and Njord is god of the sea, their divine functions make them mutually incompatible. This suggests that their break up is the best result in order for them to act as gods, and implies that divorce, among the gods at least, is a possibility.*[186]

In other words, they have no need of each other, and indeed get in each other's way.

Another way of looking at it, and probably a more historically accurate one, is to say that both are needed to make a living in the north:

> *Even though the story of the union between Njord and Skade underlines the differences between sea and mountain, I think we could interpret the story as a union between the coast and the mountain, as people in the coastal areas needed both places to make a living.*[187]

Holm thinks that the Vanir operate as a bridge between the infield and outfield (Midgard - Utgard) and perhaps hark back to a period when this division was less sharp. That

---

[186] Bennett 2009: 62.
[187] Holm 2002: 76.

Njord and Skadi

would explain why two of the Vanir men are married to giantesses.

The connection with mountains and skiing, as well as the hunting with a bow, led to Skadi being thought of as a Sami-like woman. In the chapter on Sami Parallels I have gone more deeply into the question of the conceptual similarity of Sami and jotun, based on both living in the North and East and living a similar lifestyle. As Else Mundal puts it:

> *The otherness of the Saamis and their culture and the fact that they mostly lived outside the areas where the Nordic people lived, especially in the North, but farther south also in the border areas between Norway and Sweden and in the inland of Eastern Norway, conformed to the pattern of Midgardr–Útgardr. According to the mythological map the Saamis became the Útgardr people.*[188]

Like the giants, the Sami had precious objects that the Norse wanted, notably the magical arrows that the Sami king Gusir got from his giant brother Brúni, and in turn gave to Ketill hœngr.[189]

The Skadi - Njord myth, whether you accept the Sami idea or not, clearly has to do with marriage, and the problems associated with it. One obvious problem is the one that confronts Njord: proximity and distance. We are told that Njord was married already, but his wife was also his sister. When he joined the Aesir as a hostage, he had to give up his first wife, which seems remarkably accommodating of him. (I wonder if he hadn't been promised a substitute as a reward for compliance. Skadi may not have been the only one hoping to snag an Ase for a spouse.)

It also smacks of the Roman practice of taking hostages from among tribes around the Empire and educating them in Roman ways before making them into client-rulers. (See Hostages for more on this.) If his first wife was too close, at least to human and Aesir eyes, his second wife couldn't be more distant. A jotunn, from Utgard, with completely different ways and preferences.

---

[188] Mundal 2000: 349.
[189] Mundal 2000: 349.

Njord and Skadi

As Clunies-Ross points out, the Vanir may have fought their way into a truce with the Aesir, but they joined them on the Aesir's terms. She sees them as compromises between "divine endogamy and the exchange of women that the giants desire".[190] Njord is caught in the middle of this; he will not be allowed to marry into the Aesir, and he had to give up the wife he had among his own aett; only the giants are left to him and Freyr.

Oosten notes that while the Vanir are marked by incest, the Aesir are marked by fratricide: "The opposition between alliance and war, marriage and death is also represented in the relations between the myth of Balder and the myth of the marriage of Njord and Skadi."[191] The relations between Vanir and giants was one of compensation and marriage, very different from the relations between Aesir and jotnar. "...[I]n the myths of the war between these groups we find not an exchange of women, but an exchange of men."[192]

This leads into the idea of "negative reciprocity", first defined by Marshall Sahlins in his book *On the Sociology of Primitive Exchange* in the chapter "Stone Age Economics":

> *Reciprocity is a whole class of exchanges, a continuum of forms. This is specially true in the narrow context of material transactions- as opposed to a broadly conceived social principle or moral norm of give-and-take. At one end of the spectrum stands the assistance freely given, the small currency of everyday kinship, friendship, and neighbourly relations, the "pure gift" Malinowski called it, regarding which an open stipulation of return would be unthinkable and unsociable. At the other pole, self-interested seizure, appropriation by chicanery or force requited only by an equal and opposite effort on the principle of lex talionis, "negative reciprocity" as Gouldner phrases it. The extremes are notably positive and negative in a moral sense. The intervals between them are not merely so many gradations of material balance in exchange, they are intervals of sociability. The distance between poles of reciprocity is, among other things, social distance...*[193]

---

[190] Clunies-Ross 1994: 233.
[191] Oosten: 46.
[192] Oosten: 40.
[193] Sahlins: 191.

Njord and Skadi

Clunies-Ross and Kristensen have applied this theory to relations between Aesir, Vanir and jotnar to considerable effect. When we add in Levi-Strauss' idea about marriage as an exchange of women (see Oosten, above) then we see a clear pattern of rules about who can marry whom, and who is willing to exchange with whom. In this view, the Aesir are on top, the jotnar on bottom, and the Vanir are "the filling in this uneasy sandwich"[194].

While Clunies-Ross sees the system as inherently flawed, Kristensen argues that it works just fine for the party that created it; the Aesir. Kristensen turns the focus on tensions in the kinship structure, both within the Aesir and in their relations with the giants.

He also does not see the giants as inherently evil, but rather as neutral, morally.[195] He sees the myths about relations between the different groups, and within the groups, as exploring what was permissible, and what was taboo:

> *The Old Norse myths, often preoccupied with relationships probably disallowed in the real world, thus tested various (systematically inverted) positions of the system and at the same time could explain sexual prohibitions and marriage patterns in the culture in which they were told.*[196]

John Lindow and Margaret Clunies-Ross have both written about the Njord-Skadi myth from the viewpoint of folktales and medieval customs. Clunies-Ross looks at the whole myth, Thiazi's half and Skadi's half, as based on various wondertale motifs, and the Skadi half as also a burlesque on the bridal-quest tale, with gender inversion as the order of the day. Lindow goes along with the gender inversion, and adds some parallels from medieval customs including the parading of penitents or the losers in a war barefoot, and the law against adultery that punished the woman and her lover by having them paraded through the town with her drawing him by the penis. He sees Loki as playing with status (since freemen did not have to endure physical punishments) as much as gender.

---

[194] Angela Carter, describing a stay in hospital
[195] Kristensen: 151
[196] Kristensen: 166-7.

If Lindow and Clunies-Ross see the marriage myth as a burlesque in which both parties endure humiliation, Gro Steinsland reads it very differently. To her, the marriage of god and giantess is of a very different order, a hieros gamos or sacred marriage in which the god-king fertilizes the land (giantess) and this results in the birth of a new kind of being, a divine king. Others are not convinced by this, including Clunies-Ross, whose paper "Royal Ideology" is a rebuttal of Steinsland's thesis. Others who have looked at kingship include Sundqvist and Tolley, both of whom seem unconvinced by the idea as mooted by Steinsland, and the Frazerian addendum of the ritual death of the sacred king that many have read into the poem *Yt*. Steinsland's ideas are nonetheless influential, with Else Mundal among others.

Another version of this idea comes from John McKinnell, whose book *Meeting the Other* outlines his own theory about a pattern he finds in *Ys* and other myths such as Njord - Skadi. He observes of the latter:

> *One might have expected myths about the 'sacred marriage' between the fertility god and the earth-giantess to be celebrations of a joyful union, but in fact the fundamental hostility between gods and giants was so strong that they are usually misalliances.*[197]

Among the human kings of *Ys* he sees a pattern in which the man he calls the Summer King goes to a land of winter or death where he encounters a Winter King and his daughter. The Summer King and the woman marry and have a son, but the Summer King abandons his wife, and dies because of her curse. Their son then takes the throne.[198]

Of course, in the Njord story it is Skadi who does the abandoning, leaving Njord to return to her mountains. However, Georges Dumézil has suggested that the story of Njord could be seen as a male version of the selkie or swan-maiden myth, in which a human (usually a hunter) either woos or entraps an otherworldly woman into living with him. They have a son, but either the woman finally finds her animal-skin, or her longing for home becomes too great, and she leaves her husband. The son often becomes a sort of

---

[197] McKinnell 2005: 62.
[198] McKinnell 2005: 70-1.

shaman or super-hunter, thanks to his connection to the animal world.

The swan-wife story is only one of the many folktale/fairytale elements of this story. In fact, you could analyse the Thiazi half of this story as a succession of fairytale elements, with Stith Thompson's motif-index in one hand and the *Prose Edda* in the other.

Some, including Jan de Vries, have been dismissive of the Thiazi myth and its sequel on the grounds that it is so heavily based on folktales.[199] However, the same can be said of Thor's stories, which tend to burlesque their hero as well. Clunies-Ross borrows from Vladimir Propp's analysis of folktales for her paper on Skadi, but she doesn't see the similarities as diminishing the Skadi myth at all. We are more aware these days of the ways that forms once kept separate as "high" and "low" actually flow into one another.

The second half of the myth, in fact, inverts expectations so much that its use of "low" folktale motifs may be deliberate. Skadi begins the inversion by embarking on a quest for vengeance, which turns into a bridal-quest, along with a suitor test for first her and then the Aesir. After all this drama, you would expect the deities to settle down to be married, but they keep moving around, and finally separate. The end dramatically reverses our expectations of all myths about marriage between deities - you expect them to marry and be happy, if anyone is going to.

But dismissing this myth as just a funny story ignores the way it uses humour to sneak up on some crucial issues in Norse myth: the relations between outside and inside, kinship and its obligations, and the fate of the worlds. In addition, it addresses the question of what makes for a good marriage. Not bad going for a simple nature-myth.

---

[199] de Vries 1937: 37.

CHAPTER 8

What is a Giant? Or, Risar and Thursar and Trolls, oh my!

> *In the earliest days of our lives we are all surrounded by giants, often loving, sometimes hostile and possibly dangerous, but first and foremost much larger and very different from us... Mythology would not be so potent if it did not parallel human experience. It is logical that the story of the world and the greatest mythical journey begin with giants, just like that world which is born whenever a human opens his eyes for the first time.*[200]
> (Jakobsson "Identifying the Ogre: The Legendary Saga Giants")

> *A primitive man, on meeting other men, will first have experienced fright. His fear will make him see these men as larger and stronger than himself; he will give them the name giants. After many experiences, he will discover that the supposed giants are neither larger nor stronger than himself, and that their stature did not correspond to the idea he had originally linked to the word 'giant'. He will then invent another name that he has in common with them, such as, for example, the word man, and will retain the word 'giant' for the false object that impressed him while he was being deluded.*[201]
> (Rousseau's 'Essay on the Origin of Languages')

The exact nature of a giant is one of those questions to which there is a simple answer and a much more complicated one. First, the simple answer.

A giant is a mythological being. In Norse myth, these beings live in their own territory, Jötunheim (Giant-Home). Some of them have magical abilities and knowledge, but some of them are just big brutes. Although the gods are related to the giants, they are enemies, engaged in a war that

---

[200] Jakobsson 2009: 181.
[201] Clark 2013: 11-12.

culminates with the death of the gods at Ragnarok. Giants are usually envisioned as well, big.

Now for the complicated version. First off, as the chapter title tells us, there are several different words for a giant. They can be called risi, tröll, jötunn, and thurs. There are others, but these are the four main ones.

The classic quote on these names is from the Cleasby/Vigfussion Icelandic Dictionary:

> *In popular Icel. usage risi denotes size, jotunn strength, thurs lack of intelligence; thus har sem risi, sterk sem jotunn, heimskr sem thurs, as tall as a risi, strong as a jotunn, stupid as a thurs. The ancient legends describe the risar as handsome, and a long-lived race...*[202]

Lotte Motz sums it up like this:

> *The terms, related to OI troll thus refer to magicians and their craft, those related to jotunn mainly to features of the landscape and, metaphorically, hugeness of size, those related to thurs to deficiency of intellect, while the risi-group is sparsely represented and coincides, to some extent, with words of the jotunn-group. It is thus possible, or even likely, that the giantess as hideous hag and the giantess desired for her loveliness by a god, the giant as wise teacher and the giant as dim-witted ogre had at one time belonged to different families.*[203]

Risi: are often said to be larger than a man, and handsome. *Bárdar's saga* makes a distinction between trolls and risi, the former bad, the latter good. Bardar's risar inheritance is invoked to explain his good looks and good behaviour, while another character, Dumbr, is, like his troll family, strong but also shifty and violent.

Troll: Simek offers the translation: "fiend, monster, giant". The meaning of "troll" changed over time, especially as people became Christianised, but it always indicated a hostile giant. In more Christian stories they become beings of folklore, which still live in mountains, but have magical powers.

---

[202] http://lexicon.ff.cuni.cz/html/oi_cleasbyvigfusson/b0498.html (accessed June 22, 2009)
[203] Motz 1987: 295.

Jötunn: is the most neutral term for a giant, although oddly enough it comes from the word eta, "eat", and so means something like "big eater". [204] This might explain Thiazi devouring the food that Odin, Loki and Hoenir were cooking in the Idunn myth. (This became Old English eoten, which gives us etin.)

Thurs: Like troll, thurs is one of the pejorative names for a giant. We can see this in the rune "thurs", which was used for cursing, and seems to be connected with harm to women especially. (This may be why Skirnir threatened Gerdr with three thurs runes if she refused Frey.) Runic amulets often call on Thor to drive away thursar; not surprising considering the name may mean "wounder".[205]

Flagl, Gygr, Skessa, Trollkona: all four are used of giantesses, gygr in particular appearing frequently in the Edda.

There is a great deal of controversy over just how much people ever differentiated between the varying groups of giants, or whether the categories were porous, but the four do seem to have different connotations, either indicating different groups or at least different ways of describing giants. (Riti Kroesen, for example, is dubious about Motz's categories.[206])

Ármann Jakobsson thinks that there are four main distinguishing characteristics of giants. The first is variation, that there are many kinds of monsters who can be included amongst giants. The only certainty about them is that they are different from humans. Second is closeness to nature, especially mountains. Third is ambiguity – giants can be good or bad, as in the way that Skadi received worship but her father Thiazi is definitely a bad giant if a powerful one. Fourth, that they are old and their culture is in decline. It is the time of the humans now, and the giants are throwbacks. As he paraphrases Katja Schulz, "one of the most important characteristics of giants is not being here anymore."[207]

---

[204] Simek 1996: 180. Krosen (1996: 58) disputes this.
[205] Mees 2009: 685-6.
[206] Kroesen 1996: 56.
[207] Jakobsson, 2005: 14.

This is true of the saga world of which he speaks. In the mythological poems and prose, giants are as real as gods, and as present.

Despite being nominal enemies, the gods visit giants socially, sleep with them, sometimes marry them, match wits in wisdom-contests with them, and are related to them. Even Tyr, the "straightest" Aesir, has a giant for a mother.

But they still kill them.

Especially Thor, whose mother was a giantess, Iord, and who has a giantess lover, Jarsaxa, who gave him a son. And of course, Odin has no trouble in sexually exploiting them.

Elsewhere in this book I mentioned Rasmussen's theory that the difference between the gods and the giants isn't so much that they're of different natures as that the gods made a conscious decision to be different from them. The murder of Ymir to make the cosmos was the symbol of that; not only did they kill their ancestor, but they set out to create an ordered world unlike the chaos that the giants lived in. After that there was no going back. The gods didn't create a world out of nothing, the way that Jahweh did; they killed a giant (already a symbolic act) and made the world from his body parts, thus literally creating a cosmic order from chaos.

While the giants may have been chaotic, there are signs that they were also wise, and, possibly because they'd been around longer, knew things the Aesir didn't. Two examples are the giants Bardar and Armann:

> Barðar is described as *margiss* and *forspar* — 'knowing much', 'prophetic'... he had learned much from his foster-father Dofri, also a giant; Ármann's father knew the 'old wisdom' (pagan wisdom)... the giant Arngrimr is a 'great magician'... The adjectives *frodr, alsvinnr* are applied to giants in *vaf*.[208]

Vaf being a wisdom-contest between the giant Vafthrudnir and Odin, where the two are so closely matched that Odin has to resort to trickery to win. Odin tells us in *Havamal* 142 that he learned magic songs from his uncle, a giant, and in *Harb* 20 he tells us that a thurs named Hlébarth gave him a magic wand. (Of course, Odin claims to have bested the thurs.)

---

[208] Motz 1987: 199, n. 40.

We know that they can have magical powers, great wealth, and see themselves as the equals of the gods. Thiazi, for example, checks all three boxes, having a great deal of gold, being able to shapeshift, and matching wits and magic with Odin and Loki. Several other giants are named in kennings for gold, including Thorgerdr's father Holgi, and Aegir, and in general, gold could be called the "mouth-count, and voice and word of giants."[209] As well as Thiazi, Geirrodr imprisoned Loki by magic, and the whole visit to Utgard-Loki shows a power of illusion that neatly echoes the display the Aesir put on in *Gylf*. As for equalling the gods, the giant attempts to best the gods and marry into their aett would seem to indicate that they see themselves as just as good as them. (Skadi's negotiations with the gods would fit here, too.)

One other thing we know about the giants is that they are apparently more fertile, and have the gods surrounded. These seem like extreme statements; let me justify them.

First, we know that Ymir was able to conceive asexually - from between his feet and from under his armpit. The giants therefore have two options where the gods and humans only have one. This might go some way to justifying Thor's mission statement:

> *great would be the giant-race, if they all lived:*
> *mankind would be nothing, under middle-earth.*
> *(Harb. 23, Orchard)*

Second, the dwelling-place of the giants is kept very vague in Norse myth. It seems as if there are two main locations, North and East. Even that is disputed. As John Lindow says: "Scandinavian mythology places the giants in two remote locations: on the beach, and to the east."[210] It is true that some sources simply place the giants in Utgard, and the humans in Midgard and the giants in Asgard, the last two of which are seen as central, with Utgard as surrounding it. The outlands, or outskirt-city as Jakobssson translates it, would be at least partly beach because in Snorri and other medieval sources the Ocean was seen as encircling the world. At Ragnarok the giants come from two directions,

---

[209] Faulkes: 94.
[210] Lindow 1997: 18.

from Muspellheim across the rainbow bridge, and the frost-giants by sea, in a ship.[211]

In Snorri, the giants seem to inhabit two main locales. He places Jotunheimar to the north, while the giants also live in the east. The difference seems to be that Jotunheimar is governed and inhabited by giants, as Midgard is by humans, and houses many of them, including Loki's monstrous brood. He seems to see it as the home of the frost-giants, which might explain the northern location. On the other hand, there are giants in the east, such as Utgard-loki, who is reached by leaving Asgard and travelling east to a deep forest.

When the gods go to seek them, they go in separate directions: "Thor had gone to eastern parts to thrash trolls, but Odin rode Slepnir to Giantland and arrived at a giant's named Hrungnir"[212]. (One assumes that Jotunheimar is in the North here.) However, these directions shift around, even within Snorri's own writing. The one thing that is consistent is that in the east lies trolls and deep forest.

To reach Utgard-loki, Thor and his companions must travel through the forest in the East. The forest Jarnvid (Iron-Wood) where a giantess raises wolves and giants is in the east, and in poetry Bragi the Old has an encounter with a troll-wife while travelling in the East, in a forest. And, although we don't know where it was located, Loki tricks Idunn into the forest when she is kidnapped.[213] (Note that outlaws and wolves were also associated with the forest.)

Giants are also associated with mountains; there is an entire sub-genre of berg-risi, mountain-giants. Skadi lives in the mountains, and her refusal to resettle on the shore foundered her marriage. The giant Suttungr lived on a mountain, and Thokk (a disguise of Loki's) lives in a cave. Besides that, there are many kennings that connect giants and mountains. In *Hst*, for example, Thiazi is called Fjallgylðir, mountain-howler, meaning wolf, meaning giant. Later in the poem we are told that "The Residents of the Steep Mountains" were happy - they had the apples of immortality.[214]

---

[211] Jakobsson 2009: 109.
[212] Faulkes: 77.
[213] Jakobsson 2009: 108.
[214] trans. from http://freya.theladyofthelabyrinth.com/?page_id=79

Njord and Skadi

Snorri also tells that the frost-giants live where Ginnungagap used to be. He doesn't go into a great deal of detail about this; the only thing we learn is that there's a well there, and Mimir owns it: "But under that root [of Yggdrasil] that reaches towards the frost-giants, there is where Mimir's well is, which has wisdom and intelligence contained in it, and the master of the well is called Mimir"[215]. Presumably this is the giant form of Mimir, and he must be a frost-giant too.

While the model of Utgard - Midgard seems to separate the giants in space from gods and humans, and the emphasis in the myths seems to be on what the two *don't* have in common, the giants are not totally alien.

As Clunies-Ross points out, the giants are social beings, just like the other groups they deal with. Like gods and humans, they live in families, and interact with each other and others they encounter in ways that make sense to us (and probably made even more sense to the original medieval Scandinavian audiences). Skadi and Thiazi form a family, father and daughter, and we further know that Thiazi has or had two brothers, with whom he shared the inheritance from their father. Apart from the exotic detail of how they shared out the gold in mouthfuls, nothing in that story is strange to a reader or hearer then or now. A father dies, and his sons share his goods out amongst themselves, making sure that each gets an equal share. One of them has a daughter, who inherits his property after her father dies.

While the gods and giants are in opposition to each other in a number of ways, including the major difference between them, the fact that the gods deny their kinship to the point of refusing to make alliances or marriages with them, and even killing them. Clunies-Ross suggests that a lot of the reason the giants are seen as chaotic and disruptive is because there is no possibility of a reciprocal relationship between them and the gods. This results in raiding and kidnapping, with the giants trying to take the gods' women "and symbols of order like the sun and moon"[216]. (Consider for a minute how it would look from the giants' point of view, just as in *Grendel*

---

[215] Faulkes: 17.
[216] Clunies-Ross 1994: 62.

and *Written in Venom* we are invited to see how the monster Grendel or bound Loki might see things.)

Compared to other categories of beings in Norse myth, the gods and giants have sociability in common. Both groups have families, form alliances amongst themselves, and show curiosity about others. "Apart from the dwarves, who are an all-male group, the remaining categories of supernatural beings have no clearly social organisation, though some of them engage in biological reproduction and hence have offspring who are acknowledged as theirs by supernatural society at large."[217]

This extimité, the fact that the giants are so close and yet so different, as personified in Loki, is what causes the friction between the two groups. So perhaps we should not be surprised by the children he had; it is almost as if the conflict that had reached a sort of equilibrium with his incorporation into the Aesir erupted into his monstrous and lethal children.

Loki was one test case for cohabitation of Aesir and Jotunn. I like Michael Chabon's theory that Odin made Loki his blood-brother because:

> *he brought pleasure to Odin, who with all his well-sipping and auto-asphyxiation knew too much even to be otherwise amused. This was, in fact, the reason why Odin had taken the great, foredoomed step of making Loki his blood brother - for the pleasure, pure and simple, of his company.*[218]

Skadi and Gerdr were the others. Both the daughters of predominant giant families, they if anyone would be worthy of a place in Asgard. Both resulted in losses (Freyr's sword) and gains (Saeming, Fjolnir) but in neither case did they retard Ragnarok. The forces arrayed against them were too strong.

Cult of Giants

> *The incorporation of a giant's home into the abodes of the gods is in itself remarkable. And it is even more remarkable that the circumstances have not received much attention in scholarly research. The mythical*

---

[217] Ibid: 62.
[218] Chabon: 53.

> *dwelling of a god has its counterpart in the physical shrine. And in Ls Skadi's shrines, her vé ok vangr, is mentioned... [these] are common terms for sites where a cult takes place.*[219]

I've mentioned the quote from *Lks* before, and I'll most likely mention it again, but all the same it is extraordinary for a giant to refer to her sites of worship, without any comment by any of the other characters. (We can be sure that if Skadi didn't have fields and temples dedicated to her, Loki would have mentioned it.)

We may even have the names of some of the places where she was worshipped. Place-name evidence is always a little dicey, but in the middle and south of Sweden, and the southeast of Norway we have names such as Skadevi, Skedvi, Skee, Skl, and others, which Hjamal Lindroth postulated were formed around Skedju-, the genitive or possessive form of Skedja, a feminine form of the grammatically masculine Skadi. The feminine form is linked to names for sites of worship such as vé, -hof or -lundr.[220]

Anders Hultgård takes the cautious position and says that *ve* is the only undisputed word that offers solid proof of a cult, and Skadi seems to have a few of those. However, he also says that cult places in Viking and medieval times could include:

> *natural sites such as mountains and hills (fjall, berg), groves (lundr), meadows and arable fields (vangr, akr), islands (ey), lakes (sjo☐r, sær), rivers (a☐) and springs, but also funeral barrows (haugr) and grave-fields. The designations for such sites also form part of sacral place names. At these places different constructions could be added to enhance the religious character of the site: stone- settings in the form of ships (skæið) or circles, raised stones sometimes inscribed with runes (kumbl, mærki), hearths and other constructions for ritual purposes.*

So, if we're being a little less cautious, we might want to include Skädharg, which links Skadi to Thorgerdr

---

[219] Steinsland 1986: 213.
[220] Ibid: 213-4.

holgabrudr, since one version of her name is not Holgi's bride but the horga-bride ("of the shrines").[221]

The connection between Skadi and Ullr is brought out in place-names as well, since many of the Ullevi and Ulleraker are in the same areas as the places with Skadi names. There's more on the similarities between Ullr and Skadi in their own section, but it does bring to mind Kusmenko's idea that they form a pair, with Skadi as the dark aspect and Ullr as the light one, possibly as two aspects of winter. As Welschbach observes, there are other divine pairs in Norse myth such as Freyr and Freya, Aegir and Ran, and possibly Njord and Nerthus.[222]

We also know that Skadi was referred to as the ski-dis, although whether this was just an honorific or whether she was included among the disir is not known. The disir, a broadly defined group of supernatural women, seem to have had two major functions, one involved with war in a way that recalls the swan-maidens and valkyries of heroic legend, both protective and prophetic, and another which dealt mainly with families and their destinies. In this mode they could appear to people who were doomed, for instance. Their cult may have been part of an ancestor-cult, with the disir as revered female forebears who still protected the family and its interests. (Thorgerdr and Skadi would fit in here as supernatural ancestors, although Thorgerdr is more active on behalf of her family, as far as we know.)

One giantess, Goí, apparently had a regular festival like that of the disablot, the Goíblót. I have discussed her story elsewhere, but briefly; she was the sister of Nór, who was the mythical first king of Norway. According to *Orkneyinga saga*:

> *Thorri was a great sacrificer, he had a sacrifice every year at midwinter; that they called Thorri's sacrifice; from that the month took its name. One winter there were these tidings at Thorri's sacrifice, that Goi was lost and gone, and they set out to search for her, but she was not found. And when that month passed away Thorri made them take to sacrifice, and sacrifice for this, that they might know surely where Goi was hidden*

---

[221] McKinnell 2014: Loc 7539.
[222] Welschbach: 27.

Njord and Skadi

away. That they called Goi's sacrifice, but for all that they could hear nothing of her.[223]

Or, according to *Hversu Noregr Byggðist* in *Flateyjarbók*:

King Thorri had three children; his sons were named Norr and Gorr, but the daughter Goi. Goi was lost and gone; and Thorri made a sacrifice a month later than he was wont to sacrifice; and they afterwards called that month in which this began Goi.[224]

In Joseph Anderson's translation of *Orkneyinga saga* one of the characters sets out on a voyage in the month of Goí, so we know that it wasn't just a poetic fiction.[225] According to Anderson's notes:

Goi, the fourth month of the year, corresponding to our February and part of March. The ancient mode of reckoning among the Northmen was by "winters," the year commencing on the 23rd November. Goi was sometimes called "horning-month"—the month in which the deer shed their horns; and it was also the month in which, in heathen times, the great annual sacrifice took place at Upsala, as mentioned in the Sega of King Olaf the Holy.[226]

The family seem to have come from northern Norway, and have fittingly wintry names.

The giant Fornjot was the ancestor of them all, whose name can be variously translated: as Forn-jótr, "Ancient Jutlander or poss. Giant"; For-njótr ("Early-User or Destroyer"); or Forn-njótr ("One-who-enjoys-sacrifices") or Forn-Thjótr ("Ancient Screamer").[227] He had three sons, Hlér/Sea, Logi/Fire and Kári/Wind, whose son was Jökull/Icicle (Lindow has Glacier) or Frosti/Frost, whose son was Snær/Snow. His son, Thorri, had two boys, Nor and Gor, and Goi. In another version, found in *Hversu Noregr byggðisk*, this is elaborated, with Snaer having four sons, Thorri, Fönn/Snowdrift, Drifa/Driving Snow, Snowdrift,

---

[223] http://www.sacred-texts.com/neu/ice/is3/is302.htm
[224] http://www.germanicmythology.com/FORNALDARSAGAS/HversuNoregrDasent.html
[225] Anderson: 98.
[226] Anderson: 98, n. 1.
[227] Lindow 2001: 118-9.

Njord and Skadi

Hailstorm, and Mjöll/Fresh, Powdery Snow.[228] (Although, as Lindow again points out, the last three names are feminine nouns, [229] and Motz treats them as giantesses [230], and Langeslag thinks that this is the same Drifa that King Vanlandi marries in Ys.[231])

Another giantess whom we know received worship and had temples is Thorgerdr holgabrudr. I have mentioned her already with reference to her similarities to Skadi, but for this section the most interesting thing about her is that every saga that mentions her either mentions her temples or describes an act of worship directed to her. Since all of these texts were composed after conversion, there is a definite Christian bias, with Thorgerdr's statues often being overthrown or destroyed, and her worship given a negative spin. (She is depicted often as greedy and bloodthirsty, and fickle towards her followers.)

What is not in doubt, however, is that she was seen as a powerful female figure who could reward her worshippers, and who had centres of worship where people could pray to her and leave offerings. These are described in the same terms as the temples for gods like Thor and Freyr; and while scholarly debate rages about how literally we should interpret these descriptions, and how much they are influenced by other Christian writings, especially from around the Mediterranean, we can at least say that that Thorgerdr had established centres of worship, whether in elaborate buildings or open-air. If you follow *Njals saga* and *Olavs saga Tryggvasonar*, Thorgerdr had idols in temples, which received offerings. The first part of her name, however, is sometimes spelled Horga- "of the shrines",[232] and in the sources where she has a father, he is called Holgi, which comes from the same root. (Snorri tells us that his mound was built of layers of gold and silver alternating with earth and stone.) She may very well have had both, with larger areas featuring formal temples, Roman-style, and also mounds in smaller places or as personal worship, like Ottar with Freyja.

---

[228] Langeslag: 34.
[229] Lindow 2001: 118-9.
[230] Motz 1981b: 501.
[231] Langeslag: 36.
[232] McKinnell 2014: Loc. 7540.

Njord and Skadi

As a sidelight on the worship of Thorgerdr, it should be mentioned that Jarl Hákon Sigurðarson (c. 937 – 995) was a particular follower of hers. He was a devoted enough pagan that although he was a vassal of Harald Bluetooth, Hákon ended his loyalty to Harald and Denmark rather than become a Christian. The Danes did not take this lying down, and later tried to invade, an event recorded in the *Jómsvíkinga saga*. However, the invasion, led by the Jomsvikings, was defeated. (Apart from the actual *Jómsvíkinga saga*, an account called *Jómsvíkinga þáttr* in *Flt* gives Thordgerdr and her sister Irpa the credit for repelling the invasion, after Jarl Hakon invokes their aid.)

Jarl Hakon was well-known for following Thorgerdr and Irpa, and perhaps (apart from victory in battle) the reason lies in his personal history. As Adam of Bremen put it:

> *Exceedingly cruel, this Haakon, of the stock of Ivar and descended from a race of giants...*[233]

Clearly he wishes to underline what he sees as Hakon's savagery, a pagan Northerner descended from Ivarr the Boneless (also known for cruelty) and, before that, giants. Not civilized at all, at all.

The giant he was referring to was, of course, Skadi, the mother of Saeming, the first of the Jarls of Hladir. Hakon was the de facto ruler of Norway from 975 to 995, so he was clearly someone to reckon with in the North of Europe. That may go some way to explain the descriptions of rich temples and gold and silver offerings to Thorgerdr. Davidson thinks that Skadi was popular in Halogaland because of the Sami population in Norway, and that her myth might indicate a split between her cult and the Vanic one.[234]

Skadi's father may also have had a cult, although now we're speculating. Many have seen the incident in *Hst* in which Hoenir sets the "holy table" and Thiazi, after tricking the Aesir by keeping their meat from cooking, takes most of the now-roasted ox, as a memory of a jotunn-cult. Paxson thinks that the giants' cult would have flourished in the sort of wild places normally associated with Jotunheimar[235], and similarly Lotte Motz considers that many giants were rulers

---

[233] Adam of Bremen/Tshan: 70.
[234] Davidson 1993: 61-2.
[235] Paxson 2006: 29.

of the wilderness similar to the ones found in Sami and other circumpolar cultures[236], spirits like the Inuit Sedna or Sami Meilikki.

Readers may object that Thiazi's actions were anything but helpful, and he seems to have set himself as an enemy of the gods. (The theory that holds that the problem in relations between gods and giants is the gods' unwillingness to have exchanges of goods and women with them could reply that Thiazi, having tested them, saw that the only way to get what he wanted was to steal it.) It could also be argued that Thiazi saw himself as teaching the gods to respect the rules of Utgard, and make offerings to the powers that ruled it. Motz gives other instances in which humans wandering in the wilderness were approached by giants who demanded offerings of food or warned people off taking particular animals.[237]

There are, however, many instances of jotunns being helpful to gods and humans. The giantess Gridr gives Thor a magical staff and gloves, which help him to avoid being killed by Geirrodr and his family. Thorgerdr we have already discussed, and Vargeisa gives the hero Hjalmper a wonderful sword. (Motz notes that in the same way there are spirits that form erotic relationships with hunters who are then given luck in hunting and supernatural protection.[238]) Hyrrokin is another example of a helpful giantess, who turns out to be stronger than Thor.

As Motz points out, many giants and giantesses have names that reflect natural phenomena, so perhaps they were seen as having power over them.

Skrimnir and Grimnir are two giants who cause unfavourable winds to blow ships onto the shore, while giantesses named Torfa and Hildr do the opposite for friendly humans. Thorri, a giant king, sends snow. Thorgerdr created a hailstorm to help Jarl Hakon in battle. Often, too, "darkness, fog, and sudden snow"[239] presage a meeting with a giant.

This goes with the many giant names related to weather:

---

[236] Motz 1984: esp. 175.
[237] Ibid: 179.
[238] Ibid: 185.
[239] Ibid: 183.

Leidi: fair wind,
Gusir, gustr, "gust, blast of wind"
Vindr - wind
Vindsvalir - "the cold of wind"
Hrmnir, Hrimthurs, Hrimgrimnir - hrim, "frost"
Hrimgerdr - hrim, "frost"
Mjoll, Driffa, Fonn - "snow"

Furthermore, Motz thinks that these giants tend to be localized, like the *numina* of the Sami, who also tend to protect particular areas. In the same way there are offerings to Surtr of Surtshellir, to Thorgerdr and to Thorri.[240]

There may even have been a general cult of the giantesses, to go with the cult of the disir, although once again we enter the realm of speculation here. It depends on interpretation. Apart from Skadi, there are several giantesses whose name includes the word -dis, Bergdis, Eydis, Glamdis, Skjalddis and Thordis. [241]

As I discussed in the section on Giant-Girls, there does exist evidence of what may have been a giantess-cult. But it is written as a story of Christian conversion, like the stories about Thorgerd, and it is rather late. The *Volsathattir*, included in the Flt, tells the story of what seems like either an act of very odd worship or possibly a prank, involving a horse's penis. The penis in question was supposedly sanctified to the mornir, which is the part that needs interpretation (in more ways than one). It could mean:

(1) morn, masc. sing., meaning 'sword' testified among sword-heiti in *SnE*.

(2) mornir, fem. pl., meaning "giantesses'. This meaning is best exemplified in the sources: Sn.E. Thulur; Hst 6; Thorsdrapa; Sturl. saga I, 280.

The consensus seems to favour the plural form, so we have to ask ourselves if this is some sort of cult of the giantesses, or a fertility cult of some kind. Folke Strom thinks that the mornir and disir are the same, so that it would be an offering to a collective of female powers, probably for fertility. Steinsland thinks that it is an indication of the sort of cult

---

[240] Ibid: 186.
[241] Ibid: 504.

that was associated with the giants, making offerings towards them to keep the destructive aspect of their power at bay.[242]

Both Steinsland and Welshbach think that the images found on various stones in Scandinavia may represent the giantesses. Welshbach links the "snake-witch" stone from Gotland to Skadi. As she says, it is not clear that Skadi has anything to do with the actual stone, but the image of a female holding a snake in either hand does make one think of the binding of Loki. It is easy to make a picture in the mind's eye of Loki tied down and Skadi approaching him with a snake writhing in her grip. Welshbach relates this to the little bronze statue from Grevensvænge in Denmark, of a woman in a corded skirt, which she says is holding a snake. She and Steinsland also instance the rune-stone image that is usually interpreted as an image of Hyrrokin. In the picture the woman riding the wolf has a snake for a rein, and two more snakes in her hands.[243]

The snakes themselves make a statement about the giantesses. After all, snakes have their own reputation for magic, and, to the Norse mind, the biggest snake of them all was the Midgard Serpent. As a symbol of power that can both set limits and be chaotic it can't be equalled. It also underlines the outsiderness of giantesses, who, like snakes and wolves, are wild creatures that can harm, but might also be helpful if approached properly.

In What Way Are the Giants "Chaotic"?

Justifications for the enmity between gods and giants come in several forms. We have looked at the lack of reciprocity between them, and the resulting low-level hostilities between them that result from this. This lack, and hostilities generally, are often justified on the ground that the giants are chaotic, so "it's no use trying to deal with them", so to speak.

But, from whose point of view are they chaotic? And how?

As Lotte Motz and Margaret Clunies-Ross point out, the giants live in a recognizable social world, with families and other forms of relationships that mirror our own. The Thiazi

---

[242] Steinsland 1986: 218.
[243] Welshbach: 55-7.

and Skadi stories tell us that they recognize at least some of the same legal norms, namely inheritance and the requirements of bloodfeud.

There are three reasons usually given to explain why the giants would be seen as chaotic. First, because they were created before the cosmos was, so they are chaotic by definition. (The same could be said of the Titans and Tiamat's children.) Second, because while they have various goods and specialized knowledge, they don't put them to productive use the way the gods do. A corollary to this is that when the gods and giants do interact, their giant appetites and lack of self-control militate against any sociability. Third, that their reproductive methods are an element of chaos, going against the ideology of creation.

1. The giants, like the Titans, Tiamat's children (often translated as "brood", with all its animalistic and horror-movie connotations) came first, before the cosmos was ordered, and therefore embody that inchoate, chaotic state in their own selves.

2. This obviously justifies the raiding and killing and cheating that the gods do. The wisdom of Vafthrudnir, the ale-kettle of Hymir, the mead of poetry all have to be stolen from the giants, or tricked out of them, before it can be put to good use. (The mead of poetry is a strong example, as Suttung kept it locked away in a cave, where no one could use it.) When the giants and gods do try to co-exist, as with Thiazi taking most of the ox, or Hrungnir threatening to drink Valhalla dry, or Freyja's shuddering reaction to being married to a giant, we see that their appetites overstep the mark that gods and humans must keep to. (Of course, you could argue that gods and humans, not the giants, define the bounds, which handicaps them from the start.) Aegir is the exception, being able to feast with the Aesir without incident.

3. Ymir, who represents an androgynous male being, symbolizes a state of undifferentiated sexual and physical existence. Born of venom, he and his creation have to be wrong. (Further, Uli Linke sees the "venom" that flows from Elivagar as symbolic of menstrual blood, which caused Thor such problems later. She sees the blood as contrasted with the benign milk flowing from the primaeval cow, Audhumla.)

Of course, all these points are, as I have said, concerned with limits placed by the Aesir and the humans of Midgard.

The building of an ordered cosmos with boundaries came literally at the expense of the giants; Ymir was killed and dismembered, and all but two of the rest of the giants were drowned in his blood. (From Odin's point of view, the creative power of the primeval androgyne was divided amongst the various parts of the cosmos, rather than creating mutants like the six-headed giant Ymir made.) Kristensen thinks that the gods deliberately turned their backs on their giant heritage to create an ordered cosmos, and as such Ymir and his kin had to be both figuratively and literally sacrificed to make the worlds. The creation of the cosmos, and of the categories "god" and "human" demanded it.

CHAPTER 9

Why do the Gods and Giants Interact at all?

Reading the Norse myths in Edith Hamilton's book, a much younger me wondered why the gods and giants kept getting in one another's way. After all, if Ragnarok was going to be a war between the gods and giants, wouldn't it be much wiser to stay away from each other? It always seemed to end in tears, usually for the giants.

As Clunies-Ross puts it:

> *The gods live at the self-defined centre of the world, while the giants inhabit the periphery, often conceptualized as a cold, rocky landscape that must be approached by means of a long, arduous journey. Frequently the divine journeyer to giantland must either cross a body of water or assume the power of flight in order to gain access to his giant antagonist. Why, then, do these two groups of beings come into contact at all?*[244]

The simple answer is, of course, that otherwise there wouldn't be a story. If Aristotle was right and a story needs a protagonist and an antagonist, who are in conflict over some aim, then we have to bring the two aetts together to have a story.

As Clunies-Ross goes on to say, each has things the other wants, and there is no simple mechanism of exchange by which the two parties can trade goods or knowledge. And, course, there is the exchange implied in marriage, which is totally tabooed, since the Aesir refuse to acknowledge their kinship with the giants. The Aesir want things the giants have, however. Odin comes to them for the mead of poetry, and for exchanges of lore and wisdom. Loki through his trickery gets Slepnir, among other boons. Thor, on the other

---

[244] Clunies-Ross 1989: 4.

hand, mainly fights giants, an activity he justifies as almost ecological, keeping the various species/races in balance.

The relations between the Vanir and giants are more complex in some way, because on the one hand two of the top Vanir (we have to assume) are married to giants, but the Vanir are allied with the Aesir, and we know that Freyr fights the giant Beli at Ragnarok. (If we assume that Freyr's servant did indeed kill Gerdr's brother, then the two marriages are complicated by the fact that both Vanir are implicated in the deaths of their wives' relatives.) In addition Loki says that Njord was sent as a hostage to the giants, so we have to assume that there is some degree of reciprocity among the Vanir and giants that there isn't with the Aesir.

The gods want things from the giants, but the giants also want things, or more accurately people, from the gods. Hrungnir wanted Freya and Sif, while the Master-Builder wanted Freya and the sun and moon. Thiazi wanted Idunn and especially the magical apples that went with her. (In a twist on this theme, the dwarf Alviss wanted Thor's daughter Thrud, leading to a sort of wisdom-contest between father and potential suitor.)

There are incidents of cooperation between the two groups, but they are rare. The giantess Hyrrokin is the one who pushes Baldr's boat out to sea at his funeral, after being sent for as the only one who could do it. Even then, the entire Aesir had to intercede with Thor so he wouldn't kill her. (*Gylf* 49) The other notable incident is the feast of Aegir's, which Tyr and Thor had to fetch a brewing-cauldron for in *Hymskvida*. The story of the actual feast is told at the beginning of *Skld*, as a frame for Bragi's stories about the Aesir. (The fact that most of them are about how the Aesir tricked and defeated the jotunar seems a little tactless, but Aegir doesn't seem to mind.) It is interesting that both these incidents follow Baldr's death, as if they were part of one last effort to stave off Ragnarok by easing tensions between the two groups.

Having said that, on the few occasions when giants did end up in Asgard, they were treated politely. Hrungnir, chasing after Odin, ends up riding into Asgard, where he is given ale (Freyja being the only one brave enough) and he boasts that he will take her and Sif and smash the place, which seems churlish. The Master-Builder also visited Asgard, when he made terms with the Aesir about their walls, and that seems to have gone off peacefully. (No doubt both parties went away thinking they'd tricked the other.)

Of course, there are many stories about wars between a primordial race of beings like the giants and a newer, younger race that may well be descended from the older ones. The Greek Titans, the Mesopotamian Tiamat and her offspring, the Irish Fomorians, are all examples of this pattern.

In Norse myth, the gods go to great lengths to separate themselves from the giants, going so far as to kill their maternal grandfather to construct an ordered cosmos from. The blood from his body nearly drowns all the rest of the giants, but some survive and soon there are lots more of them. So the gods build a wall around Asgard, as they took Ymir's eyebrows to make a boundary for Midgard. So you can see why they react with hostility at the giants' incursions; when you go to all the trouble of building an entire cosmos to keep your relatives out, it would be nice if they stayed out.

And of course, there is the final interaction between the two lying at the back of all of this, when both gods and giants will perish. That makes the killing and raiding between the two parties much more serious. The story can be told in two ways. First, as Odin's attempts to gather intelligence about how it will happen, Loki's efforts, finally, to bring it on, and Thor's attempts to keep the giant outside the bounds the Aesir have defined. Second, you can see it from the giants' point of view, as frustrated attempts at exchange with their own kin, leading to raiding and other harassment, which is repaid with murder.

As for the Vanir, they seem to occupy a strange position, passively inculpated in the murder of Thiazi, but apart enough that they can marry giant-women, which the Aesir will not or cannot do. Perhaps because they are not blood relations of the jotunns, their relationship with them can be less fraught with complications and bad feeling.

CHAPTER 10

Who are the Vanir?

There are really three main questions about the Vanir:

1) who are they?

2) how are they different from the Aesir? and

3) where are the rest of them?

To tackle the first, here is a quote from a dictionary of Norse myth:

> *Fertility figures, who fought a war against the Aesir, and exchanged hostages. The god Njord was one of those who was given to the Aesir, and he and his two children, although formally counted among the Aesir, maintain their affiliation with their former kin. The Vanir are also indirectly involved in the myth of the mead of poetry, since Kvasir, from whose blood the mead was made, was himself first created from the shared spittle of the Aesir and Vanir with whom the truce was formally concluded.*
> (Andy Orchard, Cassell's Dictionary of Norse Myth and Legend)

Orchard's capsule description of the Vanir includes just about all the important elements. The main myth involving them is the war between them and the Aesir, and its consequences. I have already described the aftermath in the chapter on Njord, since he was one of the hostages exchanged between the two groups.

To expand a little on Orchard, I have assembled the most important points about the Vanir in bullet form:

- "Vanir" related to Scandinavian words for "friend", and to words in other languages for "pleasure" or "desire"
- They live in Vanaheim, which is variously located (see Nine Worlds section)
- A war with the Aesir, which they either won or fought to a standstill

- Only three named Vanir: Njord, and his children Freyr and Freyja
- They exchanged hostages with the Aesir, trading either Njord for Hoenir, or Njord and Freyr for Hoenir and Mimir
- In another version, the two groups of gods spat in a vat to make Kvasir, who underwent a series of adventures of his own
- Njord had to divorce his wife after he went to live with the Aesir, because they didn't allow marriage between spouses (*Ys*)
- Loki accused Freyr and Freyja of continuing the sibling/spouse relationship (*Lks*)
- Njord will return to them at Ragnarok, but we don't know what happens to them during that apocalypse.

We know about the Aesir - Vanir war from two sources: the Eddic poem *Vsp*, and Snorri's more detailed version in his book of kingly sagas, *Hkr*. Since Snorri clearly used the poem as a source, it is worth looking at it in some detail.

Voluspa 21-4

Larrington's trans.	**Dronke's trans.**
She remembers the first war in the world,	She remembers the war, the first in the world,
When they buttressed Gullveig with spears	when Gold Brew they studded with spears
and in One-Eye's hall they burned her;	and burned her in Hárr's hall,
Three times they burned her, three times she was reborn over and over,	three times burned her three times re-born - often, unscantingly -
yet she lives still.	yet she lives still.
Bright One they called her, whenever she came to houses,	Bright Heiðr they called her at all the houses she

Njord and Skadi

the seer with pleasing prophecies, she charmed them with spells;	came to, a prophetess of good fortune - she conjured spirits to tell her.
she made magic wherever she could, with magic she played with minds,	Sorcery she had skill in sorcery she practised, possessed.
she was always the favourite of wicked women.	She was always the darling of a bad woman.
Then all the Powers went to the thrones of Fate,	Then all the Powers strode to the seats of fate,
the sacrosanct gods and considered this:	sacrosanct gods, and gave thought to this:
whether the Aesir should yield the tribute	whether Æsir should yield to exorbitant claims
or whether all the gods should partake in the sacrifices.	and all the gods should get tribute.
Odin hurled a spear, shot it over the host;	Óðinn flung and shot into the host –
that was still the first war in the world;	it was war again, the first in the world.
the defensive wall was broken of the Aesir's stronghold;	Torn was the timber wall of the Æsir's stronghold.
the Vanir, indomitable, were trampling the plain.	Vanir by a war charm were live and kicking on the plains.

It starts with Gullveig coming to the Aesir, and although it's not stated directly, most scholars assume Vanir sent her.

Njord and Skadi

The Aesir, however, attack her with spears, and then try to burn her. (The punishment for a witch, Tolley notes.[245]) In the next stanza, we hear of Heidr, who goes about to women's homes performing seidr. (Assumed to be the reborn Gullveig.[246])

In Dronke's interpretation, the Aesir then debate whether to share their tribute with the Vanir, and, unsurprisingly, vote no. So then the Aesir declare war, and the Vanir break through their wall. The Vanir are left alive (Larrington has "trampling", but Dronke and others prefer "kicking"[247]) and the Aesir debate accepting them.

Snorri's version, in the *Ynglinga saga* section of *Hkr*, goes as follows:

> 4. Odin went with his army against the Vanes but they withstood him well and defended their lands. Each of them was in turn winner; both sides harried one another's land, and did each other great scathe. And when they became weary of it, they arranged to make peace and gave each other hostages.

Snorri goes into some detail about the hostage exchange, although in this version he says that Kvasir was added to the exchange after Mimir, famous for his wisdom, was included. He doesn't say why, but says that Kvasir was the "wisest of their men" so presumably it was to keep up prestige.

The *Prose Edda*, which was intended as a manual for poets, has a more involved Kvasir-myth, in answer to the question of how poetry originated. Here, Snorri tells us:

> Bragi replied: 'The origin of it was that the gods had a dispute with the people called Vanir, and they appointed a peace-conference and made a truce by this procedure, that both sides went up to a vat and spat their spittle into it. But when they dispersed, the gods kept this symbol of truce and decided not to let it be wasted, and out of it they made a man.
> (Faulkes' trans.)

"The gods" who kept the spittle were presumably the Aesir, since when Kvasir goes missing we're told it was the

---
[245] Ibid: 22.
[246] Dronke 1969: 42.
[247] Ibid: 42.

Aesir who went looking for him. As with the Mimir story, we see the Vanir not valuing a gift that the Aesir are able to convert into knowledge.

In neither version does Snorri tell us what exactly the war was about, but he does tell us a little about how the Vanir differed from the Aesir:

> *Niord's daughter was Freyja. She was a priestess and she first taught the Asaland people wizardry, which was in use with the Vanes. Whilst Niord was with the Vanes he was espoused to his own sister (for that was lawful with them), and their children were Frey and Freyja. But in Asaland it was forbidden to wed such near kin.*

A great deal of ink has been spilled over the incestuous Vanir with their kinky magic (the "seidr" of which we know so little and have speculated about so much).

We have passing references to the Vanir in several other Eddic poems. *Alvissmal* tells us what different groupings, including the Vanir, call the sun, moon, and other natural phenomena. The Vanic ones sound rather pleasant. Clouds, for example, are Kites of the Wind.

Thrymskivida tells us that the god Heimdall has the power to foresee the future, "as the Vanir also can". As you might expect, there has been much debate on whether that means Heimdall is a Van, or if it means that he just has the same power as they do.

In *Sigrdrifumál* the Valkyrie Sigdrifa tells the hero Sigurd the mystic lore of runes. She tells him that once sacred runes were carved onto various deities and other creatures, and then "scattered with the sacred mead" (verses 15 - 18). The verse goes on to tell us that the runes are divided among the Vanir, Aesir, elves and mankind.

Unsurprisingly, *Skr* mentions the Vanir several times. When Skirnir arrives, Gerdr asks him if he an elf, or an Aesir, or of the wise Vanir. After Skirnir finally browbeats her into accepting Frey, she says, rather pathetically, that she had never expected to love one of the Vanir.

Vafprudismal refers not only to the Vanir, but also to Vanaheim, telling us that Njord was from Vanaheim, but was sent as a hostage to the Aesir, although he will return at Ragnarok.

In *Gylf*, Snorri quotes a verse about Gna, as she travels through the sky on horseback; some Vanir see her and ask what is flying up in the air. (Although in the passage, it is Snorri who mentions the Vanir, not the verse he quotes.)

What makes the Vanir different from the Aesir?

As I mentioned above, Snorri makes the Vanir's sexual arrangements and their magic distinguishing characteristics. The Aesir practice neither seidr nor sibling marriage.

Snorri's authority for both statements was probably the Eddic poem *Lks*. Loki taunts both Njord and Freyr by implying that anyone whose parents were brother and sister was never going to turn out very well, and calls Freyja a "witch": *fordeaða*. This fits with the general uneasiness about and disapproval of seidr, which colours all that we know about it. Women could get away with it, but it was seen as unmanly, and in one saga a man killed his brother because he practiced seidr.

We also know from *Ys*, which treats Njord and Freyr as kings, rather than gods, that their reigns were noted for peace and plenty. It tells us that Freyr was worshipped as a god after his death because his reign was so prosperous.

So the Vanir gods seem to have specialized in the well-being of society, whether granting prosperity or sexual pleasure, while the Aesir seem to have focused on political power, war and magic. The differences between them are sometimes more of degree than kind, but the Vanir's focus on well-being is clear.

Fertility of Beast and Soil: Frey controls sun and rain, "and through them the bounty of the earth" (Byock's trans.). He was called the "shower god", *skúrgoð*, in a face-off between his worshippers and Óláfr Tryggvason. On the other hand, Thor was also frequently invoked for good crops, but with a different spin:

> *Thor, they say, presides over the air, which governs the thunder and lightning, the winds and rains, fair weather and crops... If plague and famine threaten, a libation is poured to the idol Thor...*[248]
> (Adam of Bremen IV, 26 Tschan's trans.)

---

[248] Tschan 2002: 207. (Also quoted p. 42 of Arnold 2011.)

Njord and Skadi

In a late charm, the woman invokes Frigga and Freyja for an easy childbirth, but only Frigg (Aesir) actually helps someone overcome childlessness. Njord, as a sailor's god, is not involved here.

Control of Seas and Weather: Njord, as we know, controls the seas, the winds, and fires, all of which can menace sailors, and Frey looked after weather for farmers. When it comes to weather, though, Thor is the pre-eminent god, who could wreck their efforts with one strike (which might explain their propitiating him). The Vanir gods seem to have been more about good weather. Freyja doesn't seem to have any connection to weather.

Sexuality: On the other hand, Freyja comes to the fore here, as the Northern version of those fierce Middle Eastern goddesses such as Ishtar and Anat. We are told that she delights in love songs, and that it is good to pray to her for love. Loki (in *Lks*) accuses her of having slept with all the gods and alfs, and in the late story *Sorla thattur* she trades sex with four dwarves for her emblematic necklace/girdle Brisingamen.[249] Frey's major myth tells how he fell sick with love for Gerdr, and Adam of Bremen tells us people offered a libation to the Frey's image when they were married. He describes this image, in a temple in Uppsala, as follows: "The third is Frikko, who bestows peace and pleasure on mortals. His likeness, too, they fashion with an immense phallus."[250] Njord was married to his sister, otherwise unknown, and later married Skadi, briefly. He seems to have left sexual matters to the younger generation, who, if Loki is to be believed, carried on the incestuous family tradition. In the Saga *Herrauds ok Bósa* the guests at a wedding drink three *minnis* (religious toasts): one to Freyja, but the others to Odin and Thor (ch. 12).[251]

Battle: It's hard to know if Njord was involved in the Aesir-Vanir war or not. One has to assume he was. He is not a particularly warlike god, and his role as hostage and husband seems to point to a more diplomatic role. His children, however, seem more like the Aesir in their interest in war. Freyja gets half the slain, sharing them with Odin, and in the late *Flt* she is charged to prolong a battle until the

---

[249] although she draws the line at giants.
[250] http://en.wikipedia.org/wiki/Freyr
[251] Tapp 1956: 86.

end of time. Her dwelling, Folkvangr, is also suggestive, since it means either "Field of the People" or "Field of the Army"[252]. Freyr seems to have been the prototype of the young warrior; Ulfr Uggason referred to him as 'battle-bold", and gives his boar's name as "Battle-Tusk"[253]. (Note that Freyr rode the boar, an animal known for its fierceness.) We also know that, unlike his father, Frey fights at Ragnarok, and dies at the hands of the fire-giant Surt. Earlier, he defeats Beli using an antler. (Beli was probably another giant, since *Haustlöng* uses the kenning *bölverðung Belja* "Beli's bale-troop" to refer to giants.[254])

Wealth: Both Njord and Freyr were called wealth-giving gods. Frey was invoked for peace and abundance (*ár ok frith*), and "determined men's success in prosperity". (*Gylf*: Byock) Of Njord we are told that he was "so rich and prosperous that he could grant wealth in land and valuables to those who ask for his aid." (Ibid) Freyja weeps tears that turn to gold, and her daughter is named Hnoss, "Treasure".

Royalty: Frey and Njord were ancestral kings of the Swedes, making them both god-kings and divine patrons of their line. Frey's by-name, Yngvi, became a synonym for king, as in *Yngvi-aettir*, "rulers, kings". Freyja helped Ottar onto the throne with her magic in *Hyndluljod*, thus establishing herself as a patron of royalty. However, the ultimate ancestor of the Swedish kings was Odin, who nominated Njord to rule after him. Odin also established another royal line, the Jarls of Hlaðir, with Skadi, and his son Skiold married Gefjion and founded the line of the Danish kings. He is also the ancestor of the Volsungs. Haraldr hárfagr's lineage went back to Thor in one account. (The god who fits the other 1st function slot, Tyr, does not appear in any kingly role, or as an ancestor of kings.)

Magic: Freyja and Odin come to the forefront here, being the magic specialists among each group. We know that Freyja taught Odin the magic known as seidr, which was so disgraceful and therefore remains mysterious. Odin had his own forms of magic, such as galdr, and of course he found the runes. The was itself shows the difference in their magics: a clash between Odin's ability to unfailingly cause death

---

[252] Simek 1996: 87.
[253] known as Gullinbursti, "Gold-Bristles" elsewhere.
[254] http://en.wikipedia.org/wiki/Beli_%28Norse_giant%29

against Freyja's ability to revive the fallen, so that as fast Odin kills them, she brings them back.[255] Another possible type of Vanir magic is foreseeing the future, since we are told that Heimdall could see the future as well as any Van. (*Thrym*)

The differences between the two groups, and the war between them, have been explained in two ways. First, the historical school sees the war as reflecting a real conflict between two groups. This idea has faded away, although the new matriarchy theory of Old Europe versus patriarchal invaders has given it some new life. (Lotte Motz, too, saw the Vanir and Aesir as gods of two different groups of settlers in Scandinavia, unlike the earlier historical school who thought that the Vanir were indigenous.)

The other school follows Dumézil's theory that the war between the gods reflects the tension between the producer class (and their deities) and the warrior and aristocratic classes. The Vanir, as fertility deities, would have represented the producers, and the Aesir, whose chief gods are Thor and Odin, the other two.

In India and also Greece, the third-function gods have to fight to be recognized as equals by the other two, who see themselves as superior. Dumézil saw this as the motivation behind the war between the Aesir and Vanir. The lines in *Vsp* about sharing tribute could certainly be taken that way, and the war ends when the Vanir prove the Aesir's equals in combat.

There are problems with both theories, of course. The first one assumes a lot that isn't actually proven, since we have no records of combat between two peoples that would fit the Aesir - Vanir war. Just because Snorri talks about the two sets of gods as if they were humans in *Hkr*, doesn't mean that they are rooted in history.

The problem with the second theory is twofold. First, when you step down from broad abstractions to the details of individual deities and their stories, they tend to either contradict the deity's supposed function or overlap with others. There's a very interesting essay by Jens-Peter Schjolt which pairs up deities for each function: Thor and Frey for

---

[255] Dronke 1988: 231.

fertility, Odin and Thor for war, and Odin and Frey for sovereignty.[256] They just have differing specialities within that function: Thor protects the crops from evil forces while Frey provides the sexual power that makes them grow, for example.

Second, I'm not really convinced that you can reach across thousands of years and massive distances just like that. Most of what we have on Norse myth comes from the medieval period, which is a long time after any expansion of Indo-European peoples across the Eurasian continent. Given that, how do you know what's true Indo-European and what's borrowed from the neighbours or independently arrived at?[257]

Where are the rest of them?

Whether the Vanir are a reflection of a historical people, or a fed-up producer class demanding their share, it seems strange that we only ever learn the names of three of them. If we accept the story of the hostage exchange and Mimir's beheading, then there must have been more of them to sit in council, get angry with Hoenir's silence, and cut off Mimir's head.

There are several different answers to this question, ranging from Rudolf Simek's opinion that the Vanir as an entity are an invention of Snorri's, to the modern pagan tendency to recruit any spare deities as Vans, especially female ones.

Simek set forth his argument in a very controversial paper called "The Vanir: an Obituary", which pretty much sums up the contents. He argues that the word "vanir" is very rarely used in the poetic corpus, and he adduces Lotte Motz's argument that there is little difference between the Aesir and Vanir, and no proof that the Vanir were fertility deities. (He thinks this is a modern invention.) At best, "vanir" is just another word for "god". The expansion of the word to mean a specific set of gods comes with Snorri, who took the kenning *vanabrudr* (vanir bride) for Freyja, and the reference to vanir in Vsp, and developed a whole mythos of a group of people living in the east, who had a war with the Aesir and

---

[256] Schjødt 2012.
[257] Doniger 2008: 27.

eventually exchanged hostages. Snorri envisaged the Vanir as a parallel group to the Aesir, and that is how he writes about them. So Simek's solution to the missing Vanir problem is simple: there aren't any.

This paper, republished in the RMN Newsletter (available online) drew two responses. One, by Frog and Jonathan Roper[258], essentially agreed with Simek, adding that the Eddic mentions of "wise vans" may have owed more to alliteration (*vinir vanir*) than any real idea of a group of gods called Vanir. Clive Tolley's paper[259] sets out the contrary argument, pointing out that there is much that we don't know about Norse myth, and the Vanir's connection to shameful magic and sex makes it likely that a post-Christian society would not record a lot of their lore.

He also argues that based on place-name evidence, the cults of Njord, Freyja and Frey were popular, whether they were known as Vanir or not. He also wonders why a post-Christian author would choose to make up the Vanir, thus inventing a cult. Neither he nor Simek think that Snorri invented the kennings using the word vanir, although they can't be dated:

> ...the 11th century Þórðr Særeksson mentions Njǫrðr as a vanr in a lausavísa (Skj B1 304); Freyja is referred to as vana brúðr ['bride of the vanir'], by the 12th century Einarr Skúlason in Øxarflokkr 5 (Skj B1 450). However, kennings presented by Snorri that mention the vanir are unlikely to be anything other than genuine, though undatable as he does not cite his sources (except Þórðr): he records "vana goð/guð" ['god of the vanir'] (Njǫrðr, Freyr, Freyja), "vana niðr" ['offspring of the vanir'] (Njǫrðr, Freyr), "vanr" (Njǫrðr, from Þórðr Særeksson; Freyr), "vana dís" ['dís of the vanir'] (Freyja) (Skáldskaparmál, Ch. 6, 7, 20).[260]

These alone would establish that the Vanir were known as a distinct group. However, there is also evidence from the Eddic verses themselves, as well as skaldic poetry, as discussed above.

---

[258] Frog and Roper 2011.
[259] Tolley 2011.
[260] Tolley 2011: 21.

One good point Tolley makes is that since Norse myth never had a centralized pantheon, there's never going to a completely tidied-up mythology that answers all our questions. Another theory about the Vanir rests of this untidiness.

Schjodt agrees with this, and further argues that whether or not the term "Vanir" referred to a specific group of deities, the three we do know about share common characteristics: wealth, sexuality, and abundance.[261] While the Aesir and Vanir do overlap, there is enough evidence to show that they also were distinctive enough that no one was likely to mistake Njord and Freyr for Odin and Thor. He also points out that a living religion is rarely precise, so we shouldn't expect Norse myth to be too coherent.

Simon Nygaard[262] suggests that the vagueness of the Vanir comes from an older conception of deity: one that does not have a formalized pantheon, but rather a collective of beings that might not be sharply differentiated. This would reflect social arrangements: in a more tribal society, a looser pantheon would make sense, while the rise of chieftains would bring about a more hierarchical religion, with a clearly defined chief god and associated deities. This would explain why only the Vanir who were closely associated with the central, Aesir, religion would be defined personalities.

Nygaard sees the Vanir in general as more like the alfar (elves), who also give fruitfulness and prosperity, but who are not individual beings. You don't have to go all the way with the historical argument to see that the alfar and Vanir have a lot in common, and Freyr as god of the alfar could be seen as a personification of their benign powers. (Many writers have pointed out the continuities between alfar and Vanir, but I'm not sure how many have mentioned the undifferentiated nature of both.)

Other writers, especially modern Heathens and Pagans, have refused to allow the Vanir to go unnamed, and have proposed all manner of candidates for Vanir-dom. Some are obvious, like Nerthus, while others like Idunn, Frigg and Sif seem to reflect a gendered idea of the Vanir - Aesir divide.

---

[261] Schjødt 2012.
[262] Nygaard: 224.

Njord and Skadi

To be fair, I can understand the urge to fill in gaps in the mythology, and if we accept the story of Mimir, we have to assume there were more Vanir than just the three we know. I leave you with this thought, from an article by Alfgeir Freyjasgodhi: if Njord and Frey are "honorary Aesir" now that they are hostages in Asgard, Hoenir and Mimir (before they killed him) were "honorary Vanir". [263] Further, this may explain why Hoenir survives Ragnarok. If the Vanir are not involved, then he, like Baldr, is conveniently on the sidelines until the new world arises.[264]

---

[263] Freyjasgodhi 1988: 9.
[264] Kristensen (17) thinks the same, except that he locates Hoenir in Hel.

CHAPTER 11

Who is Njord's sister?

All we know of the goddess Nerthus, whom Tacitus refers to as Mother Earth (Latin *Terram matrem*) is to be found in his *Germania*, chapter 40:

> *By contrast, the Langobardi are distinguished by being few in number. Surrounded by many mighty peoples they have protected themselves not by submissiveness but by battle and boldness. Next to them come the Ruedigni, Aviones, Anglii, Varini, Eudoses, Suarines, and Huitones, protected by river and forests. There is nothing especially noteworthy about these states individually, but they are distinguished by a common worship of Nerthus, that is, Mother Earth, and believes that she intervenes in human affairs and rides through their peoples. There is a sacred grove on an island in the Ocean, in which there is a consecrated chariot, draped with cloth, where the priest alone may touch. He perceives the presence of the goddess in the innermost shrine and with great reverence escorts her in her chariot, which is drawn by female cattle. There are days of rejoicing then and the countryside celebrates the festival, wherever she deigns to visit and to accept hospitality. No one goes to war, no one takes up arms, all objects of iron are locked away, then and only then do they experience peace and quiet, only then do they prize them, until the goddess has had her fill of human society and the priest brings her back to her temple. Afterwards the chariot, the cloth, and, if one may believe it, the deity herself are washed in a hidden lake. The slaves who perform this office are immediately swallowed up in the same lake. Hence arises dread of the mysterious, and piety, which keeps them ignorant of what only those about to perish may see.*
> (Birley's trans.)

There is no mention of Nerthus at all in the *Eddas*, or indeed in any later writing. However, a mythos has sprung up around this figure, mainly based on etymology and the lore about Njord.

Njord and Skadi

So we can imagine that most people's mental file for Nerthus goes something like this: fertility goddess, called Terra Mater, sacred procession, sister/wife of Njord or maybe a hermaphroditic deity, same name but one Germanic, one Norse, and parents of Freyja and Frey. Further information might include an idea of Nerthus looking after the earth's fertility, while Njord did the same for the seas.

Unfortunately, most of this is supposition, not truth. We don't even know her name for sure. The original manuscript of Tacitus' *Germania* is long lost, and all we have are various copies of copies made in the fifteenth and sixteenth centuries. The source manuscript, from Fulda, was not an original itself, but a copy from the time of Charlemagne. This too was lost, and is known to us only from copies made in the 15th and 16th centuries. So it's not surprising that variations crept in.[265] As Lotte Motz puts it:

> *There are, in fact, reasons why the equation Nerthus-Njord should be questioned. Nerthus, i.e. nertun, is only one of several forms transmitted by the manuscripts: the others are necthum, neithum, herthum, Nerherthum, Verthum. The variant nertum was chosen by Grimm because it corresponds to Njord.*[266]

I suppose Grimm must have thought he solved a problem, because while some Norse deities have Germanic counterparts - Woden, Donar, Ziu, and Frowe - the Vanir don't. There is no Germanic Njord, Frey or Freyja. (Friday is named for Frigga.) The Vanir appear to have been Scandinavian deities, and very popular there. When Grimm found the version *nertun*, he must have felt quite pleased. After all, as Gardenstone points out,

> *Njord's place-names in Scandinavia [are] predominantly in three areas: in East Sweden (Ostergotland), in the east of Norway and in the coastal areas of West Norway. In Denmark there are at Funen (Fyn) and Zealand (Sjaelland) only three indications for one of the Njord names.*[267]

He thinks these few southern ones are more likely to come from the Viking age. So we still have to explain how a

---

[265] Gardenstone: 23.
[266] Motz 1992:3.
[267] Gardenstone: 44.

Njord and Skadi

god and goddess separated by a thousand years and in two separate places can be one deity.

Another problem for scholars has been the fact that Nerthus' cult, as it comes down to us, resembles Frey's more than Njord's. We have a description in *Hauks þáttr hábrókar* of Frey's image being taken around the villages in a cart, which sounds very similar to Nerthus' perambulations. Grimm shows some ingenuity in getting over this, however:

> *but Freyr is altogether like his father, and he again like his namesake the goddess Nerthus.*[268]

So Frey = Njord, and since Njord = Nerthus, everything is okay. Now all we need to do is say that Freyja is the same as Frey, and there's the Vanir done and we can all go home early. It also doesn't answer the objection that Njord isn't a god of earth's fertility, and we have no record of his statue travelling about.[269] (One contra-argument is that the Codex Regius, the original version of the Edda, describes Njord once as Vagna-Gud. Most others, however, read it as Vana-Gud, or Vanir God. Of my two copies of the *Prose Edda*, Byock says "wagon" and Faulkes says "Vanir".)[270]

However, it seems that some deities, both male and female, did occasionally go out among the public in the manner still practiced by Catholic saints and Hindu deities. In *Hauks þáttr hábrókar*, which is part of the 14th Century manuscript of *Flateyjarbók*, there are two different accounts of such perambulations, one by Frey, and another by another being called Lýtir. We don't know much about Lýtir, but:

> *King Eric of Sweden is said to have led the god's wagon to a certain place, and waited until it became heavy, the sign that the god was present within. Then the wagon was drawn to the king's hall, and Eric greeted the god, drank a horn in his honour, and put various questions to him.*[271]

Prophecy may have been Lýtir's main function, since one interpretation of his name is "lot, share, foretell", from the Swedish *liuta*, "cast lots". (The other is "blemish".)[272] His

---

[268] Grimm: 252.
[269] http://en.wikipedia.org/wiki/Cats_of_Queen_Berúthiel
[270] Gardenstone: 80.
[271] Davidson 1990: 93.
[272] Simek 1996: 199.

priests may have been *spámaðar*, or seers. Some Swedish place-names such as Lytisberg and Lytislunda suggest cult centres. Some have suggested that he is a variant of Frey; but if he is a god of prophecy, he must be a separate entity, since Freyr is never credited with foresight.

The account of Freyr's statue, and the cult attached to it, is more interesting. In *Ögmundar þáttr dytts ok Gunnars helmings*, also in *Flateyjarbók*, we are told:

> *Great heathen sacrifices were held there at that time, and for a long while Frey had been the god who was worshipped most there — and so much power had been gained by Frey's statue that the devil used to speak to people out of the mouth of the idol, and a young and beautiful woman had been obtained to serve Frey. It was the faith of the local people that Frey was alive, as seemed to some extent to be the case, and they thought he would need to have a sexual relationship with his wife; along with Frey she was to have complete control over the temple settlement and all that belonged to it.*[273]

In the story a young man named Gunnar escapes to Sweden after being suspected of manslaughter, and he meets the priestess and ends up driving Frey's wagon for her. He goes on to reveal that the pagan idol is nothing but a demon and takes over as Frey's image himself. (This story is one of a set of conversion narratives, so not from a pagan point of view.) In the story, however, the Swedes are delighted with their god, who now can eat food, accepts their gifts, and gets the priestess pregnant. (In the *Flateyjarbók*, Sweden is the place for all things pagan.[274])

The priest/ess of opposite gender, the wagon, and the idol that represents the deity, as well as its travels, are similar to the account Tacitus gives us of Nerthus. Like Lýtir, Nerthus signalled her presence (in the same manner?) and this was the cue for their travels. [275]

So far there hasn't been much evidence for Njord and Nerthus as similar deities. What about their names? Edgar Polomé throws cold water on this, with a rather impatient air:

---

[273] http://en.wikipedia.org/wiki/Freyr
[274] Heinrichs 1994: 55.
[275] West 2007: 133. Apparently when Athena steps into a warrior's chariot in the Iliad, it becomes too heavy to move.

a) *Nerthus and Njorðr are two separate divine entities, whatever similarity their names show; as Dumézil (1959) had already recognized, the latter is a sea god [which also explains his particular wealth], and the former is typically a fertility goddess; b) in spite of the similarity of their names, they reflect different derivations: Njorðr belongs to the root *ner- "plunge and emerge" with the suffix *-tu-; Nerthus is rather to be linked to Celtic *nerto.*[276]

Polomé tells us that *nerto- means, "force, strength".

Hopkins, on the other hand, thinks that the similarities of Njord and Nerthus, on the basis of "associations with wagons, bodies of water, and fertility"[277] can overcome this objection. (Presumably Hopkins is going with the "wagon-god" interpretation of the Eddic phrase.)

A more fruitful area of inquiry might be to consider goddesses that are similar to Nerthus herself, Germanic earth-goddesses. Here there are several theories which strike me as promising. Gardenstone sees links between Nerthus and Hertha, while Lotte Motz thinks that the travelling goddess is like Frau Holle and the rest, who visit households and reward or punish. This seems to me to make a lot more sense. The variant name "Herthum" would fit in here, too.

As for the mysterious sister of Njord, a new candidate has been proposed. In the December 2012 issue of RME Newsletter, Joseph S. Hopkins offers up Njǫrun for the job[278]. As he points out, she's somewhat underemployed, as she only appears a few times in the sources, mainly as kennings. In Skld she appears in a list of goddesses:

> *[Now are called the Ásynjur (Goddesses) by these names:]*
> *Frigga and Freyja*
> *Fulla and Snotra*
> *Gerða and Gefjon*
> *Gná, Lofn, Skaði*
> *Jörð and Iðunna*
> *Ilm, Bil, Njörun*[279]
> *and in Alvissmal, in a kenning for night:*

---

[276] Polomé 1999: 149.
[277] Hopkins: 43, n. 6.
[278] Ibid: 39-44.
[279] quoted by Hrafnhild: 15.

Njord and Skadi

> 'Night it's called among men, and darkness by the gods,
> the masker by the mighty Powers,
> unlight by the giants, joy-of-sleep by the elves,
> the dwarves call it dream-goddess.' [Draum-Njörun]
> (Larrington's translation)

Snorri also mentions *Draum- Njǫrun* in his *Nafnaþulur*, or lists of poetic names for various things, at the end of *Skáldskaparmál*.

Njǫrun is used as a kenning for a woman in poetry by Kormákr Ögmundarson, Hrafn Önundarson and Rögnvaldr Kali, and also in verses in in Íslendinga saga, Njáls saga and Harðar saga. Also, eid-Njorun or fire-Njǫrun as a kenning for woman appears in verses by Gísli Súrsson and Björn Breiðvíkingakappi, and hól-Njǫrun in a stanza by Björn hítdælakappi. In *Gislis saga Súrssonar* he relates a dream where a woman appeared to him, whom he uses many kennings for, including *eid-Njǫrun*:

> I thought in my sleep that the Sjofn of the silverband [woman, good dreamwoman] stood weeping over me, this Gerdr of the robe [woman, good dreamwoman] had wet eyelashes, and the noble Njorun of the wave-fire [woman, good dreamwoman] bound my wounds very quickly. What do you think was in that for me?
> (ch. 38)

In light of this, some have seen Njǫrun as a goddess of dream and night. One website posits that she is a goddess of dream, especially honoured by the dark-elves in Svartalfheim, and that her hall is a good place for prophetic dreamwork.[280] Of course, this is UPG, but it could connect up to the general feeling in Norse and Germanic cultures about the prophetic and intuitive abilities of women.

The name Njǫrun sounds a lot like Njord, and there have been attempts to link them before. Jan de Vries thought Njǫrun might be the Scandinavian version of Nerthus. Finnur Johnsson thought it might be a name for the earth-goddess, and Alfred Morey Sturtevant posited "a possible link among Njǫrun, *Nerþuz, and Njǫrðr by way of *ner-."[281]

The connection Njǫrun - Nerthus is an easy one to make, because it "sounds alike" and it would solve a lot of problems.

---

[280] http://www.northernpaganism.org/shrines/niorun/about.html
[281] Hopkins: 39.

Some have made the jump already; in Boar, Birch and Bog by Nicanthiel Hrafnhild presents Njorun as one of the faces of Nerthus, perhaps even her real name. A lot of his information is UPG, of course, although he does make some interesting points (quoted from p. 16):

> *The common Njör- stem fits the naming conventions seen elsewhere among the Vanir (Frey/Freyja, Ullr/Ullin, Njörð/Jörð).*

The -un (-n) ending is common among the names of the Ásynjur – c.f. Gefn/Gefjun (also Gefjon), Lofn, Sjöfn, Iðunn (with a doubling of the final consonant), Sigyn and Syn.

There is a possible connection with the Etruscan/Latin goddess Nerio, who was the personification of valour. If so, it would line up with the other references to the Vanir being able warriors (though non-aggressive).

The first point is the weakest, and to be fair, Hrafnhild doesn't insist on it, but admits that *Ullin is a reconstructed form and Njord/Jord not generally accepted.

The other three points are more interesting, especially the connection with Nerio, an equally obscure Roman goddess of battle. She was a personification of valour who was partnered with Mars, and occasionally equated to Bellona or Minerva. She sometimes received offerings of war booty.[282] I find it hard to imagine any Roman war-goddess being non-aggressive, but it's the name not the manner we're comparing here, and we already know that Nerthus comes from the Celtic -*nert*, "force, strength".

As Hopkins says, in Norse myth all beings and objects have names, and it would be nice to finally put a name to Njord's sister.

---

[282] Adkins and Adkins 2000: 163.

CHAPTER 12

What about Gerdr and Freyr?

It is a curious fact that the male Vanir feature mainly in two myths about marriage and wooing – both of which are highly questionable from our point of view. Njord's myth is the subject of this book; his son's Frey's wooing of Gerdr is a parallel story. In *Skr*, our main source of this myth, the author seems to be very aware of this parallel, bringing Skadi in at the beginning to emphasize the Vanir – giantess theme.

Frey, in fact, has three main myths: his appearance amongst the Aesir, marriage, and death. As John Lindow suggests, there is very little else for a god of peace and fruitfulness to do in the warlike world of the Aesir.[283] (The same applies to his father, for that matter.)

The story begins with a transgression. While Odin was away, Frey sat in Odin's high seat, Hlidskialf, and looked out at all the worlds. He looked in Jötunheim, and saw the giantess Gerdr. He was instantly smitten, and became lovesick for her. *Skr* doesn't make any comment about this, but in the *Prose Edda* Snorri explicitly links Frey's presumption with his punishment – languishing about infatuated. (There is a suggestion here that while Odin can handle the sight of seductive giantesses, and even get the better of them, Freyr can't.)

In a move reminiscent of the plot of *Hamlet*, Njord and Skadi send for Frey's servant Skirnir to find out what is wrong with their son. (In Snorri, only Njord is mentioned.) Skirnir fears he will incur his master's wrath, but instead Frey tells him his woes, and then commissions him to get Gerdr for him. To assist him, he gives Skirnir his horse and sword.

Skirnir rides off into Jötunheim, presumably with the aid of the supernatural horse, and arrives at Gerdr's homestead. She comes out, and offers him mead, although she says she

---

[283] Lindow 2001: 121.

fears he may be her brother's slayer. She asks him if he is elf, Vanir or Aesir that braves the fire to see her. He tells her he is neither, but has come from Frey. Then he offers her treasure: first eleven golden apples, and when she turns those down, the ring Draupnir, which dripped eight more rings every ninth night, and was burnt on the pyre with Baldr.

When she's not impressed, telling him she has all the gold she needs, he turns nasty. First he threatens her with the sword, saying he'll cut her head off. Gerdr is unmoved, telling him her father will give him a battle, Then Skirnir curses her with a "taming wand" (Larrington's translation). His curse is quite elaborate, but it boils down to three main points: lewdness and frenzy and unbearable desire.

Gerdr gives in; saying, "I had never thought that I should ever love/ one of the Vanir well." Skirnir then presses his point, asking her where she will meet with Frey. She tells him the place, and says she will be there in nine nights' time. The poem ends on a comic note, as when Skirnir tells Frey this, he wails that he can't wait that long.

As I mentioned above, Snorri also relates this story in the *Prose Edda*. He gives it a moralistic gloss, and plays down the ferocity of Skirnir. He has Frey tell Skirnir to ask Gerdr for her hand, while the poem leaves it open what Frey's intentions are. Frey is the threatening one in this version, telling Skirnir to bring Gerdr whether her father is willing or not. Frey gives Skirnir his sword to defend himself with, and the implication is that he did not return it, because Snorri goes on to say because of this Frey had to fight Beli with an antler, and will be unarmed at Ragnarok. We are left to assume that Frey's magic sword, which fought on its own, remained in Jötunheim, another example of a "wrong-way" transaction.

The only other mention of Frey and Gerdr is in the *Ys*, a part-legendary account of the kings of Sweden, beginning with Odin, Njord and Frey. We are told that Frey had a wife, Gerdr, and a son, Fjölnir, who became king after him. Since Snorri also wrote this saga, we can see why he might want to regularize relations between Frey and Gerdr.

The first thing to note is that whoever composed *Skirnismal* obviously knew the Njord – Skadi story. No doubt that reference to Skadi at the beginning was intended to remind the audience of that other Van – giantess encounter. (For modern audiences, it merely serves to confuse, since it refers to Skadi as Frey's mother. We can only speculate as to why.)

The next thing we notice is that the direction of travel is reversed – Skirnir goes to Jötunheim, where Skadi had to travel to Asgard in search of a husband. Also, both Gerdr and Skadi have a blood feud to deal with: Skadi has lost her father, Gerdr her brother.[284]

When Skirnir tries to bribe Gerdr into meeting Frey, he mentions eleven apples of gold. This has always been understood to be the apples of Idunn, and Gerdr's contemptuous dismissal of them suggests that she was aware of Thiazi's fate.

And, in another reversal, Skirnir threatens Gerdr with being stared at by all, in other words, subject not just to Frey's male gaze, but that of all males. Skadi seems to invert this when she sizes up the gods by their feet, but of course it rebounds on her.

Also, while *Skr* ignores Gerdr's desires in favour of Frey's, the whole action of the Njord – Skadi myth springs from Skadi acting on her own desires: first for compensation, then for a husband, and finally to be free of that husband when things don't work out.

Skadi	**Gerdr**
she seeks groom	Skirnir seeks bride
symbolic castration of Loki	threatened rape with rune-wand
marries Van willingly	marries Van unwillingly

Both Skadi and Gerdr qualify as beautiful giantesses, rather than the ugly troll-wife type. (Both are described as "shining". Michael Chabon, in an essay on Norse myth,

---

[284] Dronke 1962: 262.

notes, "everything that is beautiful is something that glints".²⁸⁵) This has influenced some writers on this subject, such as Lars Lonnroth, who argued that Gerdr wasn't "really" a giantess, or at least was a more refined type of giantess, and not at all like those troll-wives. This could be said to be a somewhat speciest argument. John Hnefnell Adalsteinsson turned this around and suggested that Gerdr's reluctance to go with Frey could be compared to Freyja's outraged reaction to the idea that she should marry a giant in *Thrymskivda*.

Both get promoted to Asynia – we have not just Snorri's authority for this, but other material as well. (Stephen Mitchell suggests that a Van of each generation is mated to a giantess in order to mediate the tensions between gods and giants that form such a large part of Norse myth.²⁸⁶) Both Skadi and Gerdr seem to have an autonomous zone in which they have some authority: Gerdr at her household while her father is away, and Skadi at Thrymheim, because her father is dead.

In *Gylf* Snorri mentions Gerdr after Iord (Thor's mother) and Rind (Vali's mother), as counted among the asyniur. What's interesting is that he begins with Gerdr's parents, Gymir and Aurboda, and then tells the story of Frey's infatuation with Gerdr. She gets her own chapter, moreover, while Skadi appears in Njord's. This may reflect her more equivocal status amongst the Aesir, as a divorcee.

Gerdr's pedigree may be less than assured, however. Paul Bibre lists several things that point to *Skr* being from the 12th century or later, including the runes used in Skirnir's curse.²⁸⁷ Another anomaly is Gerdr's father, Gymir, who seems to have been a sea-spirit in skaldic lore, and not a giant.

Although the introduction to *Lks* says the sea-giant Aegir was also called Gymir, Aegir is married to Ran and has nine daughters. Both Gymir and Aurboda are mentioned in that section of *Hyndluljod* known as *Voluspa hin skamma* or the Short Seeress' Prophecy, which is also thought to be a late work. (Hollander suggests the twelfth century.²⁸⁸) This poem

---

²⁸⁵ Chabon 2009: 48.
²⁸⁶ Mitchell 1983: 117.
²⁸⁷ Bibre 1986: 20.
²⁸⁸ Hollander 1990: 137.

Njord and Skadi

says Thiazi was kin to Gerdr's parents, and that they were all giants. Whether this was lore or simply a poet's conceit we'll never know, but linking Gerdr and Skadi makes sense.

Skadi' story is older, and her lineage assured. The only problem is, who was her mother? One of those questions that will forever be unanswered.

Indeed, some think that the Frey – Gerdr story grew out of the rich material of the Skadi – Njord myth. That story offered us two patterns: the rape of a goddess by a giant, and the marriage of giantess and god. I think that Skr has elements of both – the seduction of a giantess by a god (usually an Odinic theme) and the union of giantess and god (a Vanic theme).

Despite the Odinic theme, what stands out from this myth, as it does in the Njord-Skadi myth, is the hero's passivity. Neither Njord nor Frey take any part in their own wooing, and in fact they do very little in either story. In both cases a stand-in does their wooing for them, either Loki or Skirnir. Frey employs Skirnir deliberately, while Loki seems to have acted on his own initiative, but it comes to the same thing. There is an argument to be made that in both cases the gods use others of lower status to do things they would consider undignified, but as a result they're sidelined in their own stories.

Skadi's demand was for compensation, and she got it, in the form of Njord. It is curious that Frey loses his sword to Gerdr, who keeps it. A magical sword that fights by itself is a thing worth having, and surely not surrendered lightly. Was it wergild as well? The other interesting thing about the sword is that there are very few stories of a woman acquiring one. The main example is Hervor, of *Hervorarsaga*, who braved her father's burial mound and his own counsel to get his sword. She went on to become a warrior until she married, and eventually her sword passed to her son.

The other significant thing about Freyr's sword is that it represents a rare instance of treasure going from the gods to the giants. This may help to explain Snorri's evident disdain for Freyr's love-sickness. And not only is there the loss of the sword, but as Lindow points out, Freyr stops talking and socializing with the others, which goes against the Odinic wisdom that is found in speech, while drinking is symbolic of the mead of poetry, as well as being a ritual that functions as a social glue. In other words, even before he hands over his sword, Freyr has been incapacitated by the giants.[289]

In the "manly" world of the Norsemen, this could only read as weakness, and the *Íslendinga saga* backs this up. In it the chieftain Sturla Sighvatsson is clearly meant to be like the god Freyr, even down to his nickname, Dala-Freyr. (In theory, it meant something like "master of the Dales"[290]; in practice it was a gibe about Sturla's womanizing.) Finally, his enemies accused him of a lack of "manliness", cowardice and vanity. (The two who gave him this name were connected to Snorri Sturluson, by the way.)

Sturla is killed by Gizurr Thorvaldsson, who is explicitly compared to Odin in the same saga. Clearly both the incident of Hlidskalf and Freyr's lovesickness generally were in the author's mind. It would be interesting to know if there was competition between the two cults and their followers more generally.

Both Freyr and Skadi lay down their weapons in order to pursue their marital or at least amorous agendas. Snorri of course sees Skadi's capitulation as positive, since it means her re-feminization. She was armed and threatening in the role of honorary son, so removing the arms moves the grievance she bears towards a resolution, and removes the threat to the gods.

As I stated above, however, there is some tension in the way Freyr comes across, between what some like Lotte Motz have seen as heroic, imperious behaviour and other views of him as a weak, effeminate figure. We know that he has a horse, a magic sword, and a magic ship, and that he fights at Ragnarok, unlike his father.

We don't know if he fought at the war against the Aesir, and in the euhemeristic version of *Hkr*, his reign as king was noted for peace and fruitfulness, not war. Some have taken that and the reports of effeminate priests at Uppsala to mean that Freyr had a "womanish" side.

Motz's argument sticks closer to the view of Freyr in *Skr*, where he comes over as more forceful and less of a nice guy, whereas in *Skld* it is quite clear that Snorri thinks he's a bit

---

[289] Lindow 2008: 169.
[290] North 2009: 275.

Njord and Skadi

of a wimp, pining after a woman. (Of course, as some have pointed out, Snorri doesn't seem all that interested in romance, preferring stories of valour.) This means that Njord and Freyr are short-changed by him, although he acknowledges that they are important deities.

Lindow thinks that the nine nights that Freyr has to wait for Gerdr is a deliberate reference to the nine nights that Njord and Skadi spent at Thrymheim and possibly at Noatun. (See the section on Nine Nights for more.) In both cases, also, the residence seems to have been appointed by the goddess involved, since Gerdr is the one who chooses Barri, and Skadi's home is Thrymheim.

Both the nine nights and the golden apples lead us to think of the Skadi myth, and to agree with Gerdr that whatever Freyr is proposing, it's not likely to end well. Odin and Thor desert their giantess partners, and Freyr's father managed either twelve or eighteen nights with Skadi before they called it quits. Not a great record. That may in fact have been what the poet was getting at - Njord and Skadi's nines end in divorce, while Freyr and Gerdr are still apart at the end of *Skr*.

A last note on Gerdr and Skadi; several authors have said that both are involved in a blood feud with the gods, on the basis of verses in *Skr*.:

> 16. 'Tell him to come into our hall
> and drink the famous mead;
> though I am afraid that out here may be
> my brother's slayer.'

and:

> 25. 'Do you see this sword, girl, slender, inlaid,
> which I have here in my hand?
> Before these edges the old giant will fall,
> your father will be doomed.'
> (Larrington's trans.)

The second verse sounds more like a threat than anything else; like much of Skirnir's persuasion, it is in the conditional mood[291]. There is more meat in the first, which might well mean that Skirnir or Freyr has killed Gerdr's brother for real, either in the past or just now.

---

[291] http://en.wikipedia.org/wiki/Conditional_mood

CHAPTER 13

What is it that Giantesses Want?

The subject of Gerdr brings us to a very famous paper by Carolyn Larrington called '"What Does Woman Want?" Mær and munr in *Skírnismál*', which discussed Skirnir's threats of cursing to Gerdr, versus what we know of what women might themselves have desired, as shown in the sagas. Since most treatments of *Skr* have tended to assume that Gerdr was symbolically the fallow earth waiting to be fertilized, they didn't concern themselves with the "earth" felt about it.

There is a paper by Roberta Frank called "The Lay of the Land in Skaldic Praise Poetry", which documents the number of skaldic poems which describe a victorious ruler sexually "taking" the land, usually figured as Jord, the earth-goddess. From the 10th century alone, we have:

> ...three skaldic poems. The first by Guthromr sindri, reports Hakon the Good, king of Norway, when on campaign did not abandon "Onarr's daughter [the land] but found her another lover. Two or three decades later, a second poet, Eyvindr Finnsson, confirms the military seizure of Norway by Hakon Sigurdarson, jarl of Hladir, 'under whose arm the bride of Val-Tyr [land] lies, all the way east...'(62,15). The third skald, Hallfredr, addressing (probably) the same jarl, gives this metaphor of masculinity a vigorous workout.[292]

No doubt this sort of thing is very flattering to the king or jarl involved, and to the male reader today. But a female reader can't help but note that what we are talking about here is essentially rape. It's not like the earth is getting any choice in the matter, and no one ever seems to consider what she might think of the matter. (Lotte Motz has noted that unlike the Irish sovereignty-goddess Medb, or the Sumerian

---

[292] Frank 2007: 177.

Njord and Skadi

Innana, Jord doesn't get to pick her lovers.[293]) The only thing that makes *Skr* stand out from these narratives is that Gerdr does actually get to have an opinion, even if she doesn't get her way.

There have been honourable exceptions to this scholarly blindness, such as Jon Hnefill Adalsteinsson, who compared Gerdr's reaction to Freyr to Freyja's reaction to being married to the giant Thrym. (Although Adalsteinsson doesn't pursue the point, Freyja's comment about being the most *ragr* of women if she married a giant is neatly paralleled by Skirnir's threat to curse Gerdr with unslakable sexual desire if she refuses his master.) And, of course, Lotte Motz was very critical of the whole interpretation of Gerdr as an earth-goddess awaiting the fertilizing sky-god, seeing Gerdr as meaning something like "the one enclosed" and connecting it to a whole range of Norse goddesses and other powerful female figures.[294] Motz, who sees the giants as earlier powers supplanted by the newer gods, sees Gerdr (and Skadi) as subjugated to the gods' patriarchal power.

Frank is also very dubious about the universality or indeed even the "Norseness" of a sacred marriage between earth-goddess and sky-god:

> *The poet's central task was to catch and keep those moments in which his patron seemed illuminated by a divine force, and the drott, the prince's family, servants, clients, and armed retainers, enveloped in a new confidence. Hallfredr's four half-stanzas celebrated and legitimated a ruler's seizure of land in stereotypical phrases that fused military and erotic imagery, a metaphoric interchange sanctioned a millennium earlier by Ovid and the Roman elegists. The assumption that only archaic German myth or ritual could have produced the skald's suggestive poetry is mistaken.*[295]

I think it's a fair guess that the stanzas equating Harald with Odin were more to do with current politics than some Indo-European myth or ritual.

I'm not sure how well *Skr* maps onto that template anyway. Freyr is the Veraldagud, the World-God, not a sky-

---

[293] Motz 1996: 78.
[294] Motz 1981b: 125-6.
[295] Frank 2007: 190

god like Odin, Tyr and Thor, and Gerdr is not the earth-goddess, but a giantess. Myths that celebrate nuptials or at least sex between two deities usually have a fair bit to say about the sex and the bond between the two. This must be the only fertility myth of sky and earth in which the earth doesn't want to know, and is essentially blackmailed into giving up her autonomy. In fact, the poem ends before the two meet, which seems a bit pointless.

Further, if you accept either Clunies-Ross' idea that the giants are shut out of the gods' exchange network, or Kristensen's theory that gods are separating themselves from their chaotic giant relatives, either way the giants are the outsiders, who need to be controlled or eliminated. So it may very well be that for a medieval audience Skirnir's behaviour was okay, whereas if a representative of the giants had tried that on Freyja, Sif or Idunn the story would have a very different ending.

We see things from the vantage point of the Aesir. From the jotunar's POV, things look rather different. Gerdr and Skadi both are very clear about what they want, both negative and positive. Gerdr is the negative, since she does not want to be with Freyr, and makes this clear. Neither bribery nor threats move her; it takes a magical curse to change her mind, and even then she makes it clear that she has been browbeaten into it. Skadi, at the positive pole, states very clearly that she wants an Ase husband, and not just any Ase, but Baldr. She says this straight out, in her usual blunt fashion.

Skadi's choice from the feet is of course unsuccessful, although she does managed to reverse the usual direction of looking. She takes on the role that is usually given to Freyr or the skald Kormak, who is smitten by seeing Steingerdr's foot. Of course, he only sees her because she is peeping at him, so it becomes a bit more complicated. Skadi naturally plumps for the most attractive of the gods, just as the male giants want Freyja. Both are usually rationalized by saying that Skadi wanted position and power, and the giants the power of fertility, but maybe Baldr and Freyja are the sexiest of their genders? So naturally Skadi is disappointed to be saddled with an old man who is too stubborn to change residence.

It might be worth looking at their stories from the POV of the giantesses. As Larrington puts it, the story from Gerdr's point of view goes like this:

Njord and Skadi

> Ski☐rnisma☐l is about a woman, apparently autonomous, and with unhampered access to wealth, who is sitting at home in her hall one day when an unknown man arrives and demands that she arrange a sexual rendezvous with a second man, Freyr. She refuses. Bribes and threats are offered and rejected. Finally a violent threat to the very core of her female identity brings about her submission and she agrees to meet the importuner.[296]

Gerdr is quite clear about what she doesn't want; Freyr.

But Skirnir's rune-wand also lays out a series of curses that presumably reflect his idea of things no woman would want. He threatens her with:

a. Being invisible (26.4–6); being a public spectacle (28)

b. Unbearable sexual frustration (29; 34.5–8; 36.3–4)

c. A physically repulsive husband (31.1–3)

d. Low social status and loss of autonomy (30; 35.4–10)

e. Male, authoritarian disapproval (33)[297]

This may seem odd to us, but such curses did exist at the time this poem was being composed. One 13th century runic inscription wishes a "harmful skag-valkyrie" with the *ergi* of the "she-wolf", wishing u☐þoli (unbearable desire) on her. (The she-wolf was believed to mate with the lowest animal in the pack, also reflecting the "three-headed thurs" that Skirnir wishes on Gerdr.) In *Clarí saga*, the maiden king Séréna suffers that very fate when she is humiliated, forced to wear coarse clothing which exposes her, and live with an ogre, all to break her spirit and humble her pride.[298]

As for what women do want, their *munr*, or desire, is sovereignty, rule over themselves. The Wife of Bath, through her own example and through her tale, tells us as much. The curse on the Loathy Lady is only lifted when Gawain gives up his power to determine the course of her life, giving her back her autonomy. (Note, also, that both McTurk and Taylor saw the Wife as having similarities to Gudrun and Skadi.)

---

[296] Larrington 1992a: 5.
[297] Ibid: 7.
[298] Fridriksdóttir: 120-1.

As Larrington points out, Gerdr's choice is between Freyr and the three-headed Hrímgrímnir, but there is no other option on the table. She cannot choose not to choose. The autonomy that she seems to enjoy at the beginning of the poem, welcoming people into the hall and negotiating directly with Skirnir, as if she was without male relatives, is to end, either way. She won't be allowed to be a loose end like Skadi, who went off into the wild zone, leaving Njord behind.

Skadi's story also looks a little different if we start from her end. Her father comes home one day with Idunn and her apples, and all the jotnar are happy. Then one day Thiazi (according to Snorri) goes out fishing, and Idunn disappears. Thiazi chases Loki, and doesn't come back. Somehow, word gets back to Jotunheimar that Thiazi is dead, and the gods consider this a great feat.

Naturally, Skadi is incensed, and sets out for Asgard to see what concessions she can wring out of them by way of compensation and atonement. The Aesir seem to be reasonable, and offer her a choice of husband, but she winds up with the wrong one. Still, she decided to make the best of it, and gets to see Loki humiliated and her father's eyes cast into the heavens as stars. She and her new husband go to Thrymheim, but all he does is moan about how noisy it is. So they go to his place where the constant noise of the sea and the gulls starts to get to her. Skadi decides she doesn't, after all, want this man for a husband, not that badly, and leaves him. No husband is better than this one.

When you compare the stories of Skadi and Gerdr, you wonder if one of the reasons Skirnir was so stern with her was to make sure she didn't wriggle out the way that Skadi did. Skadi managed to hang onto her autonomy, even if she did lose in the husband stakes. Gerdr appears to have lost hers.

"The Gaze" and Norse Women

Both the myths of Skadi and Gerdr involve questions of who is looking at whom, and the power that goes with that. If we accept Motz's interpretation of her name as meaning "Enclosed", then we could argue that like Gunnlod or Menglod she was hidden away, and the many barriers between them and suitors are a way of protecting that seclusion and, like Þryð in Beowulf, controlling who can see them. [299] For Menglod it all ends happily, we assume, although cynical me can't help but think of Michael Palin's bolshy peasant in *The Holy Grail*. Things don't go so well for Gunnlodr or Gerdr, perhaps because they're giants. Perhaps coming under the gaze of an Ase or even a Van is not so good.

Skadi's story seems to completely invert that. She gazes at the gods, and chooses from among them, and the main sufferers are Njord, who ends up with no wife (again), and Loki, who's endangered his testicles for nothing. Then she retreats to her mountains, away from them all and the troublesome glances of the gods; at least until Odin happens along, if we accept that genealogy.

In the maiden king sagas we sometimes see the heroine deliberately avoiding being caught in the male gaze. In *Sigurdar saga thogla*, which Fridriksdóttir describes as one of the more violent and misogynistic stories, Sedentiana hides herself in her castle to escape male attention: "she decides to reside in her new castle, and the black one will never be able to look at her, with a view of pleasing his eyes."[300]

Vision was no innocent thing in the Middle Ages, although their theories of gazing were somewhat different from ours:

> *Vision, in the medieval period, went far beyond our modern conception of the sense. There was thought to be a physical continuity between the eye and the visible object; the eye was even considered to be able to "assimilate itself to the visible object as seen and cognized. In some sense, the eye becomes what it sees even as it sees what it sees." (Denery 2005, 89, 95)...A look could also hold baser connotations... looking was widely equated with lusting.*[301]

And no wonder, if looking was such a tactile thing. There were two competing theories of vision in the Middle Ages, one holding that the eye sent out rays that touched the object seen, while the other reversed the direction, with objects sending rays to the eye. Both types turned up in love-poetry,

---

[299] Larrington 1992a: 11.
[300] Fridriksdóttir: 127.
[301] Jacobs 2014: 154.

with either the poet seeking out the image of the beloved, or else rays from the woman's eye were sent to the poet's, often allegorized as Cupid's darts.[302] The "lowly" position of the courtly poet could be interpreted in this way, and perhaps Snorri's version of Freyr's lovesickness is his comment on romances and love-poetry.

Vision is given a specifically Norse twist in the sharp, penetrating gaze of various characters in the literature. The god Thor nearly gives himself away when he's disguised as Freya, as Thrym asks why his eyes are so terrifying. (*Thrym* 27) Among mortals, males as diverse as St. Olaf and Sigurdr Fafnisbani were noted for their sharp or extra-good vision. Like Thor, Helgi Hundingsbana's eyes give away the game when he is disguised as a woman.

The only female exception is Svanhid, who perhaps inherited it from Sigurdr. When she is sentenced to be trampled by horses, she has to have her head covered so as not to spook them. There is also the more magical side of vision: prophecy, which is mainly but not exclusively female, and sorcery, which is equal opportunity (and sorcerers were dispatched like Svanhild, so they couldn't ill-wish their executors).

In a similar way, we hear of giantesses in the *fornaldarsagas* being shot through the eyes with arrows, presumably to both kill them and neutralize their magical abilities.[303] These giantesses are usually presented as monstrous, which legitimates violence against them, of course.

Jacobs argues that Helga of *Gunnlaugs saga* reverses the conventions of the gaze, but in a very feminine way.[304] She does very little; many commentators have been surprised by how passive she seems compared to many other women in the sagas. However, her looking is emphasized throughout, at important plot-points. Her grandfather, Egil Skalla-Grimsson and her father are described as having excellent eyesight, which doesn't seem a big deal to us, but before modern medicine and contact lenses it was unusual.

---

[302] Ibid.
[303] Fridriksdottir : 67.
[304] Jacobs: 164.

The story, in brief, is that Helga loved Gunnlaug, but was married to another. Her looking, even staring, at Gunnlaug is a motor of the plot. (Compare Steingerdr staring at Kormak, and Skirnir threatening Gerdr with being stared at.) As Jacobs points out, Helga rarely speaks, so her gaze must speak for her; her continued looking at Gunnlaug is her way of asserting herself as subject, instead of the object of her father and husband's desires. Jacobs thinks that Helga's gazing does what love-poetry does for the skald, both inspired by the distance between themselves and their desire.[305]

Giant-Girls, Phalloi, and Castration

Moving right along from blinding, castration comes in three kinds in Old Norse literature: mimed, or at least, playful; religious, as in the odd rite related in *Volsa thattr*; and finally, real violence done by one man to another. (You could also include a fourth category; the magical curses laid on Kormak and Hru☐tr that prevent them from consummating their loves.)

Writers of the sacrificial king school have tended to be (perhaps worryingly) interested in the episode where Loki ties his testicles to the nanny-goat's beard. From the outer limits (Barbara Walker) to the fairly normal (Richard North) this idea keeps cropping up. The idea that Loki has tackle ripped off to amuse a goddess is not out of bounds for mythology; the gods have done plenty weirder things. (When you can trace your ancestry back to an androgyne and a cow, your normal is different.)

However, while I can see connections between Loki and Baubo, I don't think that Loki died or became a woman or otherwise "fertilized the earth" either sacrificially or sexually. I certainly don't think there was ever any ritual like this one:

> *Like Kali, Skadi had to be propitiated each year with an outpouring of male blood in primitive sacrificial rites. Her annual victim was assimilated to the god Loki, who became a "savior" by fertilizing Skadi with his blood. Loki's genitals were attached by a rope to a goat, and a tug-of-war ensued, until Loki's flesh gave way and he fell into Skadi's lap, thus bathing her loins in his blood. The gods watched anxiously to see if Skadi smiled; and*

---

[305] Ibid: 165.

when she did, it means spring could return once more to the land.[306]

Presumably Ms. Walker thinks that Skadi was pleased by the blood.

I think that John Lindow and Anthony Adams get closer to the mark. Lindow thought that Loki was playing with notions of status, since the freeborn could only be punished with fines, while slaves were normally given physical punishment, including castration.

Adams' rather more gruesome paper looks at some historical examples but mainly focuses on the blinding and castration of Órækja Snorrason. This unpleasant episode from *Íslendinga saga* (the same one that featured the killing of Sturla Sighvatsson) follows another, threatened, mutilation of Hrafn Oddsson, who escapes by submission, essentially. You could say he choose symbolic over actual castration, given the nature of masculinity as it was constructed in the medieval north.[307] While some at the time may have seen his giving in to Gizurr Thorvaldsson as cowardly, all he loses is face, while Órækja suffers terrible physical injury, social isolation, and loses his wife.

This was certainly an illegal act, since castration was considered a "major wound" like blinding someone or cutting off their ears, which warranted retribution and payment.[308] Conversely, beggars, slaves and anyone guilty of bestiality could be castrated as punishment. Could this have been what Loki was referring to: a servile man, caught in a sexual act with a nanny-goat, and being paraded like an adulterer? I could see someone laughing at that.

The incident with Loki is part of the reason that Skadi is connected with this rather bloody idea. The other is the name "Morn", which is used in *Hst* to refer to her, and in general usage means a giantess. In the *Flt*, there is a rather odd incident related in the saga of St. Olaf, which is usually called Vǫlsa þáttr. It might be an indication of a cult of the mornir, or giantesses.

---

[306] Walker: 940.
[307] Adams 2013: 189.
[308] Ibid: 199.

Vǫlsa þáttr

This all supposedly took place while St. Olaf and his men were visiting a farm. While they were there, the farmer killed a stallion, and the story goes on to describe various possible rituals that are performed with it. (The Romans at least had the decency to stick to the tail for their rites.)

The odd thing is that if you read the actual story, it seems to start as a prank, or at least incorporates an element of teasing, as when the actual penis is severed, the farmer's son takes it into the room where the women are and shakes it at them, saying:

> *Here you may see*
> *a vigorous phallus*
> *severed from*
> *a father of horses.*
> *For you, slave-woman,*
> *this Völsi*
> *is not at all dull*
> *between your thighs.*[309]

After that, however, his mother takes it and preserves it with herbs and leeks, and wraps it in linen. Much later she takes it out, lays it on her husband's knees, and says:

> *Enlarged art thou, Völsi,*
> *and raised aloft,*
> *enriched with linen,*
> *supported by leeks.*
> *May giantesses*
> *accept this holy object,*
> *but now, my husband,*
> *you must accept Völsi.*[310]

The last four lines act as a refrain as the people pass it around, each time naming the person it is being passed to. Not everyone is enthusiastic; the daughter swears "by Gefjun/ and the other gods" that she is unwilling to accept the penis, but she participates in the ritual anyway. The whole thing ends when King Olaf throws it on the floor and the dog gets it. This upsets the whole family, but Olaf converts them, of course.

---

[309] https://notendur.hi.is//~eybjorn/ugm/volsi.html
[310] https://notendur.hi.is//~eybjorn/ugm/volsi.html

It's hard to know if we're meant to take this seriously as a pagan ritual, or if it's meant to be exoticizing in the same way as Thiazi and his brothers sharing out gold by mouthfuls. You don't have to be a Freudian to see that the Loki - goat incident, the serpent set over Loki later, and then this form a phallic pattern. Presumably this where the Frazerian school is getting the idea from.

There are two objections, however. First, we don't know if this was ever a pagan ritual; it could just as easily have been a joke, or possibly the writer made it up to contrast the ignorance of pagans with the superior knowledge of Olaf, who throws the penis to the dog instead of venerating it.

Obviously the "sacred king" school and its associated pagan and Heathen adherents see the volsi as another instance of the fecundation of the earth through sacrifice and ritual. What sort of evidence can be found to support such an idea?

It's difficult to disentangle the antiquarianism that the story obviously shows from any actual residue of pagan lore and practice. The story is obviously constructed on the "strange doings by yokels" model, also found in *Gautreks saga*. As Tolley puts it:

(a) each involves a king visiting an isolated farmhouse;

(b) the setting is an out-of-the-way place remote from normal society;

(c) the local inhabitants are shown living their lives in a manner which is contrary to the norms of society;

(d) the manner of life depicted is a source of astonishment but also amusement - the yokels are looked down upon as benighted and ignorant souls;

(e) the coming of the king marks the end of this strange society, by conversion or suicide;

(f) the yokels put up no resistance to the newcomers, despite outnumbering them and being noticeably inconvenienced by them;

(g) the strangest parts of the description of the yokels' actions are highlighted by accompanying them with verses.

All of these elements tend to suggest that the writer finds the pagans funny and outlandish, which makes it more likely that the episode was invented. Tolley thinks that the author may have included just enough older material to make his story seem both genuine and old.

One of these is the lin and laukr motif. While Tolley thinks that the lin was supposed to be flax rather than actual linen, he notes that leeks (for which read any allium) were both preservative and had a medicinal function: they were said to increase semen and help women conceive.[311] The shape of a leek or the shoot from an onion or garlic bulb left to sprout may well have suggested such ideas.

The stallion sacrifice and the priapic nature of the whole rite suggest Freyr, of course, and the famous priapic statue found at Rällinge in Sweden is usually attributed to him. This is mainly due to the account by Adam of Bremen, which states that there was a statue of Freyr at Uppsala, and it was notable for its enormous penis:

> *The third is Frikko, who bestows peace and pleasure on mortals, His likeness, too, they fashion with an immense phallus.*[312]

He goes on to say that they make offerings for war to Thor, but for marriages to Frikko.

Sacred horses were kept at Freyr's sanctuary at Thrandheim in Norway. In Olaf Trggvason came there to destroy it, and happened upon a sacrificial rite: a horse was about to be killed "for Freyr to eat"[313], but the king took the horse and rode it to the temple, which was completely taboo, of course. (He attacked images of Thorgerd as well.) Horses were kept at temples of Freyr in Iceland as well, and we know that Hrafnkell had a stallion dedicated to Freyr and twelve mares as a stud. In *Vatnsdaela saga* the sons of Ingimund were followers of Freyr, and they liked to attend the horse-fights held in the god's honour. None of this demonstrates a phallic cult, but it does show a connection between Freyr and horses, especially since both Hrafnkell's horse and that of Ingimund's sons were named Freyfaxi, "mane of Freyr".

So we know that Freyr could be a phallic god, and that he was associated with horses. The other side of the equation is

---

[311] Tolley 2009: 693.
[312] Adam of Bremen/Tschan: 207.
[313] Davidson 1990: 97-8.

the word "mornir", which the horse's penis is being offered to. Tolley states that he does not see any evidence for a cult of the giantesses, but he does also say that the only giantess who is referred to as Morn is Skadi, in *Hst*, where Thiazi is referred to as Morn's father. (The poem also refers to Thor as the "waster of the morn's children"[314].) One reading of this is that the marriage of Njord and Skadi ("Njordr" read here as "strength, manliness", or else "concealment") is having a sacred wedding to Skadi. (Tolley is quoting Gro Steinsland, who has put forward a theory of sacred marriages between god/kings and giantesses as renewing the land.[315])

Tolley does make a good point about the word mornir, which could also be a masculine singular word, "sword". But I disagree with his contention that there was no cult of giantesses, as I have shown elsewhere in this book. It's not impossible that either the horse's penis was offered to them as a sacrifice or else an offering to Freyr (which would support the "sword" reading) could work.

A giantess-cult could possibly be one of the house-cults like the one *Vsp* refers to when Heidr is going about to women's houses and teaching them seidr. It is not the sort of activity that needs temples or public spaces of any kind, and this volsi-offering may well have been of the same kind. That does not mean that the author is not poking fun at it; the whole episode is too literary and patterned for it not to be a carefully-polished story. What lies behind it, what the author selected in order to make it sound convincing, is a matter for speculation. As Tolley himself points out, it still has scholars arguing over whether it was real or not, and if so what it meant.[316]

---

[314] Tolley 2009: 695.
[315] Ibid: 695.
[316] Ibid: 697.

CHAPTER 14

Why Could Skadi Claim Atonement and Compensation?[317]

> *(There is also one woman who is both to pay and take a wergild ring,* given that she is an only child, *and that woman is called "ring lady." She who takes is the daughter of the dead man if no proper receiver of the main ring otherwise exists but atonement payers are alive, and she takes the three-mark ring* like a son, *given that she has not accepted full settlement in compensation for the killing, and this until she is married,* but thereafter kinsmen take it. *She who pays is the daughter of the killer if no payer of the main ring otherwise exists but receivers do, and then she is to pay the three-mark ring* like a son, *and this until she enters a husband's bed* and thereby tosses the outlay into her kinsmen's lap.)
>
> Translation from Laws of Early Iceland: Grágás, tr. Andrew Dennis, Peter Foote, Richard Perkins (Winnipeg: Univ. of Manitoba Press, 1980), p. 181; Clover's italics.

This passage from the *Grágás* tells us under what (very exceptional) circumstances a woman may claim compensation for a crime against her family. Usually women were not allowed to do this, leading to the image of the whetting woman in the sagas, who urges her men on to revenge since she has no legal standing of her own. As we can see from Skadi's appearance at Asgard in armour and carrying weapons, she clearly feels that she is entitled to claim compensation.

There were two schedules for compensation in *Grágás*, *Baugatal* and *Vígslóði*, and both divide the kin of a slain person into four tiers, according to how closely related they were to the victim. The first is made up of the nearest kin, father, brother or son, who must pay up if their relative

---

[317] Faulkes: 56-7.

committed the crime, or collect if they are the plaintiffs. Their share is the main "ring" of the compensation. Then come lesser kinsmen, whose share of the wergild is less. The two schedules are exhaustive, tracing out all permutations of relationships. However, they are almost without exception men, aside from the "ring-lady", who gets the largest share of the compensation if there is no one else left to collect, basically.

This may not seem so unusual, but what makes it striking is that this relativeless woman fills the breach "*as a son* and even - since the clause applies only to the unmarried - as a "maiden". That the practice is of some antiquity in Scandinavia is suggested by the presence of similar statutes in the early Norwegian laws."[318] As the law-code says:

> *Now, there is one maiden who is called a baugrygr; she both pays into the baug and receives payments form it, if she is an only child and has come into an inheritance, till she is seated in the bridal chair; then she throws [the right and duty in the matter of the] inheritance back upon the knees of her kinsmen; after that she shall neither pay into, nor receive payment from, the baug.*[319]

This law claims to date from the time of King Hakon, grandson of Sverri, who enacted a new law-code in 1260 CE. This provision appears in the section on the reckoning of the wergild system.

Presumably the "ring-lady" had to be a legal man, with no living male relatives, because in Old Icelandic law women could not go to law. This is one of the very few instances in which a woman could represent herself and claim compensation in her own right. (Back then, your best bet was to be a widow if you wanted independence.) If you follow the sagas, women seem to have had a great deal of informal power, but the actual formal mechanics of the law had to proceed through a male relative, whether by blood or marriage. Since most Icelanders seem to have reckoned kin bilaterally, either would do.

The minute a woman married, however, any right to compensation she had went to her husband, since he was her legal representative. According to the law, any claim on

---

[318] Clover 1986: 46.
[319] Larson (trans.) 2011: 294. (originally 1935)

Njord and Skadi

her family for compensation went to the husband as well, but that doesn't apply here, since the right to wergild reverts to the woman's relatives on her marriage.

If you follow Clunies-Ross, this is why the gods give in to her request for a husband. Once married, as the law says, the duty of seeking compensation or continuing the feud falls to her kinsmen. Of course, they may also have wanted to settle the whole thing and have it over with - they'd had plenty of trouble with Thiazi already, and now it was coming from beyond the grave. It may well have been an attempt to better relations with the giants, thus staving off Ragnarok, from gods who'd suddenly had to face their own mortality each time they looked in the mirror or at one another. (Stephen Mitchell, for one, thinks the marriage was a way of resolving conflict.[320])

It seems counterintuitive, though, to be so keen to marry Skadi to Njord. Odin and co. must have been very sure that Njord wouldn't get "turned" so to speak, since one of the most common motifs in the sagas is that of a husband or other kinsman being goaded into avenging a wrong done to a woman. They were obviously very confident about Njord. Also, as Miller points out:

> *Practical kinship, whether based on shared blood, marriage, or even fictive kinship relationships, provided one of the chief bases for group recruitment in saga Iceland. People looked to kin and affines for aid in law and life. They avenged each other's wrongs; they invited each other to weddings and funerals; they gave each other gifts. They stood surety for each other and hired on their poorer cousins as servants.*[321]

Since the last thing that the Aesir wanted to do was associate themselves with their despised relatives, it's odd that they would agree to marrying one of them. Since Njord was a Vanir, it might not have mattered so much if he married a giantess. Perhaps the contest was rigged, because what would they have done if she had chosen Baldr?

The other parts of her compensation involve Loki humiliating himself to make her laugh, and, in a completely unexpected gesture, Thiazi's eyes being made into stars. We

---

[320] Mitchell 1983: 113.
[321] Miller 1990: 178.

notice that the gods do not offer her any monetary compensation or treasured objects. There were probably two reasons for this. First, and least pleasant, is that the gods were not in the habit of giving things to the giants, but taking them. Second, and a bit more speculative, is that Skadi had enough wealth of her own (after all, her father and his two brothers were proverbial for it) that her marriage to Njord the Wealthy would not seem incongruous. Marriage among people of unequal status or wealth was discouraged, although there were very few actual repercussions, mainly social rather than legal.[322]

The ring-lady in *Gragas* is assumed to be seeking compensation, since women did not usually seek vengeance. There has always been some ambiguity about Skadi's arrival at Asgard - it is unclear whether she is armoured and seeking to prosecute a blood-feud, or simply strengthening her claim to compensation by reminding the Aesir of what could happen if they didn't pay up. (Since it is in their interest to stave off Ragnarok as long as possible, the Aesir would not want to start a war with the giants.)

On the other hand, we know that the gods are immortal, and the only threat so far to their immortality has just died. His only issue is standing right in front of them. Still, the Aesir and giants do not have a blood-feud on the go, though Snorri seems to read their stories in that light, more than other writers.

For example, in *Gylf* we are told the story of Utgard-loki and how he deceived Thor and his companions. Immediately Gylfi/Gangleri asks how Thor revenged this, and Harr responds with the tale of Thor's visit to Hymir. Again when they get to Baldr's death, Gylfi again asks if it was avenged, and is assured that Loki will not forget it.[323]

There doesn't appear to be the sort of score-keeping that characterizes feuding among humans (although it gets slippery in long-running ones), but Lindow suggests it may be behind the pairings-off at Ragnarok. The gods, however, are immortal, and so for now the giants "must content themselves with raiding and other forms of harassment."[324]

---

[322] Ibid: 122.
[323] Faulkes 51.
[324] Lindow 1997: 58.

This is the real handicap the jotunns labour under - unlike the gods they can be killed. Thus Thiazi's theft of the apples changed the rules of engagement to their advantage.[325]

Given this, Skadi's decision to ask for compensation in the form of an Aesir husband seems odd. But, she is following the prescribed female role in asking for compensation, and for a husband. Where she is atypical is that she journeys to Asgard, across what we're told is a long distance through hostile terrain, and risks death to demand what she feels is her due. In a certain sense, she is in the same position as rich American women in the late 1800s coming to Britain. She has money, and she would like position, and the way to acquire that is through a husband.

So we have two different images of Skadi: either warrior maiden or, if not exactly peace-weaver, then someone who doesn't want the feud to escalate. As is often the case with this goddess, she manages to be outside the usual categories. This may help to explain how she got into Asgard in the first place, and how once inside she managed to broker a deal with the gods.

How powerful is Skadi?

So, the question becomes, what was so threatening about Skadi's grief that the Aesir felt they had to give in to her demands?

The first and most obvious response is that the Aesir wanted to delay the war with the giants as long as possible, to avoid the destruction of themselves and the world. But this begs the question of whether Skadi had that much power, either in herself or in her allies. She presumably has no near male relatives or else she wouldn't have been negotiating with the gods herself.[326] She may have carried some of Thiazi's prestige with her, but Thiazi was dead. We know he was rich, and powerful in magic, but Skadi doesn't appear to have inherited his abilities, only his home.

But the Aesir do negotiate with her, which suggests that either she carries a threat in herself (more on this below) or

---

[325] Ibid: 58.
[326] although Snorri tells us that Thiazi had two brothers, Idi and Gang, they don't appear in this myth.

else that Thiazi, who is described as "terrible", "powerful-minded", "mighty", or perhaps crucially, wealthy carries more clout than we know.

Another part of the answer lies in Skadi's reply to Loki's taunts about her father:

> *You know, if first and foremost you were at the killing when you attacked Thiazi,*
> *from my sanctuaries and plains shall always come baneful advice to you.*[327] *(Lks 51)*

Clearly Skadi had temples and land set aside for her cult. This cuts two ways – first it tells us that Skadi had worshippers, which gives her worldly power, and second, reminds us that there is no record of Loki having any cult. It is also significant that she is the only goddess who defends herself. The rest either try to soothe him down, or in Freyja's case, stand up for another but not herself. This suggests a forceful personality, and self-assurance.

In addition, she was given the title *dís*, goddess. As Else Mundal points out, the distinction between goddess and giantess is a lot blurrier than that of god and giant.[328] Thorgerdr Holgabrudr was a Norwegian goddess with her own temple, who was also described as a giantess.[329] This is probably because there were so many, overlapping, categories of powerful female beings, such as valkyries and the disir, who were not always well-defined but could be called on for assistance. (I always wonder, when trying to categorize all these different beings, how a medieval Scandinavian would react to my efforts. With laughter or bafflement, probably.)

So Skadi is as much a goddess as say, Freyja or Sif. They could argue, however, that in addition to their family connections, they were inherently divine, while Skadi had to "marry in". What's interesting, though, is that she retains her status even after the divorce. Perhaps godhood, like priesthood, cannot be revoked.

Ingunn Ásdísirdóttir thinks that as the Germanic tribes moved northward, they came up against the cult of Freyja, and had to incorporate her into their religion because it was

---

[327] Larrington's translation.
[328] Mundal 1990: 312.
[329] Simek 1996: 326-7.

so prevalent, even though they already had Frigg to fill that slot..³³⁰ In the same way, Skadi may have been "written into the script". This would explain the discrepancies in the material between the acknowledged power of giants and giantesses, and the fact that they're made out to be the enemies of the Aesir. This ambivalence runs all through the myths and sagas.

It also raises the point – what exactly is the difference between a giant and a god? It's not necessarily size. The many recorded instances of gods mating with giant women would be ludicrous if it were. (In the story of Hadingus, he raises this very objection to the giantess who would be his lover. She tells him she can change her size. No difficulty, then.)

The two main characteristics of giants that are significant here are monstrosity, of which large size is but one kind, and wisdom, mainly of a magical nature. In a myth-system that regarded such knowledge as powerful, that gave the giants an advantage. As Lotte Motz points out, apart from Odin, the gods tend to rely on their courage and strength to help them defeat giants. Only Odin would presume to match them in wisdom and lore.³³¹

We also know that both Skadi and Gerdr were considered beautiful, the latter so much so that Frey was smitten as soon as he saw her. Skadi is described as the "bright bride of the gods" (*Grim.*), which hardly fits the image of a mountain-giantess. Snorri tells us that Gerdr was "the most beautiful of all women" (*Gylf*). He goes on to say that when "she lifted her arms and opened the door for herself, light was shed from her arms over both sky and sea, and all worlds were made bright by her."³³² (This led Lonnroth to suggest that maybe Gerdr wasn't a giantess after all, since she far outclassed them, which seems a tautological argument.)

While I would not suggest that either giantess was powerful because they were beautiful, it suggests that the usual idea of a troll-wife does not apply, and that the two were always closer to goddesses than those who would make clear lines of demarcation would admit.

---

[330] Ásdísirdóttir 2006: 423.
[331] Motz 1982, p. 77.
[332] Faulkes: 31,

Both Skadi and Gerdr are given lineages, as well. No doubt part of that is the fact that both married (or at least had some sort of liaison with) gods, and were royal ancestors. Margaret Clunies-Ross suggests that Skadi's status as a royal ancestor of the earls of Hladir in Norway may have influenced Snorri's version of the myth, but that still implies that she was a powerful force to be reckoned with, except that her power would come from her descendants rather than her father.[333] (The line supposedly descended from Skadi and Odin's son Saeming through to the earls of Hladir, who ruled Trøndelag and Hålogaland in Norway from the 9th century to the 11th century). [334]After all, it's the first story related in *Skáldskaparmál*, which is a treatise on poetry, after all. Whatever political clout Skadi had in mythical time, in this world and that time she had pull through her family associations.

Finally, in the section on Loki's vulgarity, I discussed other myths from around the world that depict grieving deities as a threat to the world order. The most famous example is probably Demeter, who staged the world's first sit-down strike after Hades carried off her daughter. The next best-known is the sun-goddess Amaterasu, who retreated into a cave after her brother the storm-god grossly insulted her and killed one of her maids. (Obviously, I'm ranking these from my own, Western POV.) Two more are the Egyptian sun-god Ra, who refused to adjudicate between Horus and Set, when the adult Horus came to seek revenge for his father Osiris' murder by Set, and the story of the Hittite earth-god Telipinu, whose story is similar to Ra's.

The other myth, from India, is of the goddess Kannaki, whose husband dies, after which she goes into violent, prolonged mourning that is only relieved when she sees young men playing the horn game. When the horn broke, she laughed. In all these cases, obscenity or a suggestive innuendo (in the horn game it is the "male" horn which is supposed to break - one can imagine the comments from the spectators) startles the deity into laughter, which ends the mourning.

---

[333] Clunies-Ross 1987: 212.
[334] http://en.wikipedia.org/wiki/Earls_of_Lade

In all these cases, the deity's prolonged mourning is dangerous to earthly life - the sun not shining, the crops not growing, and in Kannaki's case a goddess so deranged by grief that she causes the city of Maduri to burst into flames.

It is often thought, and I think it may be a valid idea, that by making Skadi laugh, Loki hoped to neutralize her death-aspect. At any rate, he turned aside her wrath, and whether he ever followed it up by actually sleeping with her, he had broken the force of mourning and anger that propelled Skadi to Asgard in the first place.

Did Skadi win or lose?

The pressing question, of course, is did Skadi gain anything by her attempt to avenge her father, or did the gods just buy her off? She set very unusual conditions, because while she asked for atonement and compensation (the usual legal formula), the form that that compensation took was unique. The demand for a husband from among the Aesir has a certain logic to it, but the demand that they make her laugh (which she was sure they could not do) is strange enough that I will discuss it, and what I see as the pattern behind it, at some length.

Naturally I went to my books to see what those who study Norse myth for a living thought. There wasn't really a consensus: Else Mundal, Jenny Jochens, and Judith Jesch took a positive view, while John Lindow, Margaret Clunies-Ross, and Lotte Motz voted no. John McKinnell thought both parties were mauled by the process, and Carolyne Larrington had no opinion. Of three others I found online, Ross Enochs of the Marist College and Sarah Welschbach in her master's thesis voted no, while Lyn Skadidottir (in *Jötunbok*) voted yes.

Else Mundal makes a good point when she says that the gods were shamed. After all, bare feet were the mark of a penitent, and the covered faces equally convey mourning or shame. Then Loki's play with the goat is hardly the Aesir at their most virile, seeing as how he nearly castrated himself to appease her (which is probably why Loki was detailed for this job).[335] Mundal thinks that Skadi has put them in the same position as Thor in *Hyrmskvida*, and she thinks, too, that

---

[335] Mundal 2000: 355.

Loki was chosen to fool with the nanny goat as a symbol of the gods' "wounded masculinity".[336] (Lindow and McKinnell pick up on this as well, while not necessarily agreeing with the conclusion Mundal draws from it.)

Jenny Jochens points out that Skadi did, after all, become a goddess, a fate not shared by most giantesses who engaged in sex with the gods. In fact, there are two main patterns for god - giantess encounters: the Thor pattern where you kill them before they kill you, and the Odin pattern of seducing them and making off with their goods (Gunnlod) or otherwise using them (Rind). So you argue that Skadi, who was neither robbed nor killed, got off relatively lightly.

Judith Jesch sees Skadi as an in-between figure, who stands between those giantesses who are victimized by the gods, and goddesses like Gerdr, who seem to have been completely assimilated into the Aesir's world. Skadi's behaviour during her marriage to Njord seems to bear that out - they go to her place first, and when they go to his she does not scruple to complain of it.[337] We know that Skadi, despite her divorce, is invited to the gods' feasts, since she is present in Aegir's hall in *Lks*, and Snorri counts her as one of the goddesses, along with Gerdr and Jord.

Lyn Skadidottir points out that Skadi did succeed where all the other giants' bride-quests failed - she married one of the gods.[338] Thrym, Hrungnir and the Masterbuilder all failed to get Freyja, but Skadi married Freyja's father, and Thor had to stand by and watch. In the same book, Raven Kaldera says that Skadi got a seat at the gods' councils which she kept even after her divorce[339], which I presume refers once again to *Lks*, which is sometimes interpreted as the gods sitting in judgement over Loki.[340]

In the neutral zone we have Larrington and McKinnell. I put Larrington here because in her article on Scandinavia in *The Feminist Companion to Mythology*, in which she quotes Judith Jesch on Skadi as the one that got away, so to speak,

---

[336] Ibid.
[337] Jesch 1991: 139.
[338] Skadidottir: 119.
[339] Kaldera: 113.
[340] Klingenberger: 149.

but doesn't really express an opinion of her own. McKinnell does not see either party coming out of it well:

> *Similarly, Snorri's story of Njörðr and Skaði is an absurd burlesque, a: reversal of 'normal' wooing patterns in which a grotesque bride secures a husband by force and chooses him blindly, and neither husband nor wife can bear to live in the home of the other.*[341]

Both Njord, by allowing himself to be chosen like a woman, and Skadi, who allows herself to be diverted from revenge, come off badly in McKinnell's reading. He views the myth as a burlesque of the bride-quest story anyhow, so we shouldn't expect the main characters to keep their dignity, although he suggests that the judgemental aspects could be later inclusions, much as Snorri moralizes over Frey's infatuation with Gerdr.[342]

Clunies-Ross and Lindow agree that Skadi's compensation wasn't worth much, and a contemporary audience would have felt it wasn't. Clunies-Ross clearly agrees with Jakobsson's Rule: the gods always cheat[343]. In *Prolonged Echoes* she implies that Odin somehow rigged the contest so that Skadi would not get Baldr. Enochs agrees with her, saying that while various outsiders tried to bargain with the gods, the gods always got the best of the deal. As he says: "The gods took advantage of the desires of others and entrapped them."[344] (This is as true of Thiazi as of Skadi.)

Lindow feels that a marriage based on choice of legs/feet rather than worked out amongst the two families would not have been worth much to a medieval audience, and in his second paper on the subject, he goes further and says that both Skadi and Freyr were in the power position and lost it through infatuation. (Skadi fell for beautiful feet, Freyr for Gerdr's arms.)

Motz sees Skadi's position as akin to Brynhildr's. Both were tricked out of their choice of man, and she contrasts Brynhildr's refusal to have anything further to do with Gunnar against Skadi's more pragmatic approach.[345] As far

---

[341] McKinnell 2005: 8.
[342] Ibid: 64.
[343] Jakobsson 2013: 115, n. 21
[344] Enochs: 20.
[345] Motz 1993: 50-1.

Njord and Skadi

as Motz is concerned, Skadi has been deflected from her purpose: revenge. By accepting a husband instead, she has betrayed herself. (Although according to Snorri it was Skadi herself who demanded a husband from amongst the gods, and Clunies-Ross sees her action as subversive, potentially threatening the Aesir if she did get the god she wanted.) Motz does have a point when she compares Brynhildr's laughter when she achieves her vengeance with Skadi's laughter at Loki's humiliation. She thinks that heroic female characters get treated better than Eddic ones, as comparing Brynhildr/Skadi and Sigdrifa/Gunnlod shows.

Welschbach thinks that Skadi only partially succeeded, and in a very compromised manner. She doesn't see the demand for a husband in the critical light that some writers do; as she puts it:

> *Matrimony was an integral part of the ongoing power-struggle and the binding via marriage could enlarge a party's predominance or better its position of power (Andersson and Miller 1989, p. 24). In hindsight to this the act of choosing a husband has to be understood as an option for Skaði to strengthen her rule and upgrade her reputation.*[346]

Since Skadi is the only one of the jotunns who succeeds in getting a spouse from amongst the Aesir, to that extent she has won. (The Master-Builder, Thrym, and Hrungnir all get hammered by Thor for their ambitions, while Thiazi gets burned.) But instead of getting Odin's legitimate heir and the god who would rule after Ragnarok, she ends up with the hierarchically lower (and older) Njord.

Further, since the gods did make Skadi laugh, they could be said to have "won" that round. Welschbach discusses the parallel case of Bolli and Kjartan in *Laxdæla saga*. Bolli marries the woman intended for his foster-brother Kjartan, and then offers him a young stallion by way of compensation. Kjartan refuses, and the feud escalates until Kjartan's death. Welslchbach points out that as long as the relationship was unbalanced by the failure to redress Bolli's unjust act, violence is not far off.[347] After the gods have given her a husband, and made her laugh, presumably they are quits. As

---

[346] Welschbach: 28.
[347] Ibid: 31-2.

a further, gratuitous act of compensation, either Odin or Thor threw Thiazi's eyes up in the sky as stars, which confirms that he was no ordinary opponent.

Chapter 15

Sami Parallels

> *It is tempting to view the unhappy marriage between Saamis and Nordic people in the literary motifs as a symbol of the relationship between the two peoples, an inescapable life together, attraction and drifting apart at the same time. And perhaps there is a mythological superstructure for this relationship in the Old Norse myths, in the unhappy marriage between Njordr and Skadi, the giantess who went skiing and hunting like a Sami woman; she longed to return to the mountains, and left her husband.*[348]

The "Other" is a very hot topic right now. Jeffrey Jerome Cohen's book on monsters came along just as scholars were beginning to re-evaluate the role that giants played in Norse myth. Clearly there was something in the air. For your average medieval Scandinavian, giants might very well be "Other" but they were a remote other, whom they were unlikely to encounter. But there was another "other", with whom they might very well trade or otherwise interact, and these were the Sami, who are usually called *Finnar* in the Old Norse texts.

Today, the Icelandic word Finni means an inhabitant of Finland. However, in medieval times it seems that it usually meant the people who lived in Finnmork, which would be today's Finnmark, in northern Norway. Those Finnar would have been the Sami people (once called Lapps or Laplanders).

The Finns of Finland can also be called Finnar (their name in Swedish) and may be that there were two kinds of *Finnar*: Finns themselves and the Sami people.[349] The two peoples speak Finno-Ugrian languages, but are very different, the Finns having long abandoned the hunter-gatherer lifestyle, while the Sami were famous for living off the land, fishing, hunting and trading.

---

[348] Mundal 1996: 112.
[349] Aalto: 2.

Njord and Skadi

The Sami live in northern Europe, in the region they called Sapmi, which includes some of northern Sweden, Norway, Finland and the Kola Peninsula in Russia.[350] The genetic origin of the Sami is unknown, but some claim that they are aboriginal Northern Europeans, who repopulated the Sapmi region after the last ice age. Archaeologists have placed people in the region from before 8100 BCE, although the Sami languages are dated from about 2000 - 2500 years ago.

As the Nordic peoples moved further north and the Sami south, they came into contact, although they had very different lifestyles and cultures. The Nordic people were mainly farmers, while the Sami were mainly hunters and trappers up until about 1500 CE, when a crash in reindeer population led to many of them settling down. Their shamanistic religion was very different from the pre-Christian beliefs of the Norse.

There is a theory that they were driven north by incursions of Viking settlers, although there is no historical record of actual battles between them. The nature of the relations between the Norse and Sami are still being debated, but there were political alliances, although the actual people seem have had little contact apart from trading.

Lately, though, with the new interest in circumpolar religions and cultures, as well as the willingness to assume that cultural exchange between the two groups was a two-way street, the Sami have been coming to the forefront again. With this shift, we have seen a renewed interest in the idea of the giants as honorary Finns, and the Finns as honorary giants. Skadi in particular, with her skis and bow, has looked like the Finn-women who marry the Yngling kings, marriages that often go wrong. The idea that there is some Sami - Scandinavian content to the Thiazi - Skadi myth is not news. Folke Strom was theorizing along those lines before the Second World War.

As Kusemenko puts it:

> *Nobody denies the fact of great Scandinavian influence on the Sami in the Viking Age. But if we ask whether this Sami-Scandinavian contact is reflected in Scandinavian culture, we get as a rule a negative answer....The*

---

[350] http://en.wikipedia.org/wiki/Sami_history

> *Scandinavian influence on the Sami languages and on the Sami culture on the one hand stigmatization of the Sami in the 19th and beginning of the 20th centuries, which has been extrapolated to the whole period of the Sami-Scandinavian contacts on the other, has made an assumption about Sami influence on the Scandinavians impossible.*[351]

There is, however, good reason to assume that contact was a two-way street, and that while the Sami were seen as "other", these were others the Scandinavians could borrow from.

Sami - Norse Relations

The usual description of the Sami in Old Norse literature is that they were good hunters, archers, skiers, fishers, sorcerers, magicians, and healers. [352] Even the rather mundane ability to ski was given a magical spin in Saxo's account, in which at first he marvels at how fast the Sami are on skis, but later becomes more fantastical in his account of them:

> *When they [the Sami] scattered in flight... they cast three pebbles behind them, which to the enemy they made look the size of three mountains. Stunned by this cheating vision, Arngrim recalled his men from pursuit, believing himself blocked by a wall of towering cliffs. The next day they met again and were defeated, whereupon they flung down snow and gave it the appearance of a mighty river.*
> (Gesta Danorum V, Hollander's trans.)

The third time, however, the Finns had run out of magic, and Arngrim's troops carried the day.

The Sami were associated with prophecy, too. According to Saxo, when Othinus (Odin) wanted advice on how to avenge the death of his son, the Finn Rostiophus is able to tell him.

They appear in historical accounts, too, notably in the life of Harald Fairhair, who fled from his father with a Sami adviser from Hadaland. (It wasn't just pagans, either, Olaf

---

[351] Kusmenko 2009: 66.
[352] Ibid: 68.

Tryggvason visited a Sami for her prophecies when he went to Norway, although later church laws forbade others from taking advantage of this sort of advice.[353])

We have to assume that Odin, with his interest in prophecy and wisdom, learned more on Samsey than how to beat a drum (*Lks* 24). Magic in ON literature is associated with gender or ethnicity, so that people who practice it are usually either women or non-Norse, like the Sami. (This is the point of Loki's taunt to Odin about Samsey - not only doing a womanish thing, but a strange, foreign one into the bargain, as practiced by foreigners that most Norse people were wary of.)

It was not just prophecy that the Sami were credited with. They were supposed to be able to change themselves into animals, often whales or walruses. (In *Sturlaugs saga starfiama* a Finn turned himself into a dog and an eagle during a battle with a Norse magician.[354]) They could also transform into trolls. The Sami were also supposed to be able to control the weather, just as the giants could.

The Sami were well-known for these qualities, so much so that others could be described as Finns or Finnish if they also could use magic or wisdom. The prose introduction to *Volundarkvida* tells that Volund's father was a "Finnish king" and one of his brothers was named Slagfinnr. All the brothers "skied and hunted for animals"; very Sami behaviour. Another group who often came in for that comparison were the giants, who were also supposed to be wise, magical, and to live in inhospitable areas. The Sapmi lands could easily stand in for Utgard, and like the giants, they were strange, other, but at the same time had goods, magic and wisdom that the Norse wanted.

If there was prejudice or uneasiness around the Sami, it didn't stop Icelandic and Norwegian kings marrying them. Harald Fairhair, for example, was married to a Sami woman Snaefrid ("Snow-peace"), and they had four sons. Harald composed a verse about her after her death. The Danish king Gram declared war on the Finnish king Sumblus, but then fell for Sumblus' daughter and that put paid to the war. Helgi, king of Halogoland, sought to marry Thora, daughter of

---

[353] Ibid: 70.
[354] DeAngelo 2010: 275, n. 15.

Njord and Skadi

the king of the Finns. (His friend Hother helped him, a la Skirnir, because Helgi had a bad stammer.[355]) Some of these stories, especially the latter, many not be true, but they reflect what was seen to be possible. In light of these stories, it is interesting that there was a personal name *Halffinnr*, (Sami by half), and that it was usually understood to mean *finnskr at móðurkyni* (Sámi after mother).[356]

Skadi and the Sami: three generations?

Skadi has evident features which correspond to the cliché features of the Sámi in Old Icelandic literature. She goes skiing, hunts with a bow and shoots game. In skaldic poetry, she is called ondurdís, ondurgoð 'ski goddess' . She is a giantess but she belongs to the gods. She was one of Njörd's wives, but according to the Norwegian skald Eyvind Finnsson (!), she did not want to live with Njörd and did better by marrying Odin. She had many children with him. One of them, who was the ancestor of a very well-known person in Norwegian history, Hakon Jarl, was called *Sæmingr*.[357]

Not just Skadi, either. It has been argued that the name of her son *Sæmingr* also indicates Sami origin, although that doesn't seem provable one way or the other.

The etymology was put forward by the German scholar Karl Mullenhoff, who read Saemingr as "son of Sami". This etymology is pretty well discredited, but Saemingr would have been a powerful symbol of Sami-Scandinavian coexistence, just as Harald Fairhair's sons would have been.

Mundal thinks that it is a misunderstanding to see the relation between the two words Saemingr and Sami as depending on a phonetically correct derivation. She thinks that any relationship between the two would have rested on folk etymology; Saemingr could have functioned as a name derived from 'Sami' if that was what people believed.[358] Also, she says:

> We can see from a story in Vatnsdœla saga, chapter 12, that a word for the Sami people phonetically equivalent to the first part of the compound name Sæmingr was

---

[355] Book III, History of the Danes, Fisher and Davidson (trans): 71.
[356] Kusemko 2009: 71.
[357] Ibid: 79.
[358] Mundal 2009: 28.

> known among the Scandinavians. In this saga Sami men speak of themselves as semsveinar. The last part of the compound word, sveinar, is an Old Norse word for 'young men,' but the first part of the compound word must, however, be a Sami word that the Sami used about themselves.

Whether the name *Sæmingr* was made up to make associations to the Sami, whether the name existed first and the associations to the Sami were caused by the first part of the compound name, or whether the name *Sæmingr* in the Middle Ages was associated with the Sami at all, is impossible to say with certainty. We do not know whether the genealogy back to Óðinn's and Skaði's son Sæmingr was Eyvindr Finnsson's invention, but it is worth noting that Eyvindr himself was from Northern Norway.[359]

Mundal goes on to say that the Hladir themselves, Saemingr's descendants, were supposed to have been from northern Norway, and so Eyvind may have wanted to emphasize the northern connections with a name that evoked the Sami, which Saemingr would. Of course, this implies that the ruling family of Norway had Sami ancestry.

Nor does the Sami connection stop with Saemingr. Thiazi may have a counterpart in the Sami fishing god. Southern Sami *tjaehtsi*, "water", has been suggested as the origin of his name, which de Vries and Simek consider etymologically difficult, and there is a Sami god Tjatsiolmai, which looks good, however specialists may feel about it. At sites where Tjatsiolmai is honoured, there are large stones in the form of a man or large bird. One site in Northern Finland has a seven-meter stone at the shore of the lake; the lake is called Taasti-jarvi in Finnish, which corresponds to the Sami word Tjaastijauri (Tjatsi lake or Water lake).[360] Others have similar names, such as Tjatsisoulo ('Water island').

Another connection between them is that both receive sacrifices. Tjaziolmai received sacrifices so that people would have luck fishing, and the story in *Hst* and *Skld* of Thiazi demanding food from the gods is often interpreted as the giant demanding tribute. According to Snorri Thiazi was out at sea, fishing, when Loki appeared to rescue Idunn.

---

[359] Ibid: 28.
[360] Kusemko 2009: 77.

Tjatsiolmai often accepts sacrifices while in the shape of a bird, and was often represented as a bird or a man with bird feet.[361]

His name appears to vary; he has a Wikipedia article under the name Tjaetsieålmaj, meaning "men of the water" or Thjathjeolmai (singular). According to the article he controlled lakes and rivers, and in Sami mythology he gave people fortune when fishing.[362]

As I have pointed out above, Skadi certainly seems like a Sami woman, skiing and using a bow. When she appears in Asgard, however, she is taking on yet another role that the Norse gendered masculine: avenger. There were, at least in literature and probably oral lore, precedents, the *skjolmær* or shield-maiden, and the *baugrygr*, or ring-lady. (Although, Mundal points out, in real life, the ring-lady would not be expected to actually take up arms against those who had slain her kin.[363]) The fact that she behaves like a Sami tells us that we shouldn't expect conventional behaviour from her, so naturally, coming from a society with such differing expectations of the sexes, she behaves in the most masculine manner possible.

To add to this, we have examples of short-term relationships entered into (by Norse men and gods) when they were away from home. *Rigsthula* is one example, with Rigr taking the husband's place for three nights each place he stays, and *Orvar-Odds saga* is another, with the hero entering into a limited-term marriage with an Irish princess. There is information about a similar custom amongst the Sami, but it all comes from after the Reformation. Mundal suggests that if a similar custom existed during medieval times, and the Norse knew of it, then the offer of a husband for Skadi takes on a new meaning.

In real life, this was probably not an accommodation offered to women, which underscores Skadi's masculine role here. (And in turn forces the gods into a feminine role.) The fact that she chooses by feet is also significant, because in IE myth emphasis on feet or legs usually stresses the sexual

---

[361] Ibid: 78.
[362] http://en.wikipedia.org/wiki/Tjaetsie%C3%A5lmaj
[363] Mundal 2000: 352.

Njord and Skadi

nature of the hero.³⁶⁴ Mundal goes further and speculates that the Norse gods had their faces covered, which would have suggested bridal veils as well as hiding one's face from shame. This strongly suggests the transvestite Thor in *Thrym*, pretending not very successfully to be Freyja.³⁶⁵

The story of the Norwegian king Harald Fairhair's marriage is especially interesting, since the Christian Snorri asserts that it was caused by magic. Harald went on progress one winter in Uppsala, and while he was at a Yule banquet, he got word that a Finn wished to speak to him outside. At first Harald refused, but then the Finn asked again, this time with a more personal message, and the king and some of his men went to him.

When they got to the Finnish king's hall, his daughter Snjófri☐ðr poured mead for Harald, who immediately fell violently for her. She turned him down, however, saying that he could only have her after they were married. Harald did so, and they had four children. Then Snjófri☐ðr died, and her body, it seemed, did not change. King Harald sat by her for three winters, waiting for her to revive.

Finally, Thorleif the Wise persuaded Harald to have the body moved, and when it was, the decay was evident; odours of corruption came from it, as well as "all kinds of worms and adders, frogs and toads and vipers" came out of it. Snjófri☐ðr was burned (hurriedly), and Harald "swore off his folly".³⁶⁶

There are similarities here with the Freyr-Gerdr story, with both Freyr and Harald being helplessly love-struck on the instant, and both women holding them off. In addition, Snorri gets very moralistic about both, seeing both Harald and Freyr as brought low by a woman, so to speak. McKinnell thinks that the story of Harald and Snjófri☐ðr has its parallel also in the story of Njord and Skadi, as both women travel to alien lands to seek a husband.³⁶⁷ (And Snjófri☐ðr is also a Sami, which is considered akin to the giants.) He also relates it to the Summer King - Winter Bride pattern (see Theories) and says the spell that keeps Harald in

---

[364] Clunies-Ross 1989: 6.
[365] Mundal 2000: 353-4.
[366] Heimskringla, Hollander (trans.) 1964: 80-1.
[367] McKinnell 2005: 64.

mourning is a way of keeping him in the realm of death and cold.[368]

Snorri copied this story nearly word for word from an older text, the Norwegian saga of kings from around 1190 called *Ágrip af Nóregskonunga sogum*. Both in *Ágrip* and in Snorri's text, *Haralds saga hárfagra*, Snæfríðr's father is spoken of as a *finnr*, 'a Sami.' But Snorri—or a later scribe—put in the chapter heading: *Frá Svása jǫtni*, 'About the giant Svási.'[369] So the Snæfríðr story fits into two patterns - the offer of a mate, as in the Skadi story, and the temporary liaisons between a hero and a giant's beautiful daughter. (Note the description in *Hst* of Thiazi as a "mountain-Finn".)

King Nórr: Uniting Norway

> There was a king named Fornjotr. He ruled over the land which is called Finland and Kvenland, that lies to the east of the gulf which goes toward Gandvik. That is called Helsinga Bay. Fornjotr had three sons. One was called "Ocean" [Hlerr], whom we call "Sea" [Ægir], one "Flame" [Logi], and the third Kari. Kari was father of "Frost" [Frosti], who was father of "Snow the Old" [Snaer]. His son was called "January" [Thorri]. He had two sons, one called Nor and the other Gor. His daughter was called "February" [Goi]. "January" was a great sacrificer. He sacrificed each year at mid- winter, and they called that the "January sacrifice" [Thorrablot]. The month took its name from that. It happened one winter at the January sacrifice that "February" disappeared. A search party went after her, but she was not found. And when a month had passed, "January" performed a sacrifice, sacrificing for this: that they might learn where "February" had come to rest. They called that the "February sacrifice." But still they knew no more about her. Three winters later, the brothers made a vow that they would search for her, and they divided the search in this fashion: Nor would search on land, and Gor would search the out-skerries and islands. He travelled by ship.
> (Lincoln's trans, from Orkneying saga 1. 1-24)[370]

---

[368] Ibid: 76-7.
[369] Mundal 2009: 29.
[370] Lincoln 1999: 172-3.

Njord and Skadi

This story appears in three different forms: *Orkneying saga*, and two texts from *Flt*: *Hvertsu Noregr bygdist* and *Fundinn Noregr*. All three agree that Norway was united long before Harald Fairhair, by a mythical king Nórr.

As the story tell us, Nórr travelled across the land seeking his sister, on skis and shooting game to feed himself. His brother, Gor, went by sea, presumably living on fish and searching the Danish straits. They finally met near Sogn, and although they had not found their sister, they shared out the territory they had explored between them, Nórr taking the land and Gor the sea. They did not abandon their search completely, and Nórr finally found her, prisoner of King Hrolf of Bjarg. Nórr fought a duel with Hrolf, but it was inconclusive, and they decided to settle the matter by marrying each other's sisters. Norr went on to be the first king of Norway, which was named for him.

This story takes a different tack from the Njord - Skadi story, as in it the land is shown as peaceable, where people can exchange relatives to make households and families. By contrast, the sea world of Goi is turbulent and warlike, with no women aboard ship, of course. The sea wins out, however, as Nor's realm allows for so many descendants that the kingdom has to be parcelled out in smaller and smaller pieces among them, and these petty kingdoms vanish from the story. Gor's two sons (no mother mentioned, but presumably there was one) become violent sea-kings, ancestors of the earls of Orkney.

Nor and Gor came from the north originally, their ancestors being the rulers of Finland and Kvenland. As they searched, Nor conquered the Lappar, and all of Norway. When Nor found his sister, she was with Hrolf, son of King Svaði in the mountain of Dovri. Nor, of course, married Hrolf's sister, Hadda. Mundal sees a parallel between Sva☐si and Svaði, both kings connected to the mountain of Dovri, who marry their daughters to the conqueror.[371] No one in the story of Nor is said to be Sami, but the fact that Nor, Gor and Goi (February) have ancestors called January, Snow, and Frost seems to point to the Sami and the giants.

Mundal thinks that the parallels with the Sami were deliberate propaganda. It may have been important to the

---

[371] Mundal 2009: 33.

Norwegians to say that all the peoples of Norway were willing participants in the uniting of the country, even the Sami. At any rate, it gives us an origin story for the earls of Mœrir and the earls of Orkneys, starting from the north of Norway, possibly from the giants or Sami, through Halfdan the Old to Rognavald, who became earl of Møre under Harald Fairhair (yes, him again) and whose brother, nephew and two of his sons became the first earls of Orkney. (See *Orkneying saga* chs. 3 and 4, as well as the *Historia Norvegiae* and *Hkr* and also the *Fragmentary Annals of Ireland*.) The significant thing here is that Møre is in the far north of Norway, a fitting place for a family that traced its descent to that same region.

CHAPTER 16

Why is Njord so passive?

Njord doesn't have a lot of myth. So it seems strange that in the only one in which he features as a main character, he does so little. In contrast to the active, vengeful Skadi he is passive, even allowing Odin to marry him to a giantess without so much as a murmur. The only thing he does is complain that he doesn't like living in Thrymheim. (Of course, we don't know who initiated divorce proceedings.)

His passivity, along with the fact that Skadi chooses him in what is normally a Cinderella-type bride show, has led some to assume he too is taking a feminine role. In fact, many people seem to feel that Njord is somewhat less than entirely manly. The similarity of the names Njord and Nerthus has led many to theorize a connection between the god and goddess, assuming that Njord was originally the goddess Nerthus or else bisexual. They point to the masculine form of Skadi's name to prove it, assuming that she was Nerthus' husband before a sex-change. As Turville-Petre puts it:

> *The form of Skadi's name is typically masculine, but it is doubtful whether any great significance should be attached to this. The masculine forms Skuta, Sturla decline as feminine, and were probably originally nicknames. It may be that Skadi was originally a god, while her consort, Njord, was a goddess, whose sex changed because the name appeared to be masculine. If so, much remains to be explained. Why should a god, Skadi, with a masculine name, be allowed to turn into a goddess?*[372]

When I first read this, I thought it was rather sexist, as if being a god was a promotion but a goddess the opposite. However, when you consider the amount of emotional investment men had back then in not being sexually passive

---

[372] Turville-Petre 1975: 165.

or womanly – most of *Lks* consists of Loki accusing various gods of just that – you can see his point.

The Njord – Nerthus identity is a tenuous one, resting merely on the similarity of name. We might as well assume that Frey and Freyja are the same deity. Brother and sister, now, maybe. When Loki accused Freyja of having slept with all the males around, including her brother, he seemed pretty clear that they weren't the same person. The charge was incest, not onanism, same as his broadside against Njord. It isn't always worth taking Loki's word for things, but you can imagine the slurs he would have come out with had he felt that Njord and Frey were half-female.

Loki brings up another instance of Njord's passivity. He says that when Njord was sent as a hostage, the daughters of the giant Hymir urinated in his mouth. This is often explained away as the daughters of a sea-being, the rivers, emptying into the sea, but it still doesn't sound good. Perhaps we are supposed to imagine a puny Njord faced with enormous giantesses, as in several of Thor's adventures, where he is portrayed sleeping in the thumb of a giant's glove, or cowering with Tyr in a cooking-pot.

One creditable attempt to grasp the nettle appears online on a blog called "A Heathen Blog", in an article called "Njörd's Honor".[373] It is written in defence of Njord, but it faces up to the charges against him, and makes a credible attempt to refute them.[374]

Unfortunately, I cannot find that article, which seems to have vanished even beyond the power of the Wayback Machine, so I will construct my own defence of Njord, starting with the first encounter between the Aesir and the Vanir, which led to war. The few references we have to the war don't tell us what role Njord played in it, but we have to assume that as an important member of the Vanir aett, he was involved. (In *Hkr* 4, we are told that Njord and Frey are the most outstanding of the Vanir.)

Still, Njord's role as a hostage, his ability to calm storms, still winds, and put out fires on ships, and the fact that when he ruled as king of the Swedes, it was an era of peace and

---

[373] http://heathenblog.wordpress.com/2006/12/30/7/
[374] if anyone has a copy of the text, I would be really grateful if they would send it to me.

plenty, suggest that war was not exactly his main focus. Perhaps we have to assume that either he was too old for fighting, or else that he simply was more interested in peace and well-being.

None of this tells us anything about Njord's honour, of course, but perhaps place-name evidence can help us out here. There are numerous attestations of places named for Njord around the coast of Norway and inland Sweden (although the latter may be named for Nerthus - see Simek. [375]). Stefan Brink, in his survey, finds "around a dozen" places with Njord- names in Norway, all in the south, and about sixteen named for *Niærþer in Sweden.[376] (Brink thinks that *Niærþer may have been a goddess, although he also suggests that this may be because the Swedish names were assumed to be connected to Nerthus, and so were recorded that way.)[377]

This ties in with Lieberman's assertion that the Icelanders would never have tolerated a story in which Njord abased himself the way that Loki did[378]. There are no places named for Loki, after all. A society that put such great emphasis on manliness would not have accepted a god who was believed to have behaved in an effeminate or dishonourable fashion. We have to remember that *Lks* is not Gospel, and also that all the gods and goddesses get a mauling in it. If Thor could survive accusations of cowardice and cuckoldry, then presumably Njord could come out of Loki's accusations without too much damage to his reputation. After all, every other source speaks respectfully of him, calling him "prince of men" (*Grim.* 16), and both him and Frey are called the "best of men "in *Hkr.*

Perhaps it's best to accept that people had a rather different view of godhood back then, which could accommodate weaknesses and foibles as well as strengths. Another line of defence here is suggested by Andy James, who says:

> As O⬚ðinn, at least, knows, Njörðr will return to
> Vanaheim after Ragnarök, while Loki will be destroyed

---

[375] Simek 1996: 134.
[376] Brink 2007:118.
[377] Ibid: 118.
[378] Lieberman 1992: 113.

> (Vafðrúðnismál 39, 4-6). As to the claim about Hymir's daughters, one starts to wonder whether Loki really is crazy, as Freyja has just suggested. No myth survives that could be twisted, even by Loki, into this accusation. It has often been suggested that Loki may be referring to rivers flowing into the sea, which is of course Njörðr's special domain, but if so his mental processes are shown as bizarre to the point of insanity. Njörðr ignores the last claim completely, pointing out only that although sent to the gods as a hostage, he differs from Loki in being manly, and the father of the heroic Freyr.

And perhaps that is the best way to understand it. Loki has finally gone way too far, throwing wild accusations about and simply lying when he cannot twist what is already known to discredit a god or goddess. After all, we don't know that Tyr had a wife, or that Gefjon prostituted herself for a jewel, or that Idunn slept with her brother's slayer. It may be that all these are inventions. Meulengracht Sorensen thinks that all these accusations may be *nid* - in which case they don't need to be truthful, merely shameful. And of course if Loki's motive was to provoke the Aesir into violating sanctuary and attacking him, the grosser the insult the better. Truth doesn't come into it.

So in all, while Njord's role in the myths may still be a fairly quiet one, I think we can acquit him of being totally abased, however tempting it may be to assume the worst about the somewhat kinky Vanir. It may well be that Loki was insulting him precisely because of his peaceable nature and role as mediator; letting others treat you extremely badly indicates good nature taken to excess. It also may have been another side-blow at his marriage to Skadi - insinuating that Njord lets giantesses push him around, and that his status as a hostage allowed Odin to put him in the humiliating position of Baldr-substitute.

Either of these would be insulting, so we have to hand it to Loki for wrapping them both up into one pithy insult. Loki does this throughout the poem, taking shots at various goddesses for adultery, either with him or another, knowing that the aggrieved husband cannot strike back at him.[379] So if Njord is passive here, so are all the others, even Thor, who

---

[379] James 1997: 4.

despite his threats does not give Loki the thrashing he says he will.

Njord and Idunn

The only other character in this story that is as much acted on as Njord is Idunn. In a way Njord in the second half answers to Idunn in the first half, both pawns in other people's games. Thiazi stealing Idunn has its counterpart in Skadi demanding a husband from the Aesir, and getting one. Neither Idunn nor Njord are given any say in the matter. Both also end up with a giant as the result of a trick – Loki tricks Idunn into coming with him by telling her he can show her some apples that compare to hers, while Njord is one of the gods who participates in the foot show. Skadi, of course, was aiming for Baldr, and no doubt Njord did not expect to be chosen. (If you follow Clunies Ross's argument that Odin contrived the whole thing to prevent Skadi marrying Baldr, we have to assume that Njord was fooled just as much as Skadi was.[380])

There are many parallels between Njord and Idunn. Both are associated with fertility. With Idunn this connection is so strong that popular books often make her an honorary Van, as if her function usurped her other affiliations. If we assume that Thiazi desired Idunn for her apples of immortality, symbolic of the reproductive cycle, then we can also assume that when Skadi wanted to marry, she planned to have children with her husband. Thus Njord would be fulfilling the same function that Thiazi planned for Idunn, that of perpetuating the giant lineage. (Which raises the question: what would the status of their children have been?

Both are the objects of the giants' quests. Thiazi subcontracts his, so to speak, forcing Loki to do his dirty work for him. Skadi, on the other hand, goes to Asgard herself in search of compensation, which includes a husband. In neither case do they get what they want – Thiazi loses Idunn and his life, Skadi is hardly married before she's divorced. What's interesting is that neither Njord nor Idunn get any say in the matter.

---

[380] Clunies Ross 1994: 122-3.

Njord and Skadi

Finally, both Njord and Idunn had to spend time among the giants as either kidnap victim or hostage, if Loki is to be believed. Hst is silent about how Idunn spent her time among the giants, but we know that Njord was humiliated by giantesses and presumably was not happy. I think we can assume that like him, Idunn was pining for home.

CHAPTER 17

What is a Hostage?

In his book *Hostages in the Middle Ages*, Kosto lays out what he considers the definition of a hostage, as distinct from what we would think of as a hostage now. It consists of five elements[381]:

- guarantor of an agreement
- not subject to ransom
- a third party
- actually or potentially subject to loss of physical liberty
- given rather than taken

You can see that medieval hostages were quite different from what we imagine today. These days we think of those schoolgirls taken by Boko Haram, or sailors or oil-rig workers kidnapped by Somali pirates and held to ransom. (This isn't to say that similar things didn't happen in early times, just that the institution of hostages was something different from these sorts of violent acts.)

Njord's status as hostage certainly fits four out of the five criteria above, although I'm not sure about his standing as a third party. If he were involved in the war against the Aesir, he would be an interested party.

He definitely fits the first requirement and the fifth; however, as he and his son were given freely to the Aesir as part of an agreement between the two parties after they realized that neither side would win the war between them. As a guarantor of a peace agreement, he was naturally not subject to ransom. How much he was confined is an open question - if we assume that Noatun is in Asgard, then that limits his mobility, although he did go to Thrymheim with Skadi. (We also know that he returns to Vanaheim at Ragnarök, so we have to assume that the deal between the

---

[381] Kosto 2012.

two sides has expired then, or Njord feels that it has.) Although there were cases of people offering themselves as hostages conditionally, Henry II, for example, offered himself as hostage for the customs that were granted to the burghers of Namur, no one imagined that he was going into captivity.[382]

High-status prisoners in medieval and renaissance times did not share the privations that poorer people did. When you think of, for example, Mary Stuart in captivity, remember that her household consisted of fifty servants, which the English queen paid for. Another good example is Manuel II, a fourteenth-century Byzantine prince who was definitely a hostage, but not lacking for comforts.

Njord, according to the account in *Hkr*, seems to have been a hostage after the Roman model. In the early days, the Romans took hostages after or instead of battles, but as the empire grew, they adopted the practice of taking princely hostages at a young age and educating them in Roman ways. The British king Togidubnus was one such, in what was an odd sort of catch-and-release program that the Romans used to build up a network of client-kings. (The other main purpose of hostages, of course, was to demonstrate Roman might; Cleopatra and possibly Boudicca killed themselves to avoid just that fate.)

We know that when Njord went to live among the Aesir he had to give up his wife, since brother-sister marriage was not allowed among the Aesir; that seems a lot to swallow in the name of peace, but it does seem to be part of an assimilation process that also saw both Njord and Freyr being given priesthoods and being included in the Aesir's councils, just as Hoenir and Mimir were among the Vanir. (If we accept Clunies-Ross' idea that Njord was the "forced card" in the bridegroom line-up, then you could argue that the Aesir took the acculturation so far as to push Njord into another marriage.)

Another point to emphasize is that all four, or five if you count Kvasir, went freely. That is the difference between hostage-giving and hostage-taking. When Julius Caesar was kidnapped by pirates, that was hostage-taking, and all too familiar to us. (Although his haughty demeanour and

---

[382] Ibid: 17.

repeated claims to consideration as a Roman make you wonder why they didn't dump him overboard. Presumably they just kept thinking of the ransom.) Kosto, on the other hand, thinks that the institution of hostages depended on the hostage acting as a form of surety, and undertaking this willingly.

The whole idea of hostage as surety fits well with Njord in more ways than one. First because all four hostages acted as a guarantee of good behaviour by Ases and Vans, and second because of the peculiar legal status it involved. Suretyship involved an odd combination of real and personal surety, since:

> *Hostages have been understood as a mixture of the two: they are people, but from a legal standpoint they are treated as things (not unlike slaves).*[383]

When we consider the Skadi - Njord myth, with Njord and the other gods having to appear barefoot and with faces covered before Skadi, and the loss of status involved, we have to think that he was being treated in the same equivocal fashion - as a bargaining chip in a settlement, both person and thing. Further, Lindow and Mundal argue that all the gods in the line-up are being treated this way.

The use of hostages to increase one's power and prestige did not cease with the Romans, and:

> *strong unifying forces are discernible wherever a competent warlord set out to lead his co-ruling nobles into successive cycles of campaigning and the subsequent distribution of conquered land and the wider spoils of war (slaves, women, hostages, treasure, tributes, armaments)...*[384]

Which raises the question of whether, when the Vanir decided to throw in Kvasir as a third hostage besides the agreed-upon two each, they were acknowledging a superior power, or showing how generous they could be with their own. The equal distribution of Aesir and Vanir hostages would have signalled both the truce that ended the war, and carefully left both parties with equal prestige, since both got two hostages.

---

[383] Ibid: 7.
[384] Teschke 1998: 343.

The contrast between Kvasir, whom the Vanir had freely given to the Aesir and who was supposed to be the "wisest" of men, and the silent Hoenir may have been the tipping point for the Vanir; the exchange was not equal after all, and their gesture of goodwill disrespected.

A final point, which Kosto illustrates with the story of William Marshal. He had been handed over by his father, John, to King Stephen to guarantee a truce during a siege. When Stephen's men found out that John Marshal had used the truce to build up his fortifications, they advised the king to kill young William. Stephen, furious, agreed, but finally could not bring himself to have the boy killed. This, as Kosto points out, rendered William useless as a hostage, and eventually Stephen released him. This was consistent with medieval practice; even in cases where someone stood surety for bail and would have been imprisoned if the person did not appear, the guarantor usually was fined rather than actually locked up.[385]

Dr. Beachcombing's blog points out how rarely a hostage was executed, even when the hostage-givers reneged. (Which is not to say it didn't happen, but the circumstances had to be right. Inter-religious hostilities during the Crusades often ended badly, and a story from Ireland where when Diarmait of Leinster welched on the deal for the second time his son paid the price.)[386] Dr. Beachcombing also instances both Catherine of Sforza and John Marshall boasting that they could have more children.[387] It might go some way to explaining why when the Vanir cut off Mimir's head, it didn't reactivate the war, as we would have expected.

In a situation like the one the two groups of gods faced, where there was no superior arbitrator to take their case to, and no reason to trust each other, the legal guarantee offered by hostage-exchange was the best they could hope for. That's not to say that both sides wouldn't try to game the system, either.[388] But if the Aesir wanted to focus on keeping the jotunar at bay, they didn't need another enemy tying up their resources in a war against a foe that also had a reproductive

---

[385] Kosto 2012: 16.
[386] http://www.strangehistory.net/2012/09/20/hostage-taking-in-ancient-and-medieval-times/
[387] Ibid.
[388] https://tenthmedieval.wordpress.com/tag/hostages/

advantage, as well as being nearly their equal in wisdom, strength, and magic. So it was to their long-term advantage to swallow the insult offered Mimir, and, Odin-like, turn it to their advantage.

CHAPTER 18

Why did Skadi have to choose by their feet?

One of the odder features of this rather odd myth is the choice of bridegroom by his feet. Naturally the audience for this story wouldn't have thought much to that sort of marriage, and you wonder what on earth possessed the Aesir to make the offer, and Skadi to accept it. And why feet?

The first thing you would think of when contemplating a line-up of barefoot gods is that they were either showing penitence or had been defeated.[389] In medieval times those were two common times for someone to appear barefooted before another, especially someone who could certainly afford shoes. Either condition would be pleasing to Skadi, who no doubt felt that the gods should be showing remorse for killing her father, and while we can't say that she defeated them, the fact that she had penetrated into Asgard and was negotiating terms with them was a victory of sorts. Lindow tells us that:

> in the reconciliation effected in 1265 between the archbishop and city council of Cologne, the members of the latter and co-conspirators were made to face the archbishop in such garb [bareheaded, without belts, and barefoot] and to declare their sorrow over their actions.

Thus Skadi would be in the role of the authority figure, who would normally be male.

The other thing that modern Westerners might think of is fairy tales, and especially Cinderella. (Although there are Indian and Chinese versions of the Cinderella story, too.) I have already mentioned the Indian folktale in which a father and son choose their brides by their footsteps, only to find that the father has chosen the daughter and the son the mother. Stith Thompson's Motif Index has a category H365, "Bride test: size of feet". The main difference between

---

[389] Lindow 1992: 136.

Njord and Skadi

Cinderella and Njord is that while the prince wanted her, Skadi had her eye on someone completely different. Regnilda, too, got Hadingus, which was the whole point of the trick in the first place. By comparison, Skadi's choice by feet (or lower legs) seems unmotivated; there's no reason why it should be feet rather than hands or anything else. I discuss this a bit in the section on folktale parallels, but I think that John Lindow is right; Cinderella bears only a superficial resemblance to Njord.

The other major parallel in Norse literature is equally unmotivated, except at the level of love at first sight. The skald Kormak falls for Steingerdr when he gets a glimpse of her bare feet, and immediately is inspired to make a verse about it. In a later paper, John Lindow revises his opinions about the bridegroom line-up and suggests that Skadi had a similar *coup de foudre*; having been struck with sudden "mad vanic love"[390] for a beautiful foot, she justifies it by saying it must be Baldr's - no one else could be so gorgeous. (One wonders if Njord was flattered or annoyed.) Skadi is a woman, and Kormak is a man, and the other victim of sudden love is a god: Freyr. When he sat in Odin's high-seat, he saw Gerdr raise her arms, and fell for her on the spot.

As Lindow points out, neither feet nor arms are innocent in Norse myth. Both Skadi and Gerdr are giants, and the first of the giants, Ymir, conceived more beings from between his feet and the sweat in his underarm.

> *Under the arm of the frost giant they say*
> *A maid and lad grew together;*
> *One foot on the other begat*
> *The six-headed son of the giant.*
> *(Vaf. 33)*

(According to Snorri, the left armpit. He's good on those kind of details.) Lindow thinks that the gods were subtly underlining their superiority even as they acted contrite:

> When Snorri wrote that Skaði was to choose on the basis of the feet and invited his readers or listeners to imagine a scene in which all the Æsir reveal their feet to her, then, Aurgelmir's or Ymir's monstrous, promiscuous, incestuous feet present themselves inevitably. The Æsir reminded Skaði of one of the many defects in her

---

[390] Lindow 2008: 178.

> ancestry, and at the same time they showed that they had perfectly normal feet, without any sexual appetites whatever. To some extent, then, they would have mitigated the act of contrition I posited in my earlier piece on Skaði and would also have been mocking her.[391]

Later, when Loki taunted her in *Lks*, he may have been making the same point about giant sexuality being abnormal, to the point where Skadi would sleep with the people who killed her father.

As I have noted elsewhere, it is only the giants who can reproduce asexually like this, and although medieval Icelanders wouldn't have known that asexual reproduction is limited to simpler life-forms, they would have known that it was odd, and non-human. The Aesir and Vanir, who are closer to humans, reproduce the way that humans do. The versatility of the giants (since we have to assume that Thor and Odin got children on various giantesses the normal way) gives colour to Thor's justification of giant-bashing: if I didn't, there'd be no room for humans.[392] (Note also Clunies-Ross' interpretation of *Vsp*; she assumes that the gods created first the dwarves and then humans after their encounter with the three giant girls, presumably to fill up the world.[393]) We know from Freyja's reaction in *Thrym* and Skirnir's curses to Gerdr that the giants were considered sexually voracious, which gives point to Thor's words.

In fact, the creation of the first humans is an important example of the difference between gods and giants. Both Ymir's offspring and Askr and Embla are created in unusual ways, but there are significant differences. First, the gods start with actual matter, in the form of driftwood for humans, earth or stone for dwarves.

The giants start from scratch, so to speak, or at least from bodily fluids. Thus the giants' origin is entirely maculate; body heat, or sweat, brought them into being. It is up-close and couldn't be more personal. The humans, on the other hand, are created at a distance, and by some sort of magical process, one assumes, since Odin was involved. (It's also interesting that there are three gods, just as there were

---

[391] Ibid: 176.

[392] Harb 23.
[393] Clunies-Ross 1994: 166-8.

three giant-maidens; was Odin making the point that he didn't need his jotunn kin to populate the world?)

Once again, then, we see a distance being created between giants and gods, and the emphasis on feet a reminder of the sweaty, symbolically incestuous origin of the giants, which the Aesir reject. In an act of symbolic ju-jitsu, they take what would seem to be Skadi's triumph and try to turn it to their advantage.

A further possibility also focuses on physical difference, but this time between Aesir and Vanir. The Vanir are noted for their physical splendour: Freyr is the phallic god, enormously so, while his sister Freyja is so beautiful that both gods and giants desire her.[394] The Aesir are more notable for physical absence: Odin has one eye, Tyr one hand. (The story of Mimir illustrates this in a different way - after the Vanir behead him, he is reanimated by Odin, as a bodiless head that is a source of magical wisdom.) The contrast between the wise, bodiless head and the Vanir's association with the body, and especially the lower body, is pointed. Skadi chooses by selecting from the lower bodies of the gods on show - no wonder she didn't get Baldr.

---

[394] Schjodt 2008: 386.

Chapter 19

Why is Loki so vulgar?

When Skadi, disappointed in her choice of a husband, demanded that the gods make her laugh, everyone listening to the story must have thought, what will Loki do? The answer is simple, but rather shocking. He took a rope, tied one end to his testicles and the other to a nanny-goat's beard, and played tug-of-war, shrieking in pain, until the rope broke, he fell into Skadi's lap, and she laughed.

I think these days people would be offended, or a best bemused, by such bumpkin antics. The only thing I can think of that comes close is the scene is *Huckleberry Finn* where the Duke and Dauphin perform onstage naked and covered in paint. The outraged audience runs them out of town on a rail.

Loki, of course, hadn't promised anyone a performance of Shakespeare, and nobody would have expected anything refined from him. But wasn't he running the risk of offending an already angry and disappointed woman, who may well have felt that the Aesir had pulled a fast one?[395] The answer comes in four parts, and involves psychology, myth, and danger.

First of all, people seem to have had a more robust sense of humour back then. Even deities. After all, how long would you find it amusing to throw spears at Baldr? Five minutes? Most of the funny bits in the myths and sagas are pretty primitive. The Thor myths are a case in point – in one myth two giantesses try to drown him by pissing a huge river for him to cross. And I suppose really that the old sense of humour hasn't really gone away, it's just moved to South Park and Jackass. If you put Loki's antics on YouTube, it would probably get lots of hits.

Life was short and harsh back then, and perhaps the point of other people's pain was that it wasn't happening to

---

[395] Clunies Ross, of course, thinks that they did.

you. Tragedy is when it happens to you, comedy when it happens to someone else. These days we prefer to watch pain and humiliation in the form of X-Factor and Pop Idol. But in the same way that they cheerfully watched torture, executions, and bear-baiting, medieval people seem to have found pain funny in a way we don't now. The fairytale about the princess who never smiled until she saw an old woman slip and fall on ice seems shocking to most modern people.

Education, too, makes a difference. The sophisticated works of court skalds wouldn't have meant much to most people, who wouldn't have been able to unravel the kennings and involved wordplay. What circulated amongst the peasantry was a sort of lowest-common-denominator humour that probably reflected the earthy conditions of their own lives.

Second, Skadi laughed because of the way Loki was playing with status, gender and even the atonement the Aesir had promised Skadi. The most obvious thing is that the test of making the woman laugh is a suitor test - in theory, when Loki makes her laugh, it is a prelude to marrying her. The fact that the trick he uses involves binding himself and being painfully pulled along by a goat alludes to how Thiazi battered him into doing his will, and it implies that not only a powerful giant but also a nanny-goat can drag him around. Also, there was a medieval penalty for adultery, which John Lindow thinks, must have influenced this incident, in which:

> *If a man is found to be in adultery with another man's wife, then it is the law of the town, that he shall be drawn by her through the town, up one street and down another, by that same limb with which he committed the sin with her, and thus shall be finished with the matter.*[396]

This law was well-known (as you can imagine) and turned up in French municipal law from the late 11th century, where it was stipulated that both parties should be naked. The law spread through the 12th century, and reached Scandinavia from Lübeck.[397] As Lindow points out, the humiliation is public (*skamstraff*) as is Skadi's quest for compensation, and the penalty is for adultery, and she has

---

[396] Lindow 1992: 134 (his translation).
[397] Ibid: 134.

demanded a god in marriage. Further, physical punishments were reserved only for the lower classes, the thralls, while free men paid fines. Castration in particular was a punishment for thralls, and this tug-of-war would certainly bring that to mind.[398]

Going even further, if we accept the idea of the adultery penalty, Loki is posing as a penniless adulterer, whose partner was a nanny-goat. Its beard in particular is a symbol of gender ambivalence. The fact that it was generally a symbol of masculinity (this seems to have been an era when men generally went bearded, if art be believed) lent force to insults like *taðskegglingr* "little dung-beard, part of a *nið* directed towards Njall's sons in *Njals saga*. Both parties, in fact, are gender-ambivalent, since the female has a beard and the male has in the past been not just female but a mare. (Calling a man a mare was a killing matter, remember.)

When we consider that the Aesir collar Loki and threaten him when they realize that Idunn is missing, and how Thiazi abused Loki, we think of both Carol Burnett's definition of humour: tragedy plus time,[399] and Karl Marx's observation that history repeats itself, the first time as tragedy, the second time as farce.[400] (Of course, it stops being funny later, when Skadi's prediction comes true and she finally gets her revenge.)

So it would seem that part of what made Skadi laugh was the total humiliation that Loki was willing to undergo, or at least pretend to undergo.

Thirdly, this part of the Skadi myth has echoes from other myths in other parts of the world. These come from Greece, Egypt and Japan, which may seem a bit far-flung, but their themes repeat those of the European tales and bring them into the realm of myth.

From Greece comes the myth of Demeter, whose daughter Persephone was carried off by the god Hades to be his bride. In her grief and anger, she declared nothing would grow on Earth until she had Persephone back. One day she was sitting deep in depression, when a woman called Iambe

---

[398] Ibid: 135.
[399] http://www.brainyquote.com/quotes/quotes/c/carolburne166932.html
[400] https://www.marxists.org/archive/marx/works/1852/18th-brumaire/ch01.htm

came along. Iambe makes the goddess laugh, either by saying something outrageously bawdy, or by raising her skirt. In one version, she manipulates her genitals to look like a baby. Shocked, Demeter smiled.[401]

In Egyptian myth, the story of how the sun-god Ra withdrew and returned was part of the larger story of the contention of Set and Osiris. It seemed to come to a logical end when the desert-god Set murdered Osiris, but when Osiris' son Horus grew to manhood, he took up the battle and came to claim the throne of Egypt.

The sun-god Ra chairs a tribunal of the deities to decide whether Horus or Set has the better claim to rule. Unfortunately, Ra is related to Set, and keeps trying to award him the throne. But his own mother, Neith, commanded him to give it to Horus. At this the other gods become angry with him, and the baboon-god Bebon mocks him to his face, saying, "Your shrine is vacant." Ra goes away in disgust and sulks, and all the other deities are angry with Bebon, for insulting Ra so gravely. Hathor, the goddess of love and pleasure, decides to sort it out, by going to her father Ra, and dancing naked in front of him, showing her genitals to him. He laughs, and the tribunal can resume.[402]

Another myth of rude behaviour comes from further afield – Japan. The sun-goddess Amaterasu hears that her chaotic brother the storm-god wants to visit her. At first she is reluctant, but he promises to behave, and she gives him permission. His violent nature proves too strong for him, however, and he destroys her crops, piles faeces on her throne, and causes the death of one of Amaterasu's weaving maidens. Amaterasu is so offended she hides away in a cave and refuses to come out. The entire world becomes dark, and the other deities get together to decide what to do. As the anxiously confer outside her cave, one of the goddesses starts to sing and clap, then jumps up on an overturned washtub and begins a striptease, all the while singing and making bawdy remarks. The other deities roar with laughter, and one of them shouts that they now have a better goddess than Amaterasu. She takes the bait and peeps out. Outside is a mirror that shows her to herself for the first time. While she

---

[401] Foley pp. 45-6.
[402] http://reshafim.org.il/ad/egypt/texts/horus_and_seth.htm, accessed April 27, 2009.

is still dazzled, the deities immediately grab her and pull her out of the cave, and rope it off so she can never retreat there again. This story is a little different from the others, in that everyone else laughs instead of the goddess, but it does have similarities.

The why is simple enough. In each case, the deity is depriving heaven and earth of benefits only they can give. When Demeter refuses to let anything grow, famine results, and even the gods eventually decide that without humans to worship them, they can't function. In the case of Ra, he fails to recognize the justice of Horus' case, destabilizing the land of Egypt and leaving it without a ruler. With Amaterasu, the result of the sun failing to shine is obvious. In each case, grief threatens the natural order, and must be assuaged.

The bawdiness is presumably a shock tactic, to startle the grieving deity into a normal reaction. In the numbness and withdrawal of grief, ordinary measures wouldn't get through. This probably also explains the folktales discussed earlier.

Another, related, myth sheds some light on why the Aesir might want to propitiate Skadi in particular. A Tamil goddess called either Kanniki or Pattini was associated with a tug-of-war game called the horn game, which doubled as a part of a religious ritual to supplicate the goddess. There is a male horn, and a female one, and the game involves pulling on ropes hooked to the horns until one breaks. It seems that the male horn is the one that should break, for the ritual to be successful.[403] Remind you of anything?

The myth connected to this game is equally suggestive. Kannaki loses her husband, and loses herself in grief. In her madness, she tears off her left breast and throws it down, causing the city of Madurai to catch fire. She then wanders distracted, until when she stops to rest, she sees young men, including Krishna himself, playing the horn game. When the horn breaks, she laughs for the first time since her husband died.

Once again we see the pattern of excess grief, in this case leading to madness, needing to be dispelled by rude play. But there's another element here that I think is relevant to the

---

[403] Clunies Ross 1989: 11.

Skadi story. Kannaki/Pattini is a goddess of pestilence, like many Hindu village goddesses. All of them require propitiation. Skadi, whose name connects to words meaning "shadow" and "scathe" may have been someone the Aesir didn't want to fight. Carolyn Larrington contrasts the radiantly beautiful giantesses like Gerdr with the mountain-dwelling ones like Skadi. This remote location was the home of ogresses and troll-women. [404] These latter tend to be extremely hostile to the Aesir; two of them try to kill Thor.

The fact that she finally managed to revenge herself on Loki (fixing a venom-dripping serpent over his face when the gods finally bind him) suggests that she doesn't forgive or forget. Her grim nature also suggests an old folk-belief, that the dead cannot laugh.[405] Thus Loki's exuberant vulgarity is aimed at revivifying the goddess, of neutralizing her death-aspect. It may also be significant that one of her titles is "Shining bride of the gods", hinting that her passage into Asgard marked a change from her connection with the darkness and harshness of winter.

Finally, I would suggest that Loki's vulgarity is, like that of any good comedian, a comment on the situation he and Skadi find themselves in. His tug-of-war reminds of how Thiazi dragged him, stuck to a pole, across the countryside. The nanny-goat, with its beard, reminds us that Skadi is performing a traditionally male role, and his play with his testicles relates to both his role as the "unmanly" god, and may say something about what he feared Skadi would do to him. (It may be worth noting that in Snorri's list of giantess names, one is Geitla, "She-Goat".[406]) Finally, as mentioned above, the irony of the whole situation is that her husband-to-be isn't the one having to pass the traditional suitor test – it's Loki. I think we can safely assume that Njord never did succeed in making her laugh. This, as much as his falling into her lap, may explain Loki's charge to her in *Lks* that he had slept with her. When she laughed, she as good as accepted him.

---

[404] Larrington 1992b:154.
[405] http://ourtroth.weebly.com/chapter-xix-skai-gerr-earth-and-other-etin-brides.html
[406] Sayers 2009: 15.

Chapter 20

Why does Loki borrow a shape if he's a shape-shifter?

Loki's means of rescuing Idunn brings up a number of questions, including why he borrows Freyja's hawk-shape to do it. You would think a shape-shifter like Loki wouldn't need it. Further adding to the mystery is the fact that both Frigga and Freyja have bird-shapes, but the only time we hear of them is when they're loaning them out to Loki.

So I suppose the question in this section is twofold: why does Loki need a falcon/hawk shape, and why don't Frigg or Freyja ever put theirs to use? (That we know of, anyway.) But they've both got them, hanging on the back of the door until Loki borrows them.

It is doubly odd because Thiazi, a giant, can fly in the shape of an eagle, and so can Odin and another giant, Suttungr. (Odin stole the mead of poetry and flew off in the shape of an eagle, with Suttung, also in eagle form, in hot pursuit.) Also, one of Loki's by-names is Lopt, which means "air", suggesting that he should be at ease aloft.

One explanation might be that while Odin and presumably Thiazi have magical powers that allow them to shape-shift, Loki's powers lie more in his cleverness. (Although it gets him into trouble as much as it gets him out of it.) Perhaps after the incident with the giant Geirrodr he was deemed too irresponsible to have a flying-shape of his own.

In that story he borrows Frigga's shape and goes flying about, just out of curiosity[407], and ends up being captured and held hostage by Geirrodr. After being starved into

---

[407] you can see here the difference between the Norse and the Greeks, who seem to have regarded curiosity in a more positive, if cautious, light.

submission, Loki agrees to steal Thor's hammer and bring it to Geirrodr, and gets himself into more trouble as a result.

The Geirrodr myth, by the way, has a striking resemblance to *Skr*, in which Frey sits in Odin's high seat which allows him to see across the nine worlds, and sees, and falls for, the giantess Gerdr. In both cases one deity uses the legitimate power of another deity for a less than legitimate purpose, and both get into trouble for it. (Loki gets captured and held hostage, Frey has to give up the sword he would have used at Ragnarok.)

In the Thiazi myth, on the other hand, Loki is not flying because he wants to, but because he has to. The gods have threatened to bind him if he does not bring back Idunn, and he travels under compulsion. Once again Loki has to put right what he did wrong, and the bird-costume is just a plot device to get him there.

The other myth in which he borrows Freyja's "feather-cloak" is more positive. *Thrym* opens with Thor realizing his hammer is missing, and requesting Freyja's aid to help him find it. Loki takes on bird shape and goes looking for it, heading for Jotunheim where he encounters the giant Thrym. The giant not only boasts of the theft, but also demands Freyja as ransom, leaving Loki to wing it home with the bad news.

So, on balance we have one myth where Loki's flying is positive, versus one where he gets himself into trouble in his bird form, and another in which he assumes bird form to make up for trouble he's caused already. Not an impressive record.

Odin's journeys, on the other hand, are in search of wisdom and power. Odin's purposeful travelling is as far removed from idle curiosity as can be, since he wishes to find out as much about the doom to come and means of staving it off as he can.

Odin is often thought of as shamanic, and the quest for wisdom certainly fits in there, as does the flying, which is part of shamanic journeys all over the world. (Loki, by contrast, is a trickster figure.) That would explain his ability to take on bird form. We know that Thiazi can use magic, because he used it to prevent the gods' food from cooking, and to stick Loki to the pole. Suttungr we know very little about, but we do know that giants were supposed to have sources of wisdom and magic that others did not. Which brings us back around to Frigga and Freyja.

It makes sense for Freyja to have a falcon-form. She is almost Odin's female equivalent, keen on the use of magic, and equally keen on war.

Frigga, who always seems like a more stay-at-home type, is a more unlikely person to have a bird-form or have much use for it. Although in addition to the tale of Geirrodr, "queen of falcon-form" could be used as a kenning for her (*Skld* 18-9), so it was a part of her mythos.

There seems to have been some overlap between Frigg and Freyja, although if you look closely it is obvious that they are very different goddesses. Place-name and other evidence suggests that Frigga was originally a Germanic deity, with only one attested place-name in Scandinavia, on the south coast of Sweden. Freyja, on the other hand, has a very strong presence in Scandinavia, and it may well be that the confusion between them and their attributes reflects the fact that both of them, as consorts of Odin, fill similar slots, despite their very different characters.

The final point of significance about Frigga's and Freyja's falcon-shapes is the species of bird involved. Odin, Thiazi and Suttungr all take the shape of eagles. While both are impressive birds of prey, the eagle is a lot larger than a falcon, so there may be some gender marking here.

In that case, Loki's use of a goddess' plumage may very well be another instance of gender-bending.[408] This fits in several ways. First, shamanic ritual often involved an element of cross-dressing, so perhaps there's a faint echo of that here. Second, we all know that Loki is no stranger to the idea of passing as a member of the opposite sex. (See the rest of *Thrym*, where he throws himself into his role as "Freyja's" maid, although he may be doing it in part to torment Thor.) Third, the falcon-form underlines Loki's status as not-quite-one-of-us: he doesn't get to be an eagle; he has to settle for being a falcon. Fourth, in two out of the three encounters with giants in these stories, Loki gets humiliated, which underlines his lack of status.

---

[408] Clunies-Ross 2005: 95.

So in the end it makes sense for Loki to use a goddess' plumage. The fact that in two cases out of three, including one from the *Poetic Edda*, it is Freyja's falcon-form he borrows, suggests that it is Freyja's plumage that he always borrows, and it is perhaps fitting that it is the most sexual of the goddesses that this most *ragr* of gods has to borrow it from.

Chapter 21

Why Does Loki Keep Getting Stuck?

Loki suffers a great deal in the myths from his unfortunate propensity to stick to things, or alternatively to have things stick to him. He also gets taken prisoner and kept in a chest, as well as threatened with "being trapped" unless he returns Idunn, who was also a prisoner, among the giants.

As I have pointed out before, the giants take Loki prisoner twice, and both times are commemorated in the myths that make up *Hst*. While the poem does not mention Loki's captivity, preferring to focus on the climactic moment when Thor fights the giant Geirrodr, Loki's reckless flight and imprisonment set the whole plot in motion. Both times Loki is out wandering around for what seems to be no good reason. In the Geirrodr myth "curiosity" is his motive, insofar as he has one, and in the Thiazi story he and Odin and Hoenir are out exploring, or possibly just wandering around.

Both giants ensnare Loki by causing him to stick to something; both of them use some topsy-turvy to accomplish it. Thiazi uses his magic to transform the stick Loki would beat him with into the instrument of Loki's captivity and punishment, Geirrodr uses Loki's wandering against him; he sticks the god to the windowsill, then locks the footloose god in a casket for three months. Loki's curiosity is his undoing, just like Pandora and Eve. (Yes, once again Loki has a feminine failing.) To give Loki credit, he is imprisoned for so long because he refuses to identify himself to the giant. Geirrodr essentially starves him out, which has its echo in Thiazi snatching most of the meat the gods were trying to cook.

These events are part of a larger pattern of Loki being bound or trapped, all leading up to the final binding. Besides the two already mentioned, we can add the fates of his children, who are fettered, exiled to the world-surrounding

Njord and Skadi

Ocean, or cast into Hel. We can also add the incident, which makes Skadi laugh, of Loki tying himself to a goat, which may well have reminded her of his bumping along helplessly behind her father.

Lindow and Rooth would probably suggest that we add his invention of the net, which while ingenious leads to the gods reconstructing his thought and so catching him in order to bind him. As Lindow puts it: "These physical bindings suggest his actual bonds: to the jotnar (Thiazi), to strange sexuality and gender-bending (the she-goat: cf. Clunies Ross 1989, Lindow 1992) to impulsive creative intelligence (the net), and finally to chthonic powers (the rock to which he is finally bound."[409]

In *Hst*, the language continues this theme. When the gods begin to age, and they realize that Loki is somehow behind this, the verse goes:

> *— until they found ale-Gefn's [Idunn's] flowing corpse-sea [blood] hound [wolf, thief, i.e. Loki] and bound the thief, that tree of deceit, who had led ale-Gefn off. 'You shall be trapped, Loki,' the angry one spoke thus, 'unless by some scheme you bring back the renowned maid, enlarger of the fetters' [gods'] joy.'*

Note the emphasis on binding and being bound; the gods are called the fetters, which signifies many things, including the bond between gods and humans, social bonds in general, and the bonds of contract and law. [410]

These gods bind Loki and threaten him with being "trapped" unless he comes up with a scheme to free Idunn from her bondage among the giants. Ironically, the kenning used for Loki when he becomes stuck to Thiazi is:

> *Then the burden of Sigyn's arms [Loki], whom all the powers eye in his bonds, got stuck to the ski-deity's [Skadi's] forester [father, Thiassi]. The pole clung to the mighty haunter of Giantland and the hands of Hænir's good friend [Loki] to the end of the rod.*

There are two things to note here, first that Loki is the "burden of Sigyn's arms" and second that "the powers eye in his bonds" - a very unusual locution. Clearly we are meant to

---

[409] Lindow 1997: 163.
[410] Campbell: 2.

look ahead to when Loki is bound. Moreover, Loki is about to be trapped into an action that will hand Idunn over to the "illegitimate" embrace of a giant, for the benefit of the gods' enemies generally, in contrast to the legal bond between Loki and his Asynia wife.

Further, since we know that the loosing of Loki will precipitate Ragnarok, we are not surprised that the gods are keeping a close eye on him as he is bound under the earth. (There, Sigyn's arms are burdened with the bowl of poison that keeps Loki from suffering further; a poison arranged by Thiazi's daughter.)

A final comment on binding brings us back to Loki's attempt to bring about an accord with Skadi. Binding himself to the nanny-goat, he creates what medieval folk tales called a himph-hamph. As I mentioned in the section of folktale parallels, there are several types of tale that match this sort of story: AT 559 (Dungbeetle), 571 (All stick together), and 1642 (The good bargain). The Thompson *Motif Index* also has a similar category: motif H341 (Suitor test: making the princess laugh), includes H341.1 (people sticking together). There are several different kinds of story like this, but the commonality is that in all cases everyone gets stuck together in embarrassing, preferably obscene, positions. Usually but not always, the idea is to make a woman laugh.[411]

The Njord-Skadi story is often described as a burlesque, but behind the humour is something serious, as is often the way. That helps to explain why Loki chose the stunt he did to amuse Thiazi's daughter, and might also look forward to Skadi's prophecy to Loki about his eventual fate. She knows that he will be bound and that while he may be kidding around about binding now, eventually it will come true in grim earnest.

---

[411] Lindow 1992: 132

CHAPTER 22

Conclusion

Having read through this book, I hope you will understand why I wrote this book as a series of questions. There is much we just don't know, and will never know, about Norse mythology. And there is much about the Njord-Skadi myth that is mysterious.

We needn't imagine, however, that the myth simply runs through our fingers when we try to grasp it. There is a solid core of story, as narrated by Snorri and Thjodolf, and that remains to be interpreted and re-interpreted. Someone has suggested that the two deities were the prototype of a bicoastal relationship, which is certainly a post-Jet Age idea.

It is unknown to us how this myth was received in the day, although we can try to guess at what Thjodolf and Snorri were getting at. Among other things, both aimed to flatter with references to giant ancestry, which suggests that the modern view of gods = good and giants = bad is overly simplified and certainly post-Christian. In fact, Norwegian royalty in general tended to be proud of their giant background, and so did their relatives the Earls of Orkney.

The myth also brings forward Njord's role as mediator, since he goes so far in the interests of peace to actually marry a giantess. (So does Freyr, but that is through choice, whereas Njord has to take one for the team, so to speak.) This speaks to his role as hostage among the Aesir, and the giants if Loki is to be believed. (Loki may have been referring to his marriage, now I think about it, implying that Skadi and her friends humiliated Njord beyond bearing. It makes as much sense as that Njord might have been a hostage cementing peace with the giants.)

As I mentioned in the introduction, the myth in general inverts many genres, which tells us a lot about what an audience would have expected in a story back then. Njord (and Baldr) are placed in a passive role as much as Idunn was, while their wooer who has forced her way into hostile territory is a giantess come to Asgard, not a hero exploring giant-world and hoping for sex with a beautiful giant-maiden. Also, the gods murdered Thiazi, starting the blood-feud that brings Skadi to Asgard, while she appeals to the legal formula of atonement and compensation, bringing a very civilized sense of law despite being a woman and a giant.

Later, after their marriage, the reversals continue. Although Ian William Miller says there doesn't seem to have been a settled pattern for where young couples lived after marriage, they would normally settle down near one partner's family. Njord and Skadi begin with a compromise; either nine nights at each place, or nine and three. (The 9+3 indicates a serious power imbalance, with Skadi being able to dictate the terms.) The two divorce, which was not uncommon, but Skadi remains a goddess, and you have to wonder if one of the purposes of the myth was to explain how a giantess had the run of Asgard.

The Thiazi half of the myth is the more conventional one, being a typical story of a giant stealing or (in this case, kidnapping) something/one from the Aesir, and being killed for his pains. Loki's twisting and turning as he is pulled between god and giant halves (and betrays both) is a feature in many myths. The magical, powerful and rich Thiazi is not that unusual among giants, as I have shown; there are other wise and powerful giants. The only thing that's missing is any sense of Idunn as a person. Unlike Freyja in *Thrym*, who gets to give her opinion on marrying a giant, Idunn is never heard from, and it is not uncommon even in quite modern books to see her kidnap described as a theft, as if she were mere property.

Jan de Vries described the stealing of the apples as an Odinic myth, no doubt thinking of the theft of the mead. I can see the parallel, but there is very little of Odin in this story, and no Thor. (The story might have ended differently if he had been there.) The main actors are Thiazi, Loki, Skadi and Njord. Odin and Hoenir have walk-on parts, and Idunn is more acted-on than actor.

This myth, like *Lks*, has suffered from being relegated because of its humorous elements and inversions. Presumably all Norse myth has to be tragic to be taken seriously. As with the ancient Greek comedies, sometimes it is when an author is being funny that they are being most serious. Humour aside, it has been argued that any story with so many fairy-tale elements in it could not be a "real" myth. This too has been chipped away at throughout the last century, as many myths have been revealed to be made up of such elements, and indeed it is sometimes very hard to draw a line between the two genres.

The other barrier to this myth being taken seriously is the dismissive "it's a nature myth", with all the baggage that implies. First, nature myths are seen as cute, but out-dated, explanations of natural phenomena, no longer necessary now that we have science. Second, nature myths are seen as simple, just-so stories that are devoid of depth. I hope that in my section on theory I have shown just how many areas of human experience this "nature-myth" encompasses. (It is significant that nature myths are often collected in children's literature, another genre that attracts a lot of condescension.)

I freely admit that the "nature-myth" tag raises my own hackles, and I also bristle at the word "fertility". It seems too often to be a catch-all term that has little meaning. Writing a book about a myth involving the Vanir was always going to be a challenge for me. A statement that the Njord - Skadi myth is about the link between fertility and death, because the Vanir are fertile, while the giants represent winter and sterility, seems to me full of assumptions that should be carefully examined. Still, without such unfounded generalizations, I and many others would never have been spurred to write.

At bottom, this myth is about a marriage, even if it is a marriage that didn't work out. This is the part that brings Njord, who doesn't really do a lot in this myth, into focus, because this isn't his first marriage. He had a wife, who was also his sister, which the Aesir (and most readers and listeners) considered too close a relationship. So Njord had to give up his first wife.

His second, Skadi, was far more distant. The Aesir may have had family ties to the jotunns, but not the Vanir. They were taking no chances with Njord this time. From one extreme to the other, and neither one lasted. You can imagine the uses this story could be put to as marriage advice to young people. In Skadi's case: looks aren't everything, and a husband chosen by your family is a better bet than one you choose yourself.

The myth of Njord and Skadi seems to have been well-known, since it inspired both the "complaints" in the story of Hadingus, and the love-at-first-sight motif of Kormak's saga. They were probably proverbial as the couple that didn't get on, which in a society that freely granted divorce is not surprising. Everyone hearing the story could probably think of a parallel case in their own lives.

I began this book thinking that I had found a myth without a moral, but when carefully examined, this myth has several to its credit. But apart from its didactic, obvious meaning, the assumptions built into the story, both the ones that are upheld and those that are burlesqued, tell us a great deal about the mythic universe of the ancient Norse, and how that universe reflected their own lives.

Bibliography

Primary:

The Poetic Edda, Carolyne Larrington (trans.), Oxford UP, 1996

The Poetic Edda, 1962/1990: Hollander, Lee M. (trans.), University of Texas, Austin. (2nd edition, revised)

The Elder Edda: a Book of Viking Lore, Andy Orchard (trans.), Penguin Classics, London, 2011.

Poems of the Elder Edda, Patricia Terry (trans.), University of Pennsylvania Press, Philadelphia, 1990.

The Prose Edda Snorri Sturluson/Jesse Byock, Penguin Classics, 2005.

Edda, Snorri Sturluson/Anthony Faulkes, Everyman, London, 1987.

The History of the Danes, Saxo Grammaticus/ Peter Fischer, ed. Hilda Ellis Davidson, D. S. Brewer, Cambridge, 1996.

Heimskringla, Snorri Sturluson/A. H, Smith (trans.), ed. Erling Monsen, Dover, New York, 1990.

Heimskringla, Snorri Sturluson/ Lee M. Hollander, American-Scandinavian Foundation, University of Texas Press, 1992 (7th ed.)

The Haustlǫng of Þjódólfr of Hvinir Richard North (ed. and trans.), Enfield Lock, Middlesex, Hisarlik Press, 1997.

History of the Archbishops of Hamburg-Bremen, Adam of Bremen /Francis J. Tshcan, Columbia University Press, 2002.

Secondary:

Aalto, Sirpa 2003: "Alienness in the Heimskringla: Special Emphasis on the *Finnar*", in *Scandinavia and Christian Europe in the Middle Ages. Papers of the 12th International Saga Conference Bonn/Germany*, 28th July – 2nd August 2003, Simek, R. & Meurer, J. (eds.), Bonn, 1–7.

Abram, Christopher 2011: *Myths of the Pagan North: the Gods of the Norsemen*, Continuum International Publishing Group, London & New York.

Abram, Christopher 2006: "Hel in Early Norse Poetry", *Viking and Medieval Scandinavia* 2: 1-30.

Aburrow, Yvonne, 1994/1998: *Auguries and Omens: The Magical Lore of Birds*, Capall Bann, Auton Farm, Milverton, Somerset, TA4 1NE.

Acker, Paul and Carolyne Larrington, 2013: *Revisiting the Poetic Edda: Essays on Old Norse Heroic Legend*, Taylor and Frances/ Routledge, New York and London.

Acker, Paul, and Carolyne Larrington, eds. 2002: *The Poetic Edda: Essays on Old Norse mythology*, Routledge.

Acker, Paul 2013: "*Dwarf-Lore in Alvissmál*", in Acker and Larrington 2002: 215-28.

Adalsteinsson, Jón Hnefill 1990: "Gods and Giants in Old Norse Mythology", *Temenos* 26: 7-22.

Aðalsteinsson, Jón Hnefill 1998: *A piece of horse liver: myth, ritual and folklore in Old Icelandic sources*, (trans. Terry Gunnell and Joan Turville-Petre), Háskólaútgáfan, Félagsvísindastofnun, Reykjavík.

Adams, Anthony 2013: "He took a stone away": Cruelty and Castration in Sturlunga saga, in *Castration and Culture*, ed. Larissa Tracy, D. S. Brewer: 188-209.

Adkins, Lesley, and Roy Adkins 2000: *Dictionary of Roman Religion*, OUP.

Agnarsson, Larsanthony K., n.d.: "Skadhi and Ullr", at http://www.skergard.org/FB4skad.htm.

Allen, Richard 2013: *Star Names: Their Lore and Meaning*, Courier Publications. (reprint)

Anderson, Joseph (trans.) 1873: *The Orkneyinga saga*, Edmonston and Douglas.

Anderson, Sarah M., with Karen Swenson: 2002: *Cold counsel: the women of Old Norse literature and mythology: a collection of essays*, Routledge, London.

Andersson, Theodore, 1966: *The Icelandic Family Saga: An Analytical Reading*, Harvard University Press, Cambridge, Massachusetts.

Andrén, Anders, Kristina Jennbert, & Catharina Raudvere (eds) 2006: *Old Norse religion in long-term perspectives : origins, changes, and interactions : an international conference in Lund, Sweden, June 3-7, 2004*, Vägar till Midgård 8.

Arnold, Martin 2011: *Thor: From Myth to Marvel*, A&C Black.

Arnold, Martin 2002: "*Hvat er Tröll nema That?*": The Cultural History of the Troll", in Shippey.

Ásdísirdóttir, Ingunn 2006: "Frigg and Freya: One Great Goddess or Two? " in McKinnell, Ashurst and Kick: 417-25.

Atkinson, Hugh 2009: "*vpp ec þér verp oc á avstr vega*: throwing up in Ægir's hall", https://www.academia.edu/620633/vpp_ec_vpp_ec_þér_verp_oc_á_avstr_vega_throwing_up_in_Ægir_s_hall

Bader, Françoise 1986: "An I. E. Myth of Emergence", *Journal of Indo-European Studies*, 14: 39-85.

Bandlien, Bjørn 2005: *Strategies of passion : love and marriage in medieval Iceland and Norway*, trans. Betsy van der Hoek, Turnhout: Brepols.

Barnes, Geraldine, and Margaret Clunies Ross, (eds.) 2000: *Old Norse Myths, Literature and Society, Proceedings of the 11th International Saga Conference*, Centre for Medieval Studies, University of Sydney, Australia.

Beard, Mary 1999: "The Erotics of Rape: Livy, Ovid and the Sabine Women" in *Female networks and the public sphere in Roman society*, eds. Setälä, Päivi, and Liisa Savunen, Institutum Romanum Finlandiae, Rome: 1-10.

Beck, Horace 1973/1999: *Folklore and the Sea*, Castle Books, 114 Northfield Avenue, Edison, NJ, USA, 08873.

Bennett, Naomi 2009: *Peace Unwoven: Transgressive Women in Old Icelandic Heroic and Mythological Literature, and in Saxo Grammaticus' Gesta Danorum*, University of Wellington, Victoria, master's thesis. (http://researcharchive.vuw.ac.nz/xmlui/bitstream/handle/10063/988/thesis.pdf?sequence=1)

Bibre, Paul 1986: "Freyr and Gerdr: The Story And Its Myths", in Simek, Kristjánsson and Bekker-Nielsen: 19–40.

Bibre, Paul 1992: "Myth and Belief in Norse Paganism", *Northern Studies*: 1-23.

Blom, Grethe Authén 1991: "Women and Justice in Norway c. 1300 - 1600", in *People and Places in Northern Europe 500-1600: Essays in honour of Peter Hayes* Sawyer, eds. Ian Wood and Niels Lund: 225-35.

Bonnetain, Yvonne S. 2006: "Potentialities of Loki, " in Andrén, Jennbert and Raudven, 2006: 326-30.

Borovsky, Zoe 2002: ""En hond er blandin mjök": Women and Insults in Old Norse Literature", in Anderson and Swenson, 1–14.

Boyer, Régis 1995: *La Grande déesse du Nord*, Berg International.

Bragason, U. 1992: *Snorrastefna 25. - 27. Julí 1990*, Reykjavik: Stofnun Sigurdar Nordals.

Bragg, Lois 2004: *Oedipus Borealis: The Aberrant Body in Old Icelandic Myth and Saga*, Fairleigh Dickinson UP, Madison.

Brink, Stefan 2013: "Myth And Ritual In Pre-Christian Scandinavian Landscape", in *Sacred Sites and Holy Places: Exploring the Sacralization of Landscape through Time and Space*, eds. Sæbjørg Walaker Nordeide and Stefan Brink, Brepols: 20-32.

Brink, Stefan 2007: "How Uniform Was the Old Norse Religion?", in Quinn, Heslop and Wills: 105-36.

Brubaker, Richard L. 1987: "The Untamed Goddesses of Village India", in *The Book of the Goddess*, ed. Carl Olsen, Crossroad, New York: 145-60.

Bullough, Vern L. 1974: "Transvestites in the Middle Ages", *American Journal of Sociology* 70: 6: 1381-94.

Bullough, Vern L., and James A. Inundage 2000: *Handbook of Medieval Sexuality*, Routledge, London and New York.

Byock, Jesse 1982: *Feud in the Icelandic Saga*, University of California Press.

Campbell, Dan n.d.: "'The Bound God': Fetters, Kinship and the Gods", at http://www.thetroth.org/Lore/The%20Bound%20God.pdf

Chabon, Michael 2009: "Ragnarok Boy", in *Maps and Legends: Reading and Writing Along the Borderlands*, Harper Perennial, NY: 47-55.

Chadwick, H. Munro 1900: "The Ancient Teutonic Priesthood", *Folklore* 11/3: 268-300.

Chadwick, Nora K. 1950: "Þórgerðr Hölgabrúðr and the trolla þing: a note on sources" in *The Early Cultures of North-West Europe (H.M. Chadwick Memorial Studies)*, eds. Cyril Fox and Bruce Dickins, CUP: 395–417.

Chamberlain, Isabel Cushman 1900: "The Devil's Grandmother", *The Journal of American Folklore* 13/51 (Oct. – Dec.): 278-280.

Christen, Kimberly A. and Sam Gill, 1998: *Clowns and Tricksters: an Encyclopaedia of Tradition and Culture*, ABC-Clio, Santa Barbara, CA.

Ciklamini, Marlene 1968: "Journeys to the Giant-Kingdom", *Scandinavian Studies* 40/2: 95-110.

Clark, David 2012: *Gender, Violence and the Past in Edda and Saga*, OUP.

Clark, Susan 1991: '"Cold Are the Counsels of Women": The Revengeful Woman in Icelandic Sagas', in Classen: 1-27.

Clark, T. J. 2013: "Lucky Hunter-Gatherers", *London Review of Books* 35 (21 March 2013): 11-12.

Classen, Albrecht 1991: *Women as protagonists and poets in the German Middle Ages: an anthology of feminist approaches to Middle High German literature*, Kümmerle.

Clover, Carol 1986: "Maiden Warriors and Other Sons", *Journal of English and Germanic Philology* (Jan. 1986): 35-49.

Clunies Ross, Margaret 1981: "An Interpretation of the Myth of Thorr's Encounter with Geirrodr and his Daughters", in *Speculum Norroenum: Norse Studies in Memory of Gabriel Turville-Petre*, eds. Ursula Dronke, Guđrun Helgadóttir, Gerd Wolfgang Weber, and Hans-Bekker Nielsen: 379-91.

Clunies-Ross, Margaret 1987: *Skáldskaparmál: Snorri Sturluson's ars poetica and Medieval Theories of Language*, Odense University Press.

Clunies Ross, Margaret 1989: "Why Skadi Laughed: Comic Seriousness in An Old Norse Narrative", *Maal og Minne*: 1–14.

Clunies Ross, Margaret 1994: *Prolonged Echoes: Old Norse myths in medieval Northern society, vol. 1*, The Viking Society Vol. 7, Odense UP.

Clunies Ross, Margaret 2002: "Reading Thrymskvida", in Acker and Larrington: 177-94.

Clunies-Ross, Margaret 2005: "Frequent Flyers in Old Norse Myth", in *Travel and Travellers from Bede to Dampier*, eds. Geraldine Barnes, Gabrielle Singleton, Cambridge Scholars Press: 79-96.

Clunies-Ross, Margaret 2014: "Royal Ideology in Early Scandinavia: A Theory Versus the Texts", *JEGP* 113/1 (Jan. 2014): 18-33.

Colarusso, John 2002: *Nart sagas from the Caucasus: myths and legends from the Circassians, Abazas, Abkhaz, and Ubykhs*, Princeton University Press, Princeton, N.J.

Coomaraswamy, Ananda K. 1945: "On the Loathly Bride", *Speculum* 20/4: 391-404.

Davidson, Hilda Ellis 1998: *Roles of the Northern Goddess*, Routledge, London.

Davidson, Hilda Ellis 1993: *The Lost Beliefs of Northern Europe*, Routledge.

Davidson, Hilda Ellis 1990: *Gods and Myths of Northern Europe*, Penguin, London.

Davidson, Hilda Ellis 1976: *The Viking Road to Byzantium*, Allen and Unwin.

DeAngelo, Jeremy 2010: "The North and the Depiction of the "Finnar" in the Icelandic Sagas", *Scandinavian Studies*: 257-286.

de Vries, Jan 1933: *The Problem of Loki*, F. F. Communications, eds. Walter Anderson, Johannes Bolte, Uno Harva, Knut Liestøl, C. W. von Sydow, and Archer Taylor, Suomalainen Tiedeakatemima, Helsinki, vol. XLIII, no. 110.

Dillmann, Françios-Xavier 1991: "Les nuits de Njordr et de Skadi: Notes critques sur un châpitre de la *Snorra Edda*", in *Festkrift til Ottar Grønvik på 75 – årsdagen den 21. oktober 1991*, ed. John Ole Askedal et. al., Universitetesforlaget, Oslo: 174 – 182.

Doniger, Wendy 2008: "The Land East of the Asterisk", *The London Review of Books* 30/7 (10 April 2008): 27-29.

Doss-Quinby, Eglal 2001: *Songs of the Women Trouvères*, Yale University Press.

Dresbeck, LeRoy J. 1967: "The Ski: Its History and Historiography", *Technology and Culture* 8/4 (Oct., 1967): 467-479.

Drobin, Ulf 1968: "Myth and Epical Motifs in the Loki-Research", *Temenos* 3: 19-39.

Dronke, Ursula 1962: "Art and tradition in *Skírnismál*", in Norman Davis and C.L. Wrenn (eds.), *English and Medieval studies presented to J. R. R. Tolkien*, Allen & Unwin: 250-68.

Dronke, Ursula 1969: *The Poetic Edda Vol. II: Mythological Poems*, Clarendon Press, Oxford.

Dronke, Ursula 1988: "The War of the Æsir and Vanir in Voluspá" in Weber: 223-38.

Dubois, Thomas A. 2012: "Diet and Deities: Contrastive Livelihoods and Animal Symbolism in Nordic Pre-Christian Religions", in Raudvere and Schjodt, Kindle.

Dumézil, Georges 1973: *From Myth to Fiction: the Saga of Hadingus*, trans. Derek Coltman, Chicago, University of Chicago.

Dumézil, Georges 1955: "Njordr, Nerthus et le folklore scandinave des génies de la mer", *Revue de l'histoire des religions* 147: 210-26.

Edred 1999: *Witchdom of the True: A Study of the Vana-Troth and the Practice of Seithr*, Runa-Raven Press, P.O. Box 557, Smithville, Texas, U.S.A., 78957.

Edsman, Carl-Martin 2004: "Bears", (trans. Verne Moberg) in Ency. Rel.

Eggertsdóttir, Margét 2008: "The Anomalous Pursuit of Love in Kormaks saga", in Wolf and Denzin: 81-109.

Einarsson, Biarni 1969: "The Lovesick Skald: a Reply to Theodore M. Andersson", *Medieval Scandinavia* 4: 21-41.

Eldevik, Riandi 2005: "Less Than Kind: Giants in Germanic Tradition", in Shippey: 83-110.

Enochs, Ross 2004: "Ring, Fetter, Oath", in *The Journal of Germanic Mythology and Folklore* 1 (Jan. 2014): 4-24.

Eriksen, Roy 1994: *Contexts of Pre-Novel Narrative: The European Tradition*, Walter de Gruyter.

Faulkes, Anthony 1978-9: "Descent from the Gods", *Mediaeval Scandinavia*: 92-125.

Finlay, Alison, 2001: "Monstrous Accusations: an Exchange of *yki* in *Bjarnar saga Hítdœlakappa*", *alvissmal* 10: 21 – 44.

Foley, Helene P. 2013: *The Homeric "Hymn to Demeter": Translation, Commentary, and Interpretive Essays*, Princeton University Press.

Frank, Roberta 2007: "The Lay of the Land in Skaldic Praise Poetry": in *Myth in Early Northwest Europe*, ed. Stephen O. Glosecki, *Arizona Studies in the Middle Ages and Renaissance* 21: 175-196.

Frank, Roberta 1970: "Onomastic Play in Kormakr's Verse: The Name Steingerðr", *Mediaeval Scandinavia* 3: 7-34. (Also available as a reprint booklet.)

Frank, Roberta 1990: "Why Skalds Address Women", in Pároli: 67-83.

Frankki, James 2012: "Cross-Dressing in the Poetic Edda: *Mic muno Æsir argan kalla*", *Scandinavian Studies* 84/4: 425-37.

Frazer, James George 1922: *The Golden Bough: a study in magic and religion*, abridged ed., Macmillan, New York.

Freyjasgodhi, Alfgeir 1998: "The Rest of the Vanir", *Idunna: a Journal of the Northern Tradition* 35 (Spring 1988): 9 – 18.

Friðriksdóttir, Jóhanna Katrín 2013: *Women in Old Norse Literature: Bodies, Words, and Power*, Palgrave MacMillan.

Frog and Jonathan Roper 2011: "Verses versus the 'Vanir': Response to Simek's "Vanir Obituary"", *RMN Newsletter 2 (May)*: 29-36.

Gade, Kari Ellen 1985: "Skjalf", *Arkiv för Nordisk Filologi* 100: 59–71.

Gardenstone 2012: *The Nerthus Claim*, Books on Demand GmbH, Nordstedt, Germany.

Gatwood, Lynn E. 1985: *Devi and the Spouse Goddess*, Manohar Publications, 1 Ansari Road, Daryaganj, New Delhi-110002.

Gilkus, Ingvild Saelid 1997: *Laughing Gods, Weeping Virgins: Laughter in the History of Religion*, Routledge.

Glendenning, Robert James, and Haraldur Bessason eds. 1983: *Edda: A Collection of Essays*, University of Manitoba Press.

Gräslund, Anne-Sofie 2006: "Wolves, serpents and birds: Their symbolic meaning in Old Norse belief, " in Andrén, Jennbert and Raudven, 2006: 124-9.

Grimes, Yvette 2010: *The Norse Myths*, Hollow Earth Publishing.

Grimm, Jacob (George Bell, trans.) 1882: *Teutonic Mythology I*, Google eBook.

Grimstad, Karen (trans.) 2000: *Volsunga saga: The Saga of the Volsungs*, AQ Verlag, Saarbrucken, Germany.

Gudmundsdóttir, Adalheidur 2007: "The Werewolf in Medieval Icelandic Literature", *JEGP* 106: 3: 277-303.

Guerber, Hélène Adeline 1994: *Myths of the Norsemen*, Senate. (reprint)

Gundarsson, Kvedulf 2006: *Our Troth: History and Lore*, BookSurge Publishing, North Charleston, North Carolina, USA.

Gundarsson, Kvedulfr 1998: "The Wanes", *Idunna: a Journal of the Northern Tradition* 35 (Spring 1988): 33 – 41.

Gunnell, Terry 1995: *The Origin of Drama in Scandinavia*, Cambridge University Press.

Hamer, Andrew 1973: "Legendary Fiction in Flateyjarbók" in *Proceedings of the First International Saga Conference, University of Edinburgh*, eds. Peter Foote, Hermann Pálsson, Desmond Slay, Viking Society for Northern Research: 184-211.

Harris, Joseph 2009: "Myth and Meaning in the Rök Inscription", in *Analecta Septentrionalia, Papers on the History of North Germanic Culture and Literature*, eds. Wilhelm Heizmann, Klaus Böldl, and Heinrich Beck: Walter de Gruyter, Berlin, New York: 467-501.

Heinrichs, Anne 1994: "The Search for Identity: A Problem After Conversion", *alvíssmál* 3: 43–62.

Henninger, Joseph 2004: "Scapegoat", (trans. Matthew J. O'Connell) in Ency. Rel.

Henry, P. L. 1990: "Verba Scáthaige", *Celtica* 21: 191-207.

Hermann, Pernille, Jens Peter Schjødt, and Rasmus Tranum Kristensen: 2007: *Reflections on Old Norse myths, Studies in Viking and medieval Scandinavia* 1, Brepols, Turnhout.

Heslop, Kate 2009: "Seeing things in the shield poems and other skaldic ekphrases", presented at Mediale Auffälligkeit/Conspicuous mediality, Zurich, Switzerland, 14-16 September 2009, conference paper. (http://kate-heslop.com/media/seeing_things_in_the_ shield_poems.pdf)

Heusler, Andreas 1991: "The Story of the Völsi, an Old Norse Anecdote of Conversion" (trans. Peter Nelson), in Salisbury: 187-200.

Hines, John 2000: "Myth and Reality: the Conclusions of Archaeology", in Barnes and Clunies Ross: 19-39.

Holm, Ingunn 2002: "A Landscape beyond the Infield/Outfield Categories: An Example from Eastern Norway", *Norwegian Archaeological Review* 35/2: 67-80.

Hopkins, Joseph S. 2012: "Goddesses Unknown I: Njǫrun and the Sister-Wife of Njǫrðr" in *RMN Newsletter* 5 (Dec): 39-44.

Hrafnhild, Nicanthiel 2009: *Boar, Birch and Bog: Prayers to Nerthus*, Gullinbursti Press.

Hull, Eleanor 1901-3: "The Episodes in Icelandic Literature", *Saga-Book of the Viking Society* 3: 235-70.

Jacobs, M. A. 2014: "*Hon stoð and starði*: Vision, Love and Gender in *Gunnlaugs saga ormstungu*, *Scandinavian Studies* 86/2: 148-169.

Jakobsson, Armann 2008: "A contest of cosmic fathers: God and giant in Vafþrúðnismál", *Neophilologus* 92: 263–77.

Jakobsson, Ármann 2008: "The Trollish Act of Thorgrímr the Witch: the Meanings of *Troll* and *Ergi* in Medieval Iceland, *Saga-Book* 32: 39-68.

Jakobsson, Ármann 2009: "Identifying the Ogre: the Legendary Saga Giants", in *Fornaldarsagaerne: Myter og virkelighed*, Ármann Jakobsson, Annette Lassen & Agneta Ney (eds.), Museum Tusculanum Press, University of Copenhagen, 181-200.

Jakobsson, Ármann 2005: "The good, the bad and the ugly: *Bárdar saga* and its giants", *Medieval Scandinavia* 15: 1-15.

James, Alan 1997: *The Trial of Loki: A study in Nordic heathen morality*, ORA Australia, ORA, PO Box 4333, University of Melbourne, Victoria 3052, Australia.

Jennbert, Kristina 2011: *Animals and Humans: Recurrent symbiosis in archaeology and Old Norse Religion*, trans. Alan Crozier, Vägar till Midgard 14, Nordic Academic Press, Lund, Sweden. (also on Scribd)

Jesch, Judith 1991: *Women in the Viking Age*, Boydell Press, PO Box 9, Woodbridge, Suffolk, IP12 3DF, UK, 1991.

Jochens, Jenny 1986: "The Medieval Icelandic Heroine: Fact or Fiction?", *Viator* 17: 35-50.

Jochens, Jenny 1991: "Before the Male Gaze: the Absence of the Female Body in Old Norse", in Salisbury: 3-29.

Jochens, Jenny 1996: *Old Norse Images of Women*, Mariner Books.

Jochens, Jenny 1998: *Women in Old Norse Society*, Cornell University Press.

Jochens, Jenny 2008: "Romance, Marriage, and Social Class in the Saga World", in Wolf and Denzin: 65-79.

Johnson, Buffie, 1988: *Lady of the Beasts: Ancient Images of the Goddess and Her Sacred Animals*, Harper San Francisco, New York and San Francisco, USA.

Jones, Lindsay, editor-in-chief, 2005, *The Encyclopaedia of Religion*, MacMillian Reference, Detroit, USA.

Kaldera, Raven 2007: *Jotunbok: Working with the Giants of the Northern Tradition*, Asphodel Press.

Kalinke, Marianne 1990: *Bridal-Quest Romance in Medieval Iceland*, Islandica XLVI, Cornell University Press, Ithaca.

Kaplan, M., and T. R. Tangherlini 2012: *News from Other Worlds: Studies in Nordic Folklore, Mythology and Culture*, North Pinehurst Press.

Karlsdottir, Alice 1992: "Njordr and Skadhi: the Marriage of Light and Darkness", *Mountain Thunder* 7 (Winter): 19-21.

Kellogg, Robert 1973: "Sex and the Vernacular in Medieval Iceland", in *Proceedings of the First International Saga Conference, University of Edinburgh*, eds. Peter Foote, Hermann Pálsson, Desmond Slay, Viking Society for Northern Research: 244-58.

Klingenberger, Heinz 1983: "Types of Eddic Mythological Poetry", in Glendenning and Bessason: 13-64.

Krappe, Alexander H. 1943: "Yngvi-Frey And Aengus Mac Oc", *Scandinavian Studies*, Vol. 17, No. 5, pp. 174-178.

Kress, Helga 2002: "Taming the Shrew: The Rise of Patriarchy and the Subordination of the Feminine in Old Norse Literature", in Anderson and Swenson: 81-92.

Kries, Susanne 2002: "Laughter and Social Stability in Anglo-Saxon and Old Norse Literature" in *A History of English Laughter: Laughter from Beowulf to Beckett and Beyond*, ed. Manfred Pfister, Rodopi: 1-15.

Kristensen, Rasmus Tranem 2007: "Why was Oðinn Killed By Fenrir? A Structural Analysis of Kinship Structures in Old Norse Myths of Creation and Eschatology", in Hermann, Schjødt, and Kristensen: 149-69.

Kroesen, Riti 1996: "Ambiguity in the relationship between heroes and giants", *Arkiv för nordisk filologi* 111: 57-71.

Kurman, George 1974: "Ekphrasis in Epic Poetry", *Comparative Literature* 26/1 (Winter 1974): 1-13.

Kusemko, Jurij 2009: "Sámi and Scandinavians in the Viking Age", in *Approaching the Viking Age: Proceedings of the international conference on Old Norse literature, mythology, culture, social life and language 11–13 October 2007, Vilnius, Lithuania*, eds. Ērika Sausverde and Ieva Steponavičiūtė, Vilnius University Publishing House: 65-94.

Lady Gregory 1904: *Gods and Fighting Men*, Forgotten Books.

Langeslag, Paul Sander 2012: *Seasonal Setting and the Human Domain in Early English and Early Scandinavian Literature*, University of Toronto, thesis. (http://hdl.handle.net/1807/32801)

Larrington, Carolyne 1992a: ""What Does Woman Want? ": Maer and munr in *Skirnismal*', *alvissmal* 1: 3–16.

Larrington, Carolyne 1992b: "Scandinavia", in *The Feminist Companion to Mythology*, Pandora Press: 137-61.

Larrington, Carolyne 2006: "Loki's Children" in McKinnell, Ashurst and Kick: 541-50.

Laurence Marcellus Larson (trans.) 2011: *The Earliest Norwegian Laws*, The Lawbook Exchange, Ltd. (reprint)

Lieberman, Anatoly 1995: "A Laughing Teuton", in *Across the Oceans: Studies in Honor of Richard K. Seymour*, eds. Irmengard Rauch and Cornelia Niekus Moore, University of Hawaii Press: 133-50.

Lieberman, Anatoly 1992: "Snorri and Saxo on Útgardloki, with Notes on Loki Lafeyjarson's Character, Career, and Name", in *Saxo Grammaticus: Tra Storiografia e letteratura: Bevangna, 27-29 settembre 1990*, ed. Carlo Santini, Editrice "Il Calmo", Rome: 91 – 158.

Lieberman, Anatoly 2002: "What Happened to Female Dwarfs?", in Simek and Helzmann, 257-63.

Lincoln, Bruce 1999: "*Gautrek's Saga* and the Gift-Fox", in *Theorizing Myth*, University of Chicago, 1999. (Reprinted from *The Ship as Symbol in Prehistoric and Medieval Scandinavia*): 171-82.

Lindow, John 1992: "Loki and Skadi" in S*norrastefna*, ed. Ulfar Bragason, Stofnunn Sigurdar Nordals, Reykjavik: 130–141.

Lindow, John 1997, *Murder and Vengeance Among the Gods: Baldr in Scandinavian Mythology*, FF Communications 262, Helsinki: Suomalainen Tiedeakatemia/Academia Scientiaram Fennica.

Lindow, John 2001: *Norse Mythology: A Guide to the Gods, Heroes, Rituals and Beliefs*, OUP, New York and Oxford.

Lindow, John 2008: "When Skaði Chose Njǫrðr", in Wolf and Denzin: 165-81.

Litvinskii, B.A. 2005: "Sheep and Goats" (trans. Syvia Juran), in Ency. Rel.

Lönnroth, Lars 2002: "The Founding of Miðgarðr (Völuspá 1-8)", in Acker and Larrington: 1-26.

Lothursdottir, Alfta Svanni 2003: "Loki: Friend of Othinn", http://www.northvegr.org/northern/book/loki.php.

Luhrmann, T. M. 2001: "The Ugly Goddess: Reflections on the Role of Violent Images in Religious Experience", *History of Religion* 41/2: 114-41.

Malm, Mats 2000: "Baldrs draumar: literally and literarily", in Barnes and Clunes Ross: 277-89.

Malm, Mats 2007: "The Notion of Effeminate Language in Old Norse Literature", in Qunin, Heslop and Wills: 305-20.

Marinatos, Nanno 2000: *The Goddess and the Warrior: The Naked Goddess and Mistress of the Animals in Early Greek Religion*, Routledge and Kegan Paul.

Mártinez-Pizarro, Joaquín 1990: "Woman-to-Man "Senna"", in *Poetry in the Scandinavian Middle Ages, The Seventh International Saga Conference*, Presso la Sede del Centro Studi, Spoleto: 339–350.

McGrath, Caroline 2012: "The Apple in Early Irish Narrative Tradition: A Thoroughly Christian Symbol?", *Studia Celtica Fennica* 7: 18-25.

McGrath, Sheena 1998: "Are the Vanir Fertile?" *Idunna* 35 (Spring 1998): 42.

McGrath, Sheena 1997: *Asyniur: Women's Mysteries of the North*, Capall Bann, Auton Farm, Milverton, Somerset, TA4 1NE.

McKinnell, John 2000: "Encounters with Völur", in Barnes and Clunies Ross: 239-51.

McKinnell, John 2007: "*Ögmundar þattr.* Version, Structure and Ideology" in Hermann, Egilsdóttir, and Simek: 159-74.

McKinnell, John 2002: "Thorgerdr Högabrúdr and *Hyndlúljód*", in Simek and Helzmann, 265-90.

McKinnell, John 1994: *Both One and Many*, Il Calamo, Rome.

McKinnell, John 1996: "The Trouble with Father: Hervararkvida and Cross-Sexual Encounters with the Other World", in *Myth and its Legacy in European Literature*, eds. N. Thomas and F. Le Saux, Durham : University of Durham: 63-92.

McKinnell, John 2014: *Essays on Eddic Poetry*, with eds. Donna Kick and John D. Shafer, University of Toronto Press, Toronto, Buffalo, London.

McKinnell, John, David Ashurst and Donata Kick (eds.) 2006: *The fantastic in old Norse/Icelandic literature: sagas and the British Isles,* 13th International Saga Conference: Durham and York, Durham University Press.

McKinnell, John 1986-9: "Motivation in *Lokasenna*", *Saga-Book*, XXII: 234 – 262.

McKinnell, John 2005: *Meeting the other in Norse myth and legend*, .D.S. Brewer, Woodbridge.

McKinnell, John, and Rudolf Simek, with Klaus Düwel, 2004: *Runes, magic and religion: a sourcebook*, Fassbaender, Wien.

McLeod, Mindy, and Bernard Mees 2006: *Runic Amulets and Magic Objects*, Boydell Press, London.

McTurk, Rory (ed.) 2005: *A companion to Old Norse-Icelandic literature and culture*, Blackwell, Malden, MA, USA.

McTurk, Rory 1974-7: "Sacral Kingship in Ancient Scandinavia: a Review of Some Ancient Writing", *Saga-Book of the Viking Society* XIX: 139-69.

McTurk, Rory 2005: *Chaucer in the Norse and Celtic Worlds*, Ashgate, Aldershot.

Miller, William Ian 1990: *Bloodtaking and Peacemaking: Feud, Law and Society in Saga Iceland*, University of Chicago Press, Chicago.

Mees, Bernard 2009: "*Alu* and *hale* II: 'May Thor bless'" in Ney, Williams and Ljungqvist: 683-90.

Mitchell, Stephen 1983: "*For Scírnis* as Mythological Model: frid at kaupa", *Arkiv för Nordisk Filologi* 98: 108 – 122.

Mitchell, Stephen 2007: "*Skírnismál* and Nordic Charm Magic", in Hermann, Schjødt, and Kristensen: 75-94.

Mosher, Arthur D. 1985: "The Story of Baldr's Death: The Inadequacy of Myth in the Light of Christian Faith", *Scandinavian Studies* 55: 305-15.

Motz, Lotte 1975: "The King and the Goddess: An Interpretation of *Svipdagsmal*', *Arkiv för nordisk filologi* 90: 133-150.

Motz, Lotte 1979-1980: "The Rulers of The Mountain: A Study of the Giants of the Old Icelandic Texts", *Mankind Quarterly* 20: 393-416.

Motz, Lotte 1980: "Sister in the Cave: the stature and the function of the female figures in the *Edda*", *Arkiv för nordisk filologi* 95: 168–182.

Motz, Lotte 1981a: "Aurboda-Eyrgjafa: Two Icelandic Names", *The Mankind Quarterly* 22: 93-105.

Motz, Lotte 1981b, "Gerdr: A new interpretation of the Lay of Skirnir", *Maal og Minne*: 121 – 136.

Motz, Lotte 1981c: "Giantesses and their Names", *Frühmittelalterliche Studien* 15: 495-507.

Motz, Lotte 1982: "Giants in Folklore and Mythology: A New Approach", *Folklore* 93/1: 78 –84.

Motz, Lotte 1984: "Giants and Giantesses: A study in Norse mythology and belief", *Amsterdamer Beitärge zur Ältern Germanistik* 22: 83–108.

Motz, Lotte 1987: "Old Icelandic Giants and Their Names", *Frühmittlealterliche Studien* 21: 295–317.

Motz, Lotte 1992: "The Goddess Nerthus: A New Approach", *Amsterdamer Beiträge zur älteren Germanistik* 36: 1-19.

Motz, Lotte 1996: "Kingship and the Giants", *Arkiv för nordisk filologi* 111: 73–88.

Motz, Lotte 1993: *The Beauty and the Hag: Female Figures of Germanic Faith and Myth*, Fassbaender.

Motz. Lotte 1987: "The Families of Giants", *Arkiv för norsdisk filologi* 102: 216-36.

Mundal, Else 1990: "Position of the Individual Gods and Goddesses in Various Types of Sources - With Particular Reference to the Female Divinities", in *Old Norse and Finnish Religions and Cultic Place Names*, ed. Tore Ahlback, Almqvist & Wiksell Internat: 294-315.

Mundal, Else 1996: "The perception of the Saamis and their religion in Old Norse sources" in Pentikäinen: 97-116.

Mundal, Else 1994: "Women and Old Norse Narrative", in Eriksen: 135-51.

Mundal, Else 2000: "Coexistence of Saami and Norse culture – reflected in and interpreted by Old Norse myths", in Barnes and Clunies Ross: 346-56.

Mundal, Else 2002: "*Austr sat in aldna...*: Giantesses and female powers in *Völuspá*", in Simek and Helzmann, 185-95.

Mundt, Maria 1990: "*Hervarar saga ok Heiðreks konungs* Revisited", in Pároli.

Nässtrom, Britt-Mari 1992: "The Goddesses in *Gylfaginning*" in Bragason.

Nässtrom, Britt-Mari 1996: "Freyja and Frigg – two aspects of the Great Goddess" in Pentikäinen: 81-96.

Nielsen, Niels Age 1969: "Frey, Ull, and the Sparlosa Stone" *Mediaeval Scandinavia* 2: 102-28.

Nordal, Sigurdur (trans. B.S. Benedikz and J. S. McKinnell), 1978: "Three Essays on *Völuspá*", *Saga-Book* 1: 78-135.

Norrman, Lena 2000: "Woman or Warrior? Gender in Old Norse Myth" in Barnes and Clunes Ross: 375 – 385.

North, Richard 1997: *Heathen gods in Old English literature*, Cambridge University Press, Cambridge.

North, Richard 2000: "*god geyja*: the limits of humour in Old Norse-Icelandic paganism", in Barnes and Clunies Ross: 386-95.

North, Richard 2001: "Loki's Gender: Or, why Skadi Laughed", in Olsen and Houwen: 141-51.

North, Richard 2009: "Sighvatr Sturluson and the authorship of *Viga-Glums saga*", in *Analecta Septentrionalia. Beiträge zur nordgermanischen Kultur- und Literaturgeschichte. Festschrift an Kurt Schier*, ed. Wilhelm Heizmann and Astrid van Nahl, Ergänzungsbände zum Reallexikon der Germanischen Altertumskunde (Berlin: Walter de Gruyter, March 2009), pp. 20-36.

Notopoulos, James A. 1938: "Mnemosyne in Oral Literature", *Transactions and Proceedings of the American Philological Association* 69: 465-93.

Nygaard, Simon 2015: "Between Bog Bodies and High Halls: Changes in Spatial Focus and Religious Conceptions in the Pre-Christian North", in *Sagas and Space: the 16th International Saga Conference Pre-Prints*, eds. Jürg Glauser, Klaus Müller-Wille, Anna Katherina Richter and Lukas Rölsi, Schweizerische Gesellschaft für Skandinavische Studien, Abteilung für Nordische Philologie, Deutsches Seminar Universität Zürich, abstract: 224.

O'Donoghue, Heather 2007: *From Asgard to Valhalla: the Remarkable History of the Norse Myths*, I. B. Tauris, London.

Odhinnsdaughter, Riastlin 1998: "She Who Slays", *Brigid's Hearth* 1. (also at: http://www.geocities.com/Athens/Forum/3567/ GG10.html #SheWhoSlays)

Ólason, Vésteinn 1994: "The marvellous North and authorial presence in the Icelandic fornaldarsaga", in Eriksen: 101-34.

Ólason, Vésteinn 2000: "The Un/Grateful Dead - From Baldr to Bagifotr", in Barnes and Clunies-Ross: 153-71.

Olsen, Karin E. and Luuk A. J. R. Houwen (eds.): 2001: *Monsters and the Monstrous in Medieval Northwest Europe*, Peeters Publishers, Leuven.

Olsen, Karin 2001: "Bragi Boddasson's *Ragnarsdrápa*: A Monstrous Poem" in Olsen and Houwen: 123-139.

Oosten. Jarich G. 1985: *The war of the gods: the social code in Indo-European mythology*, Routledge & Kegan Paul, London; Boston.

Orchard, Andy, 1998/2002: *Cassell's Dictionary of Norse Myth and Legend*, Cassell, London.

Orton, Peter 2005: "Pagan Myth and Religion", in McTurk 2005a: 302-19.

Orton, Peter 1998-2001: review of "Kommentar zu Leideren der Edda", in *Saga-Book of the Viking Society* 25: 226-9.

Östvold, Torbjörg 1969: "The War of the Aesir and Vanir - a Myth of the Fall in Nordic Religion", *Temenos* 5: 169-202.

Pálsson, Hermann, and Paul Edwards (trans.) 1986: *Seven Viking Romances*, Penguin Classics.

Pálsson, Hermann, Ásdís Egilsdóttir, and Rudolf Simek: 2001: *Sagnaheimur: studies in honour of Hermann Pálsson on his 80th birthday, 26th May 2001*, Fassbaender, Vienna.

Paplauskas-Ramunas, Maria 1952: *Women in Lithuanian Folklore*, University of Ottawa, diss. (www.ruor.uottawa.ca/handle/ 10393/21153)

Pároli, Teresa (ed.) 1990: *Poetry in the Scandinavian Middle Ages: the seventh international saga conference*, Centro italiano di studi sull'alto Medioevo, Spoleto.

Paxson, Diana 2002: "Skadhi, Wilderness Woman", *Sagewoman* (Summer). (http://hrafnar.org/articles/dpaxson/asynjur/skadi/)

Paxson, Diana 1992: "Utgard: the Role of the Jotnar in the Religion of the North", *Mountain Thunder* 5. (http://hrafnar.org/articles/dpaxson/norse/utgard/)

Pentikäinen, Juha ed. 1996: *Shamanism and Northern Ecology, Religion and Society* 36, de Gruyter.

Pluskowski, Aleskander 2006: *Wolves and the Wilderness in the Middle Ages*, Boydell Press, Woodbridge.

Poli, Diego 1990: "Concord and Discord in the Icelandic Banqueting Hall", in Pároli: 597-608.

Polomé, Edgar 1969: "Some Comments on Voluspa, Stanzas 17 -18", in *Old Norse Literature and Mythology: A Symposium*, ed. Edgar C. Polomé, University of Texas Press: 265-90.

Polomé, Edgar 1999: "Nerthus/Njordr and Georges Dumézil", *Mankind Quarterly*, vol. XL, no. 2.: 143 – 154.

Poole, Russell 2007: "Myth and Ritual in the Háleygjatal of Eyvindr Skáldaspillir", in Quinn, Heslop and Willis: 153-76.

Poole, Russell 1997: "Composition Transmission Performance: the First Ten *lausavísur* in Kormáks saga" in *alvíssmál* 7: 37-60.

Power, Rosemary 1984: "Journeys to the north in the Icelandic Fornaldarsögur", *Arv* 40: 7-25.

Price, Neill 2006: "What's in a Name? An archaeological identity crisis for the Norse gods (and some of their friends)", in Anders and Jennebert: 179-183.

Puhvel, Jaan 1989: *Comparative Mythology*, John Hopkins University Press, Baltimore and London.

Quinn, Judy 2000: "Dialogue with a *völva*: *Hyndluljóð, Baldrs draumar* and *Völuspá*", in Acker and Larrington 2002: 245-74.

Quinn, Judy 2013: "Mythological Motivation in Eddic Heroic Poetry: Interpreting *Grottasöngr*" in Acker and Larrington 2013: 159-82.

Quinn, Judy, Kate Heslop and Tarrin Wills, 2007: *Learning and understanding in the Old Norse world : essays in honour of Margaret Clunies Ross*, Brepols, Turhout, Belgium.

Raudvere, Catharina, and Jens Peter Schjodt 2012: *More Than Mythology: Narratives, Ritual Practices and Regional Distribution in Pre-Christian Scandinavian Religions*, Nordic Academic Press. (available on Scribd)

Roe, Anthony 1998, "The Sacred Archer", *White Dragon* (Samhain).

Rooth, Anna Birgitta 1961: *Loki in Scandinavian mythology*, C.W.K. Gleerups, Lund.

Ross, Anne 1967: *Pagan Celtic Britain: A Study in Iconography and Tradition*, Constable, London.

Rossi, Michael 2013: "Consider Jack and Oskar", *London Review of Books* 35 (February 7): 27-8.

Røthe, Gunnhild 2006: "The Fictitious Figure of Þorgerðr Hölgabrúðr in the Saga Tradition", in *Proceedings of the Thirteenth International Saga Conference*, Durham and York, 6th-12th August, 2006: pdf. (http://www.dur.ac.uk/medieval.www/sagaconf/ rothe.htm)

Røthe, Gunnhild 2007: "Þorgerðr Hölgabrúðr – the fylgja of the Háleygjar family", *Scripta Islandica* 58: 33-56.

Rubin, Gayle 1975: The Traffic in Women: Notes on the "Political Economy" of Sex." *Toward an Anthropology of Women.* ed. Rayna Reiter: 157-210.

Ruggerini, Maria Elena 2001: "Binomials in *Skírnirsmál*", in Pálsson, Egilsdóttir and Simek: 209 - 27.

RuneWolf 2005: "Jötna-Rúnir: The Mysteries of the Jötnar", *Witchvox* (www.witchvox.com/va/dt_va.html?id=9850), posted Aug. 28th 2005.

Sahlins, Marshall 1972: *Stone Age Economics*, Aldine-Atherton Inc.

Salisbury, Joyce 1991: *Sex in the Middle Ages: A Book of Essays*, Garland Publishing, London.

Sävborg, Daniel 2006: "Love among gods and men: *Skírnismál* and its tradition", Andrén, Jennbert and Raudven: 336-40.

Sax, William S. 1991: *Mountain Goddess: Gender and Politics in a Himalayan Pilgrimage*, OUP, Oxford.

Sayers, William 1992: "Soundboxes of the Divine: Hœnir, Sencha, Gwalchmai". *Mankind Quarterly* 33: 57-67.

Sayers, William 2002-3: "Gender Ambiguity in Medieval Iceland: Legal Framework and Saga Dynamics", *Scandinavian-Canadian Studies/ Études scandinaves au Canada* 14: 1-27.

Sayers, William 2009: "Snorri's Troll-Wives". *Scandinavian-Canadian Studies / Études scandinaves au Canada* 18: 1-11.

Schjødt, Jens-Peter 2008: *Initiation Between Two Worlds: Structure and Symbolism in Pre-Christian Scandinavian Religion* (trans. Victor Hansen), The Viking Society Vol. 17, Odense UP.

Schjødt, Jens-Peter 2012: "Odin, Thorr and Freyr: Functions and Relations" in Kaplan and Tangherlini: 61-91.

Schütte, Dr. Gudmund 1909: "The Cult of Nerthus", *The Saga-Book of the Viking Society*, vol., 7 & 8.

Sheehan, John 1989/90: "A Viking-Age Silver Arm-Ring from Portumna, Co. Galway", *Journal of the Galway Archaeological and Historical Society*, 43: 125-30.

Sheffield, Ann Gróa 2007: *Frey, God of the World*, 2nd edition, Lulu.com.

Shippey, Tom (ed.) 2005: *The Shadow-Walkers: Jacob Grimm's Mythology of the Monstrous*, Medieval & Renaissance Texts & Studies 291, Arizona Center for Medieval and Renaissance Studies in collaboration with Brepols, Tempe, Arizona.

Simek, Rudolf (trans. Angela Hall) 1996: *Dictionary of Northern Mythology*, D. S. Brewer, Cambridge.

Simek, Rudolf, 1986: "Elusive Elysia, or, Which Way to Glæsisvellir?" in Simek, Kristjánsson, and Bekker-Nielsen.

Simek, Rudolf, 2001: "Lust, Sex and Domination: *Skírnirsmál* and the Foundation of the Norwegian Kingdom" in Pálsson, Egilsdóttir, and Simek: 229-46.

Simek, Rudolf, 2010: "The Vanir: An Obituary", RMN Newsletter 1 (Dec.), www.helsinki.fi/folkloristiikka/English/RMN/archive.htm

Simek, Rudolf, and Wilhelm Helzmann (eds.) 2002, *Mythological Women: Studies in Memory of Lotte Motz*, Studia Medievalia Septentrionalia 7, Fassbender, Vienna.

Simek, Rudolf, Jónas Kristjánsson and Hans Bekker-Nielsen (eds) 1986: *Sagnaskemmtun: Studies in Honour of Hermann Pálsson*, Hermann Böhlaus Nachf., Graz: Wien.

Simpson, Jacqueline 1962-5: "Mímir: Two Myths or One?", *Saga-Book of the Viking Society* XVI: 41-53.

Skadidottir, Lyn 2013: "Working with Skadi" (http://www.northernpaganism.org/shrines/skadi/writing/working-with-skadi.html)

Słupecki, Leszek P. 2011: "The Vanir and ragnarok", *RMN Newsletter*, 3 Dec. 2011: 11-3.

Słupecki, Leszek P. 2012 : "Who Has to Perish in ragnarök?", in *Pre-Prints of the Fifteenth Saga Conference*: 289-90. (http://sagaconference.au.dk/fileadmin/sagaconference/Preprint-online.pdf)

Smith, Michael J. 2003: *Ways of the Astatru: Beliefs of the Modern, Northern Heathens*, Harvest-Moon Publishing, Athelingulf Fellowship. (www.geocities.com/athelingulf)

Sørensen, Preben Meulengracht (trans. Joan Turville-Petre) 1983: *The Unmanly Man: Concepts of sexual defamation in early Northern society*, Odense University Press.

Sørensen, Preben Meulengracht 1988: "Loki's *Senna* in Aegir's Hall", in Weber: 239 – 259.

Steinsland, Gro 2011: "Origin Myths and Rulership. From the Viking Age Ruler to the Ruler of Medieval Historiography: Continuity, Transformations and Historiography", in Steinsland, Rekdal, Sigurðsson and Beuermann: 15-69.

Steinsland, Gro 1987: "Giants as Recipients of Cult in the Viking Age? ", in *Words and Objects: Towards a Dialogue between Archaeology and Religion*, ed. Gro Steinsland, Norwegian University Press/ Institute for Comparative Research in Human Culture, Oslo: 212–222.

Steinsland, Gro, Jón Viðar Sigurðsson, Jan Erik Rekdal and Ian Beuermann, eds. 2011: *Ideology and Power in the Viking and Middle Ages: Scandinavia, Iceland, Ireland, Orkney and the Faeroes*, Brill, Leiden & Boston.

Straubhaar, Sandra Ballif 2011: *Old Norse Women's Poetry: The Voices of Female Skalds,* D.S. Brewer.

Strom, Folke 1956: "Une divinite-oiseau dans la mythologie Scandinave?" *Ethnos* 1-2: 73-84.

Strom, Folke 1973: *Nið, Ergi and Old Norse Moral Attitudes,* The Dorothea Coke Memorial Lecture in Northern Studies, Viking Society for Northern Research, London.

Ström, Folke 2001: "Poetry as an instrument of propaganda: Jarl Hákon and his poets" in *Speculum Norroenum: studies in honour of Hermann Pálsson on his 80th birthday,* 26th May 2001, Fassbaender: 440-58.

Sturtevant, Alfred Morey 1952: "Etymological Comments Upon Certain Old Norse Proper Names in the Eddas", *PMLA* 67/7: 1145-1162.

Sundqvist, Olof 2005a: "Aspects of Rulership Ideology in Early Scandinavia with particular references to the Skaldic Poem *Ynglingatal*', in *Das frühmittelalterliche Königtum: ideelle und religiöse Grundlagen,* ed. Franz-Reiner Erkens, Hubert & Co.

Sundqvist, Olof 2005b: "Sagas, Religion, and Rulership: The Credibility of the Descriptions of Rituals in Hákonar Saga Góða", *Viking and Medieval Scandinavia* 1: 215-50.

Svartesól 2009: *Visions of Vanaheim,* Lulu Enterprises Inc. 860 Aviation Parkway, Suite 300, Morrisville, NC 27560.

Tapp, Henry L. 1956: "Hinn Almáttki Áss: Thor or Odin?", *JEGP* 55/1 (Jan. 1956): 85-99.

Tepper, Leo 2001: "The Monster's Mother at Yuletide", in Olsen and Houwen: 93-102.

Teschke, Benno 1998: "Geopolitical Relations in the European Middle Ages: History and Theory", *International Organization* 52/2 (Spring, 1998): 325-358.

Thomson, David 1996/2001: *The People of the Sea: Celtic Tales of the Seal-Folk,* Canongate Classics, Edinburgh.

Tolley, Clive 2011: "In Defense of the Vanir", RMN Newsletter 2 (May): 20-8.

Tolley, Clive 2009: "Volsa þáttr: Pagan Lore or Christian Lie?" in Heizmann, Böldl and Beck: 680–700.

Tulinius, Torfi H. 1992: "Inheritance, Ideology and literature: *Hervarar saga ok Heiðreks*", in *From Saga to Society: Comparative Approaches to Early Iceland,* ed. Gísli Pálsson, Hisarlik Press, Middlesex: 147-60.

Turville-Petre, E. O. G. 1969: "Fertility of Beast and Soil in Old Norse Literature", in *Old Norse literature and mythology: a symposium*, ed. Edgar C. Polomé, Dept. of Germanic Languages of the University of Texas at Austin by the University of Texas Press, Austin, 1969: 244-64.

Turville-Petre, E. O. G. 1975: *Myth and Religion of the North: The Religion of Ancient Scandinavia*, Praeger.

Valeri, Valerio 1994: "Wild Victims: Hunting as Sacrifice and Sacrifice as Hunting in Huaulu", *History of Religions* 34/1: 101-31.

Vestergaard, Torben A. 1991: "Marriage Exchange and Social Structure in Old Norse Mythology", in *Social Approaches to Viking Studies*, ed. Ross Samson, Cruithne Press, Glasgow: 21-34.

Vigfusson, Guðbrandur, and Frederick York Powell 1883: *Corpus poeticum boreale: Eddic poetry v. 2. Court Poetry*, Clarendon Press.

von Schnurbein, Stephanie 2000: "The Function of Loki in Snorri Sturluson's Edda", *History of Religions*, 40/2: 109 – 124.

Walker, Barbara 2007: *The Women's Encyclopaedia of Myths and Secrets*, Harper and Row.

Wanner, Kevin 2009a: "Cunning Intelligence in Norse Myth: Loki, Óðinn, and the Limits of Sovereignty", *History of Religions* 48/3: 211-46.

Wanner, Kevin J. 2009b: "Off-Center: Considering Directional Valences in Norse Cosmography." *Speculum* 84/1: 36-72.

Weber, Gerd Wolfgang 1988: *Idee, Gestalt, Geschichte: Festschrift Klaus von See. Studien zur europäischen Kulturtradition*, Odense University Press.

Weinstock, John 2004: "Saxo Grammaticus", in *Ency. Rel.*

Welschback, Sarah 2012: ""Frá mínom véom oc vǫngom" - an examination of literary representations of the mythological figure of Skaði", *MA thesis, University of Iceland*. (http://skemman.is/stream/get/1946/12863/31204/1/MTSKadi.pdf)

West, M. L. 2007: *Indo-European Poetry and Myth*, OUP.

Whitaker, Ian 1981: ""A Sack for Carrying Things": The Traditional Role of Women in Northern Albanian Society", *Anthropological Quarterly* 54/3 (Jul., 1981): 146-156

Windele, John 1851: "On the Ring-Money of Ancient Ireland. No. II", *Transactions of the Royal Society of Antiquaries of Ireland*, 1/3: 328-33.

Wolf, Kirsten and Johanna Denzin (eds.): 2008: *Romance and Love in Late Medieval and Early Modern Iceland: Essays in Honor of Marianne Kalinke, Islandica* 54, Cornell University Library, Ithaca, NY.

Young, Jean 1933: "Does Rigsthula Betray Irish Influence?" *Arkiv för nordisk filologi* 49: 97-107.

Zerries, Otto (trans. John Maressa) 2004: "Lord of the Animals", in *Ency. Rel.*

Index

A

Aesir 10, 12-15, 18-20, 22, 24, 27, 29, 34, 37-39, 41, 43, 54, 58, 59, 62, 64-66, 68-70, 72, 76, 78, 82-84, 87-91, 96-98, 102, 103, 117-119, 121, 125, 126, 129, 134, 138, 140-149, 151, 152, 154, 155, 163, 164, 166, 168, 172, 174, 185-187, 189, 191, 192, 194, 208, 210, 211, 213-216, 218-224, 226, 227, 235-237, 244, 245, 255
Álfar 96
Alvaldi 76
Alvis 95
Amaterasu 190, 225, 226
Anat 149
Angry Queen 111
apple. 12, 14, 15, 25, 26, 78, 82, 84-90, 127, 141, 164, 165, 169, 174, 187, 211, 236
Asgard 12-14, 22, 24-27, 30, 31, 37, 39, 48, 52, 62, 64, 66, 68, 70, 80, 87, 89, 90, 92-94, 96-98, 126, 127, 129, 141, 142, 155, 165, 174, 183, 186, 187, 191, 202, 211, 213, 218, 227, 236, 254
Asyniur 6, 9, 89, 91, 251
Atlas 86
Atli 57, 59
Audhumla 63, 94, 138
Aurnir 77
Aurvandil 79

B

Balder ... 26, 90, 91, 92, 118
Baldr. 13-15, 21, 32, 48, 49, 62, 63, 69, 70, 72, 74, 77, 92, 104, 141, 155, 164, 172, 185, 186, 193, 210, 211, 219, 221, 222, 235, 250, 252, 254
Bebon 225
Bellona 162
Beowulf 175, 249
Bergelmir 64
Berúthiel 111, 112, 158
Bestla 63, 94
Bifrost 67, 83, 93, 97
boar 150
Bolthorn 63
Bragi Boddason.. 16, 17, 23, 24, 25, 65, 74, 78, 84, 127, 141, 146, 254
Brigantia 6
Brisingamen 19, 149
Buri 63, 94
Byleistr 68

C

Castor and Pollux 13, 32
castration 165, 177, 178
cat 111
cauldron 24, 39, 141
chariot. 21, 47, 83, 156, 159
Cinderella. 91, 92, 108, 207, 218
Codex Regius 33, 47, 158
Codex Trajectinus 33, 34
Codex Upsaliensis 33, 34
Codex Wormianus 33, 34
cooking fire 82

cow 63, 94, 138, 177

D

Demeter. 190, 224, 226, 245
disarblot 56, 58
disir 56-58, 131, 136, 188
dog 69, 179, 180, 199
dragon 86, 90
Driffa 136
dróttkvætt....................... 17
Durga 110
dwarf 90, 95, 141

E

eagle . 12, 18, 20, 25, 51, 65, 78, 82, 83, 199, 228, 230
Eddas 65, 66, 156, 259
Eyvind ..23, 29, 30, 50, 200, 201

F

Færeyinga saga 60
Falastur........................ 111
falcon.20, 26, 228, 230, 231
Farbauti................19, 66, 67
feet 7, 13, 25, 26, 41, 63, 69, 90-93, 104, 105, 107, 108, 126, 165, 172, 191, 193, 202, 218, 219, 221
Fenris 69
fishing.......39, 42, 114, 115, 174, 196, 201, 202
Flagl 124
Flateyjarbok..8, 47, 53, 134, 136, 149, 178, 205
Fonn 136
Fornjot......................... 132
Frey .. 16, 20, 37, 41, 42, 49, 106, 107, 124, 147-151, 153, 155, 157-159, 162 - 167, 189, 193, 208, 209, 229, 253, 257
Freya 15, 22, 37, 38, 39, 41, 46, 116, 131, 141, 176, 241
Freyja 26, 36, 40, 43, 44, 50, 54- 58, 62, 63, 82, 83, 87-89, 133, 138, 141, 144, 147-150, 152, 153, 157, 158, 160, 162, 166, 171, 172, 188, 192, 203, 208, 210, 220, 221, 228-231, 236, 253
Freyr .. 9, 28, 36, 37, 39, 40, 42-47, 49, 54, 59, 77, 88, 90, 91, 107, 114, 116, 118, 129, 131, 133, 141, 144, 148-150, 153, 154, 158, 159, 163, 167-169, 171-173, 176, 181, 182, 193, 203, 210, 214, 219, 221, 235, 241, 257
Frigg. 44, 46, 50, 62, 64, 83, 84, 88, 149, 154, 189, 228, 230, 241, 253
Frigga... 32, 36, 55, 69, 149, 157, 160, 228, 230
fylgur 57

G

Gaia 86
Gefjon 36, 160, 162, 210
Geirrod........ 62, 69, 79, 100
Geirrodr 126, 135, 228-230, 232
Gemini 13, 32, 109
Gerdr ... 7, 9, 36, 58, 59, 77, 84, 88, 90, 91, 100, 106, 107, 114, 124, 129, 141, 147, 149, 161, 163-167, 169-174, 177, 189, 190, 192, 193, 203, 219, 220, 227, 229, 241, 252
Germania 43, 156, 157
giantess.... 9, 18, 27, 40, 47, 50, 52, 53, 57-59, 63, 67, 69, 76, 78, 89-91, 94, 103, 106, 120, 123, 125, 127, 131, 133, 135, 136, 141, 163, 165-167, 169, 172, 178, 182, 185, 188, 189, 192, 196, 200, 207, 227, 229, 235, 236

giants..9, 10, 12, 14, 15, 18, 20-23, 25, 27, 34, 39, 58-60, 63-65, 68, 69, 72, 75-84, 87-90, 92-94, 96-99, 103, 117-120, 122, 124-129, 134-142, 149, 150, 161, 166, 167, 171, 172, 175, 185-187, 189, 192, 196, 197, 199, 203, 205, 206, 211, 212, 219, 220, 221, 229, 230, 232, 233, 235- 237, 248, 249
Ginnungagap 93, 128
Gna 83, 148
goat ..13, 21, 26, 47, 53, 83, 97, 107, 108, 177, 178, 180, 191, 222- 224, 227, 233, 234
Goi......... 131, 132, 204, 205
Gor 132, 204, 205
Grimnir........................ 135
Grimnismal.......8, 38, 48, 57
Grjottunggard 20
Gula-Thing 17
Gullveig 144, 145
Gusir 117, 136
Gygr.............................. 124
Gylfaginning ...8, 23, 24, 27, 28, 33, 37, 48, 56, 64, 66, 67, 72, 78, 84, 89, 93-98, 116, 126, 141, 148, 150, 166, 186, 189, 253

H

Hadingus 101-104, 109, 111, 189, 219, 238, 244
Haleygjar 59
Haleygjatal............ 8, 29, 61
Haraldr hárfagri 16
Harbardsljod...8, 13, 32, 62, 72, 83, 98, 125, 126, 220
Hárfagra 16
Harthgrepta 103
Hathor 225
Hati 58
Hattatal 23

Haustlöng. 8, 12, 16, 17, 22, 23, 30, 31, 48, 53, 65, 66, 69, 71- 73, 75, 76, 78, 81, 83, 87, 88, 90, 99, 127, 134, 136, 150, 178, 182, 201, 204, 212, 232, 233
hawk 21, 85
Heimdall..... 39, 40, 67, 147, 151
Heimskringla.. 8, 16, 23, 37, 39, 41, 50, 51, 115, 144, 146, 151, 168, 203, 206, 208, 209, 214, 239
Hel ... 55, 57, 68, 69, 84, 95, 96, 99, 155, 233, 239
Helblindi 68
Helgi.......... 58, 59, 176, 199
Hera 86
Hildr...................... 18, 135
Hindu.................... 158, 227
Hjálmþér 53
Hladir... 23, 30, 51, 59, 134, 170, 190, 201
Hoenir.... 12, 14, 18- 20, 39, 41, 63- 65, 70-75, 79, 89, 124, 134, 144, 152, 155, 214, 216, 232, 236, 257
Hǫlgi......................... 59, 60
horse 18, 22, 40, 42, 47, 53, 57, 58, 83, 136, 163, 168, 176, 179, 181, 182, 240
Horus............ 190, 225, 226
howling 114
Hrimgerdr 58, 59, 136
Hrimthursar.................... 59
Hrmnir 136
Hrungnir 20, 21, 22, 127, 138, 141, 192, 194
human sacrifice.............. 61
Husdrapa 17, 67
Hymir..... 19, 24, 38, 39, 97, 138, 186, 208, 210
Hymiskvida 24
Hyndluljod 8, 17, 40, 49, 57, 68, 77, 150, 166
Hyrrokin........ 135, 137, 141

I

Idun .... *See* Idunn
Idunn 10, 12, 14, 15, 18, 20, 22, 23, 25, 50, 55, 66, 69, 76, 78, 82-90, 99, 103, 124, 127, 141, 154, 165, 172, 174, 201, 210- 212, 224, 228, 229, 232-236
Innana 171
Inuit 135
Irish 45, 53, 85, 86, 100, 142, 170, 202, 251, 261
Irpa 60, 61, 134
Ishtar 149

J

Jómsvíkinga saga 60, 134
Jötnar 96, 256
Jotunheim 12-14, 19, 22, 26, 66, 79, 83, 90, 96, 99, 100, 127, 134, 174, 229
jotunn 48, 117, 123, 134, 221
Jötunn 124

K

Kannaki. 190, 191, 226, 227
Kormak 23, 51, 105-107, 172, 177, 219, 238
Kreppvör 40
Krishna 226

L

Laufey .... *See* Nal
Leidi 136
Loathly Lady 53
Lodur 73
Lokasenna 8, 24, 32, 38, 48, 61, 84, 99, 130, 144, 148, 149, 166, 188, 192, 199, 208, 209, 220, 227, 236, 251
Loke .... *See* Loki
Loki 9, 10, 12-15, 18-20, 22, 24, 31, 32, 38, 39, 48, 49, 52, 53, 56, 63-79, 81-84, 86-88, 90, 92, 95, 97, 100, 107, 108, 113, 119, 124, 126, 127, 129, 130, 137, 140-142, 144, 148, 149, 165, 167, 174, 175, 177, 178, 180, 185, 186, 188, 190-192, 194, 199, 201, 208-212, 220, 222-224, 227-236, 241, 244, 248-250, 254, 256, 258, 260

M

magic wand 125
Matres 57
Matronae 57
mead 78, 89, 138, 140, 143, 147, 163, 167, 169, 203, 228, 236
Menn 96
Midgard 7, 39, 64, 69, 93, 94, 96-100, 116, 126-128, 137, 138, 142, 248
Minerva 162
Mjoll 136
moon 21, 58, 69, 87, 128, 141, 147
Morn 19, 20, 48, 53, 76, 178, 182
mound 20, 60, 88, 133, 167
Muspellzheimr 93, 96

N

Náir 96
Nal .... *See* Laufey
Nanna 91, 92
Neith 225
Nerthus 43-47, 54, 131, 154, 156-162, 207-209, 245-247, 253, 255, 257
Niflheimr 93, 96
nine sisters 40
nine worlds . 74, 93- 95, 229
Njord ... 4, 10, 13-16, 23, 24, 26-29, 31- 50, 65, 70, 91, 92, 97, 102-107, 10-120, 131, 141, 143, 144, 147-

150, 153-169, 174, 175, 182, 185, 186, 192- 194, 203, 205, 207- 215, 219, 227, 234- 238
Noatun.... 13, 26, 28, 33, 37, 38, 41, 100, 169, 213
Nor .86, 102, 132, 201, 204, 205
nut 12, 26, 82, 84, 87

O

Odin .. 12-15, 18, 19, 21-23, 25, 27-29, 31, 34, 37, 40- 42, 47, 50-52, 57, 61-66, 68- 75, 78-80, 82, 83, 87, 89-97, 99, 124-127, 129, 139-142, 145, 146, 149- 152, 154, 163, 164, 168, 169, 171, 172, 175, 185, 189, 190, 192-195, 198- 200, 207, 210, 211, 217, 219-221, 228-230, 232, 236, 257, 259
Orion 79
osprey 85, 86
Ottar..57, 70, 133, 150, 244
ox 12, 18, 19, 22, 25, 65, 66, 72, 76, 79, 80, 82, 134, 138

P

penis........53, 108, 119, 136, 179-182
Poetic Edda...11, 24, 37, 57, 68, 94, 95, 231, 239, 240, 244, 245
Prose Edda....11, 16, 23, 24, 27, 33, 40, 65, 93, 116, 121, 146, 158, 163, 164, 239

R

Ra.................190, 225, 226
Radvör 40
Ragnarok 14, 39, 58, 62, 69, 70, 84, 91, 97, 123, 126, 129, 140, 141, 144, 147, 150, 155, 164, 168, 185, 186, 194, 209, 213, 229, 234, 242
Ragnarsdrapa...... 16, 18, 78
Ragnvald 16
rape............... 165, 167, 170
Regnilda 101-104, 109, 111, 219
Rigel................................79
ring 20, 21, 35, 102, 104, 164, 183, 184, 186, 202
Risi............................... 123
Rokkur 9

S

Saeming . 23, 29, 30, 50, 51, 129, 134, 190
Saga 16, 23, 36, 42, 51, 105, 122, 149, 239-244, 246-259
Sami. 7, 30, 55, 56, 61, 115, 117, 134-136, 196-205
Sami mythology.............202
Sappho............................86
sea 20, 21, 26-29, 37, 40, 45, 46, 47, 50, 91, 94, 98, 101, 102, 104, 111, 113, 114, 116, 127, 141, 160, 166, 174, 189, 201, 205, 208, 210, 233
seagull..................... 35, 114
seidr 63, 146, 147, 148, 150, 182
serpent........ 17, 39, 69, 137
Set 190, 225
shapeshifting............. 82, 86
ships 35, 114, 115, 130, 135, 208
Sif 15, 22, 50, 141, 154, 172, 188
singing 114, 225
Skadi4, 9-15, 19, 22-37, 40- 43, 46-61, 66, 69, 70, 75- 79, 83, 90-92, 102-111, 113-121, 124, 126-131, 133, 134, 136-138, 149, 150, 163-169, 171-175,

177, 178, 182, 183, 185-197, 200-207, 210, 211, 213, 215, 218-224, 226, 227, 233-238, 243, 244, 250, 254, 258

Skaldskaparmal... 8, 17, 18, 23-25, 27, 29, 40, 50, 60, 66, 67, 69, 72-74, 78, 88, 141, 160, 161, 168, 190, 201, 230, 243

Skessa 124

Skirnir 49, 58, 59, 84, 88, 90, 107, 124, 147, 163, 164, 165-167, 169-174, 177, 200, 220, 252

Skirnirsmal.....8, 36, 37, 49, 84, 92, 99, 147, 163, 165-171, 229

skis.............................. 115

Skrimnir 135

Snaefrith....................... 16

snake 48, 137

Snorri Sturluson 10, 13, 16-18, 23, 24, 27-31, 39, 40, 48, 50, 56, 57, 59, 60, 66-68, 72, 73, 76, 78, 79, 84, 87, 89, 93-99, 102, 104, 126-128, 133, 144, 146-148, 151-153, 161, 163, 164, 166-169, 174, 176, 186, 187, 189, 190, 192-194, 201, 203, 204, 219, 227, 235, 239, 243, 250, 257, 260

star 79

summer ..35, 109, 113, 114, 115

Summer King.........120, 203

sun 59, 69, 87, 95, 128, 141, 147, 148, 190, 191, 225, 226

swan 74, 120, 121, 131

sword....29, 53, 63, 90, 107, 129, 135, 136, 163, 164, 167-169, 182, 229

T

Tamil............................ 226

Telipinu 190

Terra Mater 43, 46, 114, 157

Thialfi........................ 22, 81

Thiazi 10, 12-15, 18, 19, 22-25, 27, 30-32, 35, 41, 47-49, 51, 58, 60, 63-66, 69, 71-84, 87, 89, 92, 100, 103, 108, 119, 121, 124, 126-128, 134-138, 141, 142, 165, 167, 174, 180, 182, 185, 187, 188, 193-195, 197, 201, 204, 211, 223, 224, 227- 230, 232-234, 236

Thjasse...................... 26, 27

Thjodolf............. 23, 78, 235

Þ

Þjóðólfr of Hvinir.. 16, 17, 18

T

Thor .. 13, 17, 18, 20-22, 24, 31, 32, 34, 39, 44, 47, 59, 62, 64, 69, 72, 78, 79, 81, 83, 89, 90, 93, 95, 97-99, 121, 124-127, 133, 135, 138, 140-142, 148-151, 154, 166, 169, 172, 176, 181, 182, 186, 191, 192, 194, 195, 203,208-210, 220, 222, 227, 229, 230, 232, 236, 240, 252, 259

Thorgerdr holgabrudr 59, 131, 133

Þ

Þorgerðr Hǫlgabrúðr 59

T

Thorlief.......... 17, 18, 20, 22

Thorri... 131, 132, 135, 136, 204

Thrud 22, 141

Thrymheim 7, 13, 26- 28, 33, 34, 36, 47, 48, 53, 65, 75, 100, 166, 169, 174, 207, 213
Thrymskvida ...8, 37, 39, 87, 97, 151, 171, 176, 192, 194, 203, 220, 229, 230, 236, 243
Thulur 67, 136
Thurs 124
Tiamat 138, 142
Tjatsiolmai 201, 202
toe 79
Torfa 135
Troll 123, 240, 247, 257
Trollkona 124

U

Uppsala . 149, 168, 181, 203
Ursa Major 79
Utgard 80, 81, 116, 117, 126- 128, 135, 186, 199, 255

V

Vafthrudnir .37, 38, 95, 125, 138
Vafthrudnismal.... 8, 37, 39, 80, 95, 97, 125, 219
Vafthurdnir 63
valkyries21, 57, 83, 88, 131, 188
Vanaheim 14, 37-39, 43, 93, 96- 98, 143, 147, 209, 213, 259
Vanir .. 9, 13, 16, 29, 38-41, 46, 47, 57, 77, 89, 90, 96- 98, 107, 116, 118, 119, 141-149, 151-155, 157, 158, 162-164, 185, 208, 210, 214-216, 220, 221, 237, 244-246, 251, 255, 258, 259
Ve 63, 73, 94, 99
Venus 79
Villi 73
Vindsvalir 136
Vingnir 21
Virgin Mary 31
Volsung 88
Voluspa 8, 62, 68, 73, 74, 77, 94, 95, 99, 144, 151, 152, 166, 182, 220, 255

W

wagon-god 47, 160
walnut 87
wand 164, 165, 173
wedding 87, 185
winter 35, 60, 113-115, 120, 131, 203, 204, 227, 237
Winter Bride 203
witch 51, 107, 137, 146, 148
wolf 28, 35, 69, 114, 127, 137
World-Serpent 69

Y

Ymir 63, 64, 93, 94, 97-100, 107, 125, 126, 138, 139, 142, 219, 220
Ynglinga saga . 8, 23, 28, 29, 41, 60, 96, 97, 120, 133, 144, 146, 148, 164
Ynglingatal 8, 16, 23, 30, 50, 57, 61, 120, 259
Ynglings 29
Yngvi-Frey 29, 249

Z

Zeus 86

Published by Avalonia
www.avaloniabooks.co.uk

www.ingramcontent.com/pod-product-compliance
Lightning Source LLC
Chambersburg PA
CBHW032038150426
43194CB00006B/334